The Visitor's
to
YORKSHIRE D
& NORTH PEN

INDEX TO 1:50 000 MAPS OF GREAT BRITAIN

Reproduced from the Ordnance Survey map with the permission of the
Controller of Her Majesty's Stationery Office, Crown copyright reserved.

Shading indicates maps used in this guide.
See page 25 for details.

THE
VISITOR'S GUIDE TO
YORKSHIRE DALES
& NORTH PENNINES

BRIAN SPENCER

MPC

HUNTER
PUBLISHING INC

Published by:
Moorland Publishing Co Ltd,
Moor Farm Road,
Airfield Estate,
Ashbourne,
Derbyshire DE6 1HD
England

British Library Cataloguing in
Publication Data:
Spencer, Brian, *1931-*
  The visitor's guide to the
  Yorkshire Dales. - 2nd ed.
  1. North Yorkshire. Dales -
  Visitor's guides
  I. Title
  914.28'404858

ISBN 0 86190 349 8 (paperback)
ISBN 0 86190 348 X (hardback)

Published in the USA by:
Hunter Publishing Inc,
300 Raritan Center Parkway,
CN 94, Edison, NJ 08818
ISBN 1 55650 236 2 (USA)

Colour and black & white
origination by:
Scantrans, Singapore

Printed in Hong Kong by
Wing King Tong Co., Ltd.

Cover photograph: *Swaledale,
near Keld* (MPC Picture Collection).

Illustrations have been supplied as
follows: R. Harries: pp 35 (bottom),
58-9, 58 (inset), 78, 158, 162
(inset), 187, 195 (bottom), 202,
215; MPC Picture Collection: pp
15, 39, 43, 62, 110 (both), 111
(bottom), 118, 119, 122 (both),
123, 126, 127 (top), 130 (top), 134
(both), 139 (both), 143 (bottom),
147, 150 (inset), 154 (both), 162-3,
163 (inset), 174, 178 (top), 179,
182 (top), 183 (top), 190-1 (and
inset), 195 (top); R. Scholes: pp 47
(top), 51, 66-7, 82-3, 99, 102, 127
(bottom), 138-9, 143 (bottom), 178
(bottom); B.C. Walker: p 130
(bottom).

All other illustrations are from the
author.

THE AUTHOR

Brian Spencer has had many
years' experience of walking and
camping in the Yorkshire Dales,
Lake District, Wales, Scotland
and the Peak District. He is
closely involved with the Youth
Hostels Association and a former
chairman of the Peak region
branch. An experienced tour
leader, he has led mountain tours
in Britain, The Alps, North
Africa and the Himalayas. He is
also the author of *The Visitor's
Guide to the Lake District, The
Visitor's Guide to the North York
Moors, Walking in the Alps,
Walking in Switzerland, Walking
in Austria,* and has contributed
to *Off the Beaten Track: Austria,*
all published by MPC.

CONTENTS

Key to Symbols Used in Text Margin and on Maps

 Recommended walk

 Parkland

 Archaeological site

 Nature reserve/Animal interest

 Birdlife

 Garden

 Skiing facilities

 Caves

 Church/Ecclesiastical site

 Building of interest

 Castle/Fortification

 Museum/Art gallery

 Beautiful view/Scenery, Natural phenomenon

 Other place of interest

 Sailing

 Interesting railway

 Industrial archaeology

Key to Maps

 Main road

Motorway

 Railway

River

Town/City

 Tourist Information

 Town/Village

Lake/Reservoir

Canals

Pennine Way

Settle-Carlisle Railway

PREFACE

What and where are the Yorkshire Dales? Certainly there is an area of land which fits this title within the boundary of the Yorkshire Dales National Park, but surely the dales do not stop just at the boundary of the National Park, for they continue north and south. To the north lies some of the wildest and least inhabited countryside in England, an area which has been rightly honoured with the title of 'The North Pennines Area of Outstanding Natural Beauty'. South of the Yorkshire Dales National Park the dales and moors are more rugged than their sisters within the park and possibly as a result are not quite so well known. I do not accept these rigid boundaries as we are all of the same race and speak the same language. Of course customs and dialects change and long may they remain, but I believe that the dales occupy most of the Pennine chain and for that reason I decided to expand my original brief to include the northern dales.

A few years ago I did a photographic essay of the Pennine Way and to get the shots I wanted I spent months wandering up and down the length of the Pennines, not just along the 'Way' but also through the side dales and valleys. One of the things which came out of this exercise was a realisation that it is impossible to put any form of boundary on the Pennines before the Newcastle-Carlisle gap. This then confirms my decision.

I was almost born in Lancashire, and certainly my upbringing owed allegiance to the Red rather than the White Rose; however my wife and I spent the first 8 years of married life across the moors from Haworth and this is when my real affection for the dales began. We spent every free weekend and holiday exploring the delights of the southern dales and gradually became aware that this part of our country never ceases to provide new sights and experiences for those who are prepared to look around.

One April, during my early courtship with the fells and dales, I took an American friend over my favourite hill, Penyghent. We were lucky to find the purple saxifrage in full bloom on the limestone outcrops near Penyghent Pinnacle and then on the journey back to Horton we stopped to look at Hunt Pot. My friend gazed into its depths and then told me that if this had been America there would be a fence round the hole, with a guide permanently in residence to stop people falling into it and also to give lectures on its mysteries. This horrified me, as there are too many controls as it is. Let's pray that we never reach the stage where we are organised like that. I only hope he was exaggerating, but his statement made me determined to write my guide in such a way as to encourage readers to go out on voyages of exploration and not to be led everywhere by the hand.

One thing which came out clearly while preparing this guide, was the friendliness of the people who live in the dales, and as you wander through them I hope you will enjoy meeting them as much as I did.

Brian Spencer

INTRODUCTION

This book is about part of that highland mass which forms the backbone of England known as the Pennines. The range is made up of a loosely linked series of hills reaching to almost true mountain height but keeping mostly to broad rolling moors with an average height well below 2,000ft. Although the Pennines have only a few distinctive summits above this height, it must be clearly stated that their character is closely linked to mountain masses when it comes to weather, especially in winter. The different character of individual dales and valleys which carve their way into the moors, often separated by high-level roads, is still apparent even with the standardisation of farming methods. This character variation has, to a large extent, withstood the population changes brought about by economic demands or the easier transport of the twentieth century.

The Pennine Dales are often thought of as being solely within the confines of the Yorkshire Dales National Park boundary, but their character extends much further north and south of what are mostly limestone dales within the park. The Pennines can be regarded as starting north of Derby, and include the Peak District, whose high gritstone moors continue north of its official boundary into the mass of bleak uplands between the M62 and Calderdale. Beyond Calderdale the character of the countryside changes slightly and soon the industrial valleys give way to broader and more pastoral dales. These in turn narrow and deepen as limestone begins to dominate the Craven district north of Skipton. Limestone, hundreds of feet thick, dominates the landscape northwards to Swaledale where gritstones and coal-bearing shales which have capped the fell-tops further south, take over.

Across Stainmore, and beyond the A66, the broad fastness of the Teesdale and South Tyne uplands differ in appearance from their southerly cousins, but still have an essential Pennine character. This is different from say, the Lake District or the Cheviot and even the Peak District. For these reasons therefore the dales about to be explored are those valleys draining the high ground north of Calderdale and on as far as the South Tyne Valley.

The dales have long excited the imagination; Delius, Yorkshire's major composer looked to the high tops for inspiration and literary brilliants such as J.B. Priestley and Cardiff-born Howard Spring used a dales' background for a number of their novels. Much travelled Turner captured the ever changing moods of the dales in a number of his paintings and Wordsworth, forsaking his beloved Lake District, was a frequent visitor.

The word 'Pennine' originated in a forgery produced by Charles Bertram, a professor of English at Copenhagen University. In 1747 he claimed to have discovered a fourteenth-century manuscript *De Statu Britannica*, a treatise on Roman Britain which said that the country, *Britannia Maxima*, was divided into two equal parts by a chain of hills known as the *Alps Penina*. No doubt the name was a fanciful link with the Appennines of Italy. Until 1822 no one bothered to group the individual heights under a single heading and it was two geologists, Conybeare and Phillips, who decided to use the name when writing about the rocks of northern England, and ever since, the word Pennine is used to describe the backbone of England; anything else would be unthinkable.

The hills and dales of the Pennines are not the same as they used to be; change, though slow, is the only constant thing about them. The rock layers which formed the dales have not always been in the same latitude and longtitude known today and once enjoyed a tropical climate before earth movements slowly brought them to their present locality. The time scale over which the Pennines evolved spans 300 million years, but even by that scale is nothing compared with the 4,000 million and more years that the earth has taken to develop. When ancient mountain ranges were being worn down to become the muddy floor of a tropical sea, volcanoes were active to the north. These formed the basis of the Cheviot and other rounded hills of Lowland Scotland and the Borders. Life in the sea was prolific with countless millions of tiny organisms and shell fish living and dying in a warm environment. Gradually their bodies built up layer

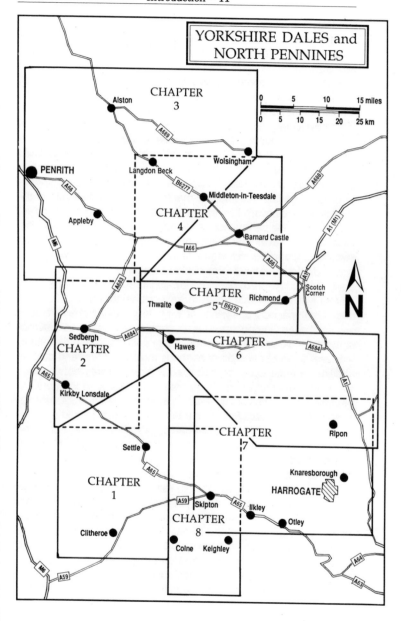

YORKSHIRE DALES and
NORTH PENNINES

upon layer into limestone, often to a depth of hundreds of feet, sometimes around coral reefs, but usually on the flat muddy remains of the ancient, or Silurian mountains. A huge continent far to the north was drained by a mighty river emptying into this shallow sea, and gradually a delta appeared slowly filling the sea with a fine mud which eventually packed down to become shale, covering the limestone remains of the earlier sea creatures. This action was not at a constant rate and allowed mud flats to develop with lagoons in between. More limestone accumulated in these lagoons before it too was covered by more mud and silt. As the delta moved further south, larger particles of sand or grit were left behind by the river and these in their turn compacted to make Millstone Grit. As an indication of the quantities involved, it has been estimated that the Millstone Grit layers of the Pennines once covered an area of more than 25,000sq miles and are the results of the destruction of a mountain range 6,000 miles long, 20 miles broad at the base and 2 miles high. As the delta developed, swamps appeared which supported tree-like plants, and when they in turn died the remains were compressed in peaty swamps, eventually through massive pressure forming coal.

During the time that these rocks were being formed, the earth underwent periods of violent activity. From deep down mineral solutions were forced upwards through weak points in the rock structure and on nearing the surface began to cool, creating veins of lead ore, fluorspar and other minerals including silver and gold. In addition, a huge sheet of molten rock thrust its way between the surface shales and over a large area of limestone in the northern Pennines. This intrusion, now known as the Great Whin Sill, extends westwards from Cross Fell to the Farne Islands and is responsible for the dramatic crags on which Hadrian built the Roman wall from Tyne to Solway Firth. In the Pennines it appears at such important features as the waterfalls of High Force and Cauldron Snout, and also in the columnar crags around High Cup Nick.

When all this activity was taking place there was no sign of any of the dales as they are known today. In fact the folds and cracks which eventually became the dales are the result of earth movements which also made the Alps and the Himalayas. These movements were active between 70,000 and 1,000,000 years ago. After this uplifting, rivers flowed down the folds and gradually deepened them into valleys. Later the various Ice Ages covered all, except the highest summits of the Pennines, with huge sheets of ice which ground their way in massive glaciers down the valleys, constantly widening and deepening them. As the ice melted with the return of warmer times, vast amounts of water gave further shape to the dales, sometimes held back for centuries by temporary natural dams, or disappeared beneath the softer limestones to form cave systems and potholes. Sometimes glacial action wore away the softer top layers to expose older rocks as is the case at Malham Tarn where a lake nestles incongruously amongst limestone. The rock beneath the tarn is slate and completely impervious to water. Rock and clay debris from retreating glaciers were left behind to further alter the shape of the landscape and is usually seen in the form of elongated low humpy hillocks such as those found below Gargrave in Craven and in Upper Ribblesdale. Other earth movements resulted in such unique features as can be found in the Malham area where the layers of rock below the Cove actually started life on the same level as the summit of Fountains Fell some 400ft higher. These later movements, or faults, are again a major feature of the modern landscape, such as the Mid-Craven Fault which is responsible for the line of limestone cliffs east of the A65 Skipton to Ingleton road. The local name for these weather worn outcrops of surface limestone is 'scar', an apt description.

After the last major upheaval finally settled, and the glaciers gave their last polish to the contours of the dales, the pattern known today was left behind. This pattern of twisted and bent folds radiates roughly from a line which starts at Cross Fell and continues southeast beyond Great Shunner Fell.

Hills make valleys, or as is the case of the Pennines, hill ranges make the dales. The Ribble begins on the north-eastern flanks of Ingleborough, and to the north the Lune drains south from the Howgills. The River Eden's source is within half a mile of that of the Ure but Cross Fell and the Lakeland Fells force it into a northwards course while the Ure flows east, down Wensleydale. The far northern dales of Tees, Wear and South Tyne originate in a geological complex east of Cross Fell known as the Alston Block. Further south another complex, the Askrigg Block, generates the main rivers of the dales, Swale, Ure, Wharfe and their tributaries.

The Ribble and Eden drain almost unpolluted into the Irish Sea and are excellent sporting rivers for the angler who can often find salmon as well as trout in them. In the north the valleys of Teesdale, the Allendales, Weardale and the Derwent Valley have beautiful rivers for most of their length but are unfortunately disfigured by industry along their lower reaches. The main rivers of Yorkshire's dales, the Swale, Ure, Wharfe, Nidd and Aire all drain into the Ouse, then into the Humber. With the exception of the Aire they have relatively clean waters all the way to the sea. The Aire, despite its lovely birth, becomes a disgraceful record of man's industrial callousness in its lower reaches. Although pollution has been reduced there is still much to be done before the sparkling beauty of Malhamdale's Aire continues along the whole of its course.

When a warmer climate returned after the last Ice Age, mosses gradually colonised the bare rocks, in turn providing soil for small alpine-type plants which later gave way in the valley bottoms to a forest which once covered the whole of the non-limestone part of the Pennines. Trees of the higher regions were dwarf birch and mountain ash, while pines lower down gave way to oak and beech woods, with the limestone region supporting grasses and alpine flowers. An interesting link with the vegetation of pre-Ice Age times can be found in the shaded fissures of limestone pavements such as that above Malham Cove. In these recesses plants normally found in dense woodland, survivors of those obliterated by the scouring ice which killed off the ancient forests and removed sustaining soil, can still find the ability to live. Here you can find woodland plants like dog's mercury and hart's tongue fern surviving happily way beyond their normal environment.

Man came late on the scene and, some would say, with disastrous results. The first men were purely nomadic hunters able to exploit the prolific game abounding on the Pennines. Their first permanent homes were in caves such as Victoria Cave above Settle where the remains of reindeer and grizzly bear have been found. An abundance of these animals normally now found in sub-arctic tundra regions suggests that the weather was not unlike that of today. When later man became more sophisticated he built settlements and grew crops. With this came the need for a calendar to regulate the year, and ensure that crop planting coincided with the correct season. This problem seems to have been overcome by the erection of stones aligned with sun or star rise at specific times of the year. Later refinements lead to complex stone circles and possibly the enigmatic stone carvings on Ilkley Moor.

About this time man settled the sparsely wooded and limestone area, and with the pressures of a growing population the first of the

Wharfedale, near Grassington

forest clearances took place, a development which continued well into monastic times and which has only been reversed recently through reafforestation. As time progressed, a primitive consumer society grew, first with trade in simple artifacts, then with more complex metals, furs and pottery. Trade was particularly strong between Ireland and Europe and the natural easy route through the Pennines, known as the Aire Gap, between the Ribble and Airedale — a link from the Irish Sea to the North Sea — was on the direct way between the two areas of population. Craven and the area around Skipton became a busy centre very early on in this island's history. A natural progression from what was essentially a semi-nomadic event led to a calendar of fairs throughout the region. Originally for major bulk buying, especially wool in medieval centuries and hiring labour, fairs have in comparatively recent times become an excuse for fun and games. Only the annual Horse Fair at Appleby retains its original purpose.

The Pennine's greatest mineral asset, lead ore (exploited by early man and later the Romans), continued to be mined in medieval days, but the main expansion of lead mining occurred during the eighteenth and nineteenth centuries when improved water supply and roofing the burgeoning industrial towns and cities created a greater need for this versatile material.

The Romans left many relics in the remote dales, and in fact they would appear to have lived in fear of the wild Brigantean tribes who inhabited the area at that time. They built a fort in Wharfedale on the site of modern Ilkley and quite probably the southern part of the dales was settled by peaceful tribes. Further north things were much different and their east-west road across Stainmore (a route which is still followed by the modern A66) was heavily defended. One of the native leaders who did not accept Roman domination was Venutius. He and his followers built a fort on the summit of Ingleborough as their headquarters. Such was the importance of the site that after its capture, the Romans turned it into a signal station; the perimeter wall and foundations of several huts can still be seen. By AD74 Venutius was defeated and many of his followers ended their days as slave labour traditionally working for Rome in the Greenhow lead mines near Pateley Bridge.

With the withdrawal of the Roman legions, the dales, as with the rest of Britain, entered a period known as the Dark Ages. At Mallerstang in the Upper Eden Valley, Pendragon Castle has links with the Arthurian legend. It was during this time that Celtic missionaries from Ireland began to spread Christianity through the dales. Their usual method was to link the new beliefs into old pagan ways in the hope of gradually overcoming the old with the new. So strong however, were some of these old faiths, that even though their origins are lost in the mists of time, there are still traces around to this day — customs like the Easter Pace Egg ceremonies at Heptonstall in Calderdale, or the pagan fire festivals of the far northern dales.

From the sixth century onwards successive waves of people came from the European mainland, land-hungry, to northern Britain. Angles, Vikings and Norsemen all subsequently became settlers, bringing their own farming methods, cultures, and languages. Place names having the Anglo 'ley' ending indicate a forest clearing, for example Otley, Ilkley and Wensley. The Danes' settlements are identified with their 'by' ending, following the name of the owner, like Thoralby, Melmerby etc. If there was a church nearby the name became Kirkby as in Kirkby Lonsdale. Norsemen left the names of features, which have gone into our vocabulary such as 'skeli' or 'scale' for outlying farms like Winterscales and Summerscales, but their major impact on our vocabulary was to leave words of natural features such as fell, gill, beck, mere, moss, heath, ling and foss.

Two of the most visible links with early times which can still be seen around the dales villages are cultivation terraces known as lynchets, and the narrow strip field systems which resulted from the necessity to plough long furrows with heavy cumbersome ox-drawn ploughs of the time. Good examples of these can be seen around Grassington and Burnsall, in Wharfedale or near Aysgarth in Wensleydale, and in Coverdale.

No sooner had Harold, king of England killed his Norse enemy and namesake at Stamford Bridge in 1066, then he too was killed at Hastings. This left the country open to the cruel Norman tyranny under William the Conqueror and forced the unruly people of the North to accept an unpopular regime. The solid castles which guard the dales and command the major routes throughout the North are Norman relics. Much of the Pennines was preserved as royal hunting forest from this time and terrible punishments were enacted on anyone caught poaching the royal game. Many ancient offices were set up to control the forest which though having no power today, are still remembered and their customs preserved. One of them is the curfew horn which is still blown every winter's night in Bainbridge.

During the Norman influence monastic orders grew in size and importance and the abbeys became some of the major landowners in the dales. It was during this time that the final clearances took place and forest gave way to hill pasture to feed the growing flocks of sheep. Living standards were improving all the time and monastic fortunes were made on wool. Even the fourteenth-century ravages of the Black Death which wiped out a tremendous part of the population in Europe had only a momentary effect on this trade, and the monasteries continued to prosper. As the size of the abbeys and cathedrals increased so did the demand for lead for their roofs and so monastic orders who were never slow to realise an asset, developed those lands where lead could be found. This in turn meant more felling of forest to provide fuel for the smelters, and an alternative fuel was sought. Coal found on Fountains Fell and around Tan Hill was mined in shallow bell-shaped pits, but even these could not satisfy later demands and eventually coal had to be carried in along the packhorse ways which developed around the dales.

In the sixteenth century Henry VIII broke the power of the monasteries by taking away their lands, treasure, and eventually destroying the magnificent abbeys. The result of this action remains to be seen in the now mellow ruins made tranquil by time and weather.

From about 1300 to 1600 the dales were vulnerable to marauding bands of Scots who came south, well into Craven, on their cattle raids. These forays were mostly carried out by small bands of men, sneaking into the more remote corners of the dales, stealing and generally making a nuisance of themselves; the small skirmishes which developed have gone down into folklore as though they were huge battles. A fray in Weardale for instance, honoured by a folk song of thirty-seven verses, was fought between only a few dozen men. The pele tower, a square defensive farmhouse, was developed about this time and allowed both animals and family to share the same roof in safety until danger passed. Nappa Hall, in Wensleydale, and Mortham Tower near Barnard Castle, are two fine examples of pele towers incorporated within a subsequent building.

As times became more civilised and the rural population started to move towards towns and cities a more peaceful Scot began to arrive on the scene. Increasing demands for fresh meat by town dwellers made good markets for Scottish beef cattle and gradually a trade developed with animals being brought on the hoof from the

The delivery van provides an important grocery service for local people

Highlands. Many of the old drove roads and pack-horse ways, some of them following Roman roads and monastic ways, are still recognised rights-of-way which can be followed for miles on foot or horse-back across the fells. G.N. Wright's *Roads and Trackways of the Yorkshire Dales* (MPC 1985), describes them in detail.

During the Civil War, the dales suffered badly in the king's cause. Many of the castles which were still homes of the nobles and lesser gentry, were besieged (sometimes for months on end) by troops led by Cromwell in support of parliament. Skipton Castle, which suffered badly, was owned by the Clifford family, and in quieter and more peaceful times after the restoration of the monarchy, Lady Anne Clifford set about rebuilding it and other family properties throughout the north of England. She was an indefatigable traveller who covered hundreds of miles on horse-back at an age when lesser mortals normally put their comfort before any other consideration.

A prominent feature of the Dales' landscape is the enormous number of stone walls. Hundreds of miles of them snake up and down fell-sides, pattern valleys and form small fields near old villages. Most are at least a hundred years old, dating from the period of Parliamentary Enclosure Acts between about 1770 and 1840, and some —

mainly those forming irregular boundaries to tiny crofts behind houses in old villages — are of the sixteenth century or maybe even earlier.

With the steady growth of industry throughout the north, the move to the towns and cities was never constant, but the effect of the Industrial Revolution was to give it new impetus. Subsequent decline of lead mining caused mass movement away from the dales. The demand for dairy produce and wool has given stability to dales farming, and mechanisation and increased mobility have brought marked changes to life in the dales. A few villages have declined; some closer to centres of industry have actually grown as commuters make their homes in them. Some provide holiday homes, and most rely to some extent on tourism.

Dales architecture has been slow to change, and most dales' buildings date from between the mid-seventeenth to late nineteenth centuries. Many houses and barns have outside stairs and a few fortified towers are incorporated into later farmhouses. Several dales have a proud castle or a ruined abbey usually in a riverside setting. Stone continues to be the one constant material used in every type of building, and strict planning control ensures that new domestic buildings are in harmony with the old. Modern farm structures, however, are outside such control, and some intensive rearing structures are particularly aggressive in the landscape.

Transport has always played a major part in the dales scene, from ancient trackways to Roman roads connecting regional headquarters like York and Lancaster. Wealthy monastic orders created routes between their vast sheep walks and granges, linking them with the main priories and abbeys. Later came the cattle drovers whose roads can still be traced, often as walled green lanes. Countryfolk often travelled miles on foot or horse-back from one dale to another to reach a nearby market. Likewise, the bulk produce of wool, carried on the backs of ponies on its outward journey to the weaver, would meet returning pack trains laden with finished goods for sale, or salt to preserve winter meat. All these ancient methods of transport created their own roads and where they cross the remoter parts of the dales or the high moors, can still be easily followed often for miles, from one linking motor road to another.

The road system began to improve with the Turnpike Acts around the mid-eighteenth century, when good quality roads were built by private enterprise. These roads were a vast improvement on the old trackways and helped speed movement between the centres of population by allowing wheeled vehicles to travel more easily on their superior surfaces. The turnpikes often built on the route of an ancient trackway, in their turn became the foundations of today's motor road system.

Between 1770 and 1790 the Pennines were crossed by a canal between Leeds and Liverpool, but its effectiveness was soon to be challenged by steam locomotion. In the second half of the last century railways spread to the remoter parts of the dales. Most of these lines are now abandoned but the most scenic of them all, between Settle and Carlisle, is still open. Despite attempts by British Rail to close the line, carefully organised counter arguments seem to be winning the battle.

Industry came early to the Pennines with the discovery and exploitation of lead and other metallic ores, and production came to a peak in the late eighteenth and early nineteenth centuries. Until then most mining was carried out by small teams of men who would only work proven veins, but gradually the concessions were bought up by various companies, some with strong Quaker foundations. With it the pattern was set for paternalistic employment with good standards of housing, and an education for the miners and their families. In recent times lead mining areas, which declined through competition from cheaper imports, found a new lease of life with the demand for fluorspar used as a flux in steel making. Once a waste product it is now a much sought-after material, particularly in the Weardale area.

Agriculture is the oldest industry, and the beginnings of planned farming came with the growth of the monasteries. The monks developed new and improved strains of sheep yielding more wool of better quality, and specialised breeds appeared in the dales. Of late, the rearing of sheep as a cash crop has diminished with a reduced demand for home-bred wool and the distinctive local breeds have mingled more with general purpose crossbreeds. Domestic industry such as the manufacture of hand-knitted stockings, once so important, has vanished and likewise few farms now make any cheese for sale.

Quarrying stone for building thrived locally at the end of last century. Today, increased demand for limestone for road-stone and cement has become concentrated in parts of Craven and Weardale. Mountainous regions are providers of water, but only the part not on

The Fox & Hounds, Starbotton

limestone is suitable for this. The major catchment areas are therefore Bowland, Nidderdale, Baldersdale, the Upper Teesdale and the Derwent Valley, where reservoirs introduce a new element into the Pennine scene. In line with current water authority policies, many reservoirs are stocked with fish or are available to sailing enthusiasts.

Today's demands on the dales are more intense than ever before. Easier transport means that more people go into the hills either as day or holiday visitors, and a significant number commute from those villages within reasonable distance of the major towns. The most attractive areas are unfortunately the most popular and heavily used. Malham, for example, can become very crowded during a holiday period as can Grassington, Ingleton, Settle, Hawes and Aysgarth. On busy weekends these are places to avoid by those seeking solitude. The quieter areas are around the Howgills north of Sedbergh and in the northern dales, or the lonely little side valleys which no motor road reaches.

With the passing of the National Parks Act of 1949, consideration was given to the setting up of a National Park in the Yorkshire Dales; by 1953 the boundaries had been decided and the area of 680sq miles enclosed by them was designated as a National Park. While the boundary encloses all the major dales, by some strange bureaucratic anomaly, Nidderdale is outside the National Park and the Howgills, a virtually unexplored range of hills between the Lake District and the Dales, are cut in half by the park's boundary.

The National Park is controlled by a committee of the North Yorkshire County Council, which is augmented by members of the three district councils whose areas encroach into the park (Craven, Richmondshire and South Lakeland), by a representative of Cumbria County Council and perhaps, most importantly, by eight members with specialist skills or interests (one-third of the total committee) appointed by the Secretary of State for the Enviroment to represent the national interest in this national asset.

In accordance with the 1949 Act, the committee is charged with two prime objectives: to 'preserve and enhance the natural beauty of the area' and 'to promote opportunities for (suitable) outdoor recreation'. At the same time, the committee has a declared policy of carrying out its main responsibilities with the interest of the local population in mind. Obviously, within these guidelines there is often conflict; in such cases decisions are generally weighted in the favour of good conservation practice. The demands of Time-Share interests, while hovering the wrong side of the horizon are kept well under control, but the threat is one which the park authority must watch carefully if local needs are to come first.

If criticism is to be levelled at the Yorkshire Dales it is the apparent lack of access agreements. Miles of open moors and fell-tops, apart from 'rights-of-way' footpaths, are officially out of bounds to walkers. Several fells have rights-of-way only as far as their upper boundaries where a law abiding walker is left with the tantalising view of the fell before returning by the same path. The fell is in all probability common land, but only commoners with shared grazing rights may use it. It is a great pity that open country in the Dales is not available to all, and it is hoped that the day is not too far away when Access Agreements are negotiated throughout the National Park. A precedent already exists on the Duke of Devonshire's grouse moors around Bolton Abbey. The moors are freely accessible to walkers except during the grouse shooting season, or at times of high fire risk. An arrangement which seems to work well for all interests.

The National Park Authority has responsibility for planning and development control in the park, but its main contact with visitors is through its 'field services': the warden service is responsible for footpath maintenance, patrol and guidance at sites popular with visitors, public and educational liaison and the liaison with local farmers; National Park Information Centres in the Dales, manned by staff capable and ready to answer the tremendous variety of questions which visitors ask; and on guided walks which are organised throughout the summer season.

Dales roads tend to be narrow and winding, but can add a new dimension to motoring enjoyment providing necessary care and attention is given to other road users. For the same reason cyclists must be particularly vigilant, especially on some of the notoriously steep hills in the area.

The walker is well catered for in the Dales. There is a wide variety of accommodation, from campsites to hotels, from Youth Hostels to bunkhouse barns, from caravan sites to warm and friendly village inns. It is calculated that there are about a thousand miles of public footpaths and bridleways in the National Park alone; the Pennine Way traverses the Dales on its route from Edale to Kirk Yetholm, while the Dales Way links Leeds with the Lake District, and the Ribble Valley Way traces the river from its source to the sea.

In the following chapters, the routes of walks have been carefully selected and graded. None are too difficult for anyone who is reasonably fit. The choice of footwear and clothing will depend on the individual, but novice walkers would do well to read *Rugged Country Rules* (from National Park Centres). Watch the weather, and leave a note of your route before setting out.

Places are dealt with, as near as possible, in a logical sequence and places to visit are set out in separate boxes progressively through each chapter. Symbols are used to highlight special features. At the end of each chapter short walks, suitable for all age groups, and scenic car drives are shown separately.

As a guide, this book is not to be used as a constant reference piece, but has been written to encourage both the first time visitor and also those more familiar with the region, to seek out for themselves all that is worthwhile and interesting.

Note on the Walks Described

The walks suggested in this book are not intended to be a field-by-field guide, but recommendations for the best routes. Many have been chosen so that they avoid the popular and crowded areas, while some are more interesting or give better views than the well known routes. Although most are suitable walks for all the family, walkers must be equipped according to the severity of the terrain: strolling along woodland walks requires only stout shoes and weather protection, but high level moorland walks need proper boots and clothing, map and compass and the ability to use them correctly.

The method used in describing the walks assumes that the walker will carry a map of 1:50,000 scale (about $1^1/_4$ in to the mile) or better still 1:25,000 (about $2^1/_2$ in to the mile). These latter are available as Ordnance Survey Outdoor Leisure Maps, giving cover to much of the Pennines. It is, of course, important that the walker is familiar with the use of maps, especially the use of the Grid Reference.

Maps

The maps drawn for each chapter, while comprehensive, are not designed to be used as route maps, but rather to locate the main towns, villages and places of interest. The Ordnance Survey maps which cover the area of this book are: 1:50,000 Landranger Series, sheets 87, 90, 91, 92, 97, 98, 99, 102, 103, 104, 110; 1:25,000 Outdoor Leisure Series, The Three Peaks, Malham and Upper Wharfedale, South Pennines and Teesdale.

Rights-of-Way

A number of walks described in this book are across open moors or limestone pavements. Although in some instances official rights-of-way do not exist, all the routes have been walked for many years by countless people without hindrance, are still regularly used and feature in most local guidebooks. It is hoped that in the near future formal agreements can be arranged for free access.

WHERE TO GO IF IT RAINS

Northern Dales
Aysgarth — carriage museum
Barnard Castle — Bowes Museum, Raby Castle (A688 north-east of
  Barnard Castle)
Castle Bolton — castle, restaurant
Darlington — railway museum, Georgian houses
Durham — cathedral, museums
Hawes — folk museum, information centre, ropeworks
Reeth — folk museum
Richmond — Georgian theatre, abbey, museum

Eastern Dales
Harrogate — cinema, exhibitions, theatre, gardens
Knaresborough — castle, caves
Ripley — cathedral, Newby Hall (4 miles south of Ripon)
York — minster, museums, Jorvik Viking Centre

Southern Dales
Bradford — museums
Haworth — Brontë museum, Worth Valley railway line
Keighley — Worth Valley railway line, art gallery
Leeds — art galleries, museums, Harewood House (A61, 8 miles
  north of Leeds)
Skipton — castle, museum

Western Dales
Blackpool — seaside resort
Carnforth — Steamtown Railway Museum, Levens Hall
Kendal — museums, theatre
Morecambe — seaside resort
Settle — Settle to Carlisle Railway line

1
RIBBLESDALE

Although born in Yorkshire the Ribble is, in its maturity, very much a Lancastrian river. It has long been a favourite outdoor recreational area for people from the nearby industrial towns of North Lancashire, and as a result farmhouse and coaching inns of earlier times have developed a tradition providing food of excellent quality. Their close proximity to each other in the Ribble and Hodder valleys ensures a spirit of competition and consequent high standards.

Lancashire's Ribble is a favourite amongst picnickers, motorists and fishermen. Downstream of Ribchester the river is noted for its sea trout and the occasional salmon are caught on their return journey to spawning grounds upstream. Apart from one or two popular places such as Edisford Bridge near Clitheroe or at Ribchester, nowhere does the river get overcrowded, even on busy Bank Holidays.

As this guide is essentially dealing with dales which are mostly in Yorkshire, it is only logical to move upstream, describing Ribblesdale from the sea to its source at Ribblehead. Here the Ribble is well and truly a Yorkshire river.

Working upriver from Preston, the first place of note is the Roman fort of *Bremetennacum* on the edge of **Ribchester**, a quiet town of interesting old weavers' cottages. Roman galleys sailed up the river as far as this fort and later shallow draughted longboats based on Ireland brought marauding Vikings to Ribblesdale. A grass bank outlines the outer walls of the fort, but only the ruined walls of the granary are left of what would have been an important centre at the crossroads of east-west and north-south routes. The site was well chosen to command a safe river crossing over the Ribble, although now a large part of the southern defences have been washed away by changes in the river's course. The late thirteenth-century church of St Wilfred occupies most of the site.

Nearby **Longridge Fell** is a favourite haunt of devotees of hang gliding and if you want to watch this graceful sport there is an easy walk following any of the paths across the fell above Hurst Green. These will give you views of Bowland to the north and the whole length of Ribblesdale to the south and east.

Stonyhurst College above Hurst Green is a Catholic college run by the Jesuits. It was founded in 1593 as a school for English Catholics, but due to repressive laws against them during the reign of Queen Elizabeth I, it was set up at St Omers in the Low Countries. After a chequered history and many moves, in 1794 following the French Revolution, the college made its way to Stonyhurst, a Tudor country house closely linked with an important local family, the Shireburns. Since then the building and college have prospered and it is now one of England's leading Catholic schools. The oldest part of Stonyhurst College dates from 1337, but there have been additions in every century, especially the nineteenth, right up to the present day. Oliver Cromwell stayed here, and slept fully clothed on a table during Civil War fighting in Lancashire. The college is situated at the end of a sweep of a magnificent avenue and is open to the public by arrangement with the assistant bursar, to whom application should be made by letter.

The river which flows round the base of Longridge Fell is the Hodder. Sleepy unspoilt villages and prosperous farms are spaced along its length. This is the boundary between Lancashire and Yorkshire and the villages have that indefinable Yorkshire character; here is another world from the industrial towns not so very far away, south of the Ribble. Village industry is essentially rural, linked mainly to farming services, but chair making based on traditional methods is still carried out in Longridge and Chipping. Witches' spells were once an everyday event in this district and these along with Celtic superstitions still linger in people's minds. A roof-high holly of great age outside Thornley Hall near Chipping will never be cut down in case it brings ill luck.

Almost hidden down a side street of **Whalley** are the ruins of Whalley Abbey, now a quiet setting for the Blackburn Diocese Conference Centre and Retreat House. The abbey was built between 1330 and 1440 and at the Dissolution of the Monasteries in the 1530s

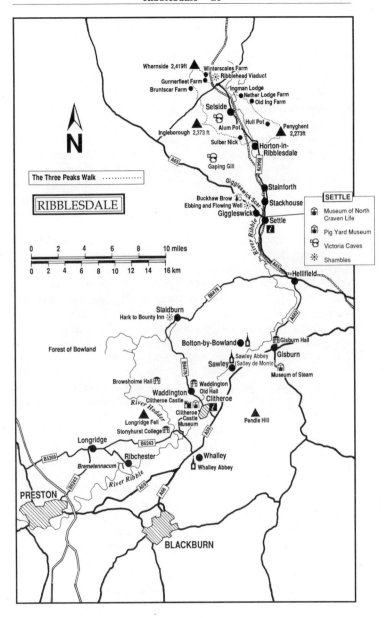

it passed into the hands of the Assheton family, who converted the abbots lodgings into a manor house. It is this section which remains as a conference centre with the ruined part of the abbey set off by banked flower gardens. At Dunsop Bridge, move temporarily into Yorkshire where the village, together with its neighbours Newton and Slaidburn, have an atmosphere that is almost feudal. Visit the Hark to Bounty Inn in **Slaidburn** and in an upstairs room you will be shown a courtroom where a primitive justice was handed out until more enlightened times. The inn is named after a famous hound from a local pack which had a distinctive cry. St Andrew's Church down the road is mostly Jacobean and has some interesting family pews. North of the Hodder Valley the **Forest of Bowland**, an upland area where jealously guarded access has only recently been eased, presents a forbidding aspect on a winter's night but in summer, especially when the heather is in full bloom, the picture is one of glorious freedom from the pressures of town life. Only two roads cross the Bowland fells; one is from Slaidburn to Bentham in the Lune Valley and the other climbs from Dunsop Bridge to Lancaster by way of the Trough of Bowland. Harrison Ainsworth's tragic *Witches of Pendle* were taken across this high pass on their way to Lancaster Castle and eventual execution.

The red sandstone Jacobean building of **Browsholme Hall**, on the minor road from Dunsop Bridge to Clitheroe, is home of the Parker family, ancient guardians of the 'Park' of Bowland, and bow-bearers of the forest. Standing above an attractive terrace the graceful sixteenth-century stone house which replaced an earlier timber and daub structure, looks out over delightful gardens towards Longridge Fell. Added to by subsequent generations, Browsholme has a pleasant homely appeal and is open to the public who can enjoy its collections of furniture, tapestries, china and works of art.

From Slaidburn the road goes south across Waddington Fell past the Walloper Well (SD 717483) where you can make a wish, towards Clitheroe and back into Lancashire. Waddow Hall on the Clitheroe road outside Waddington is owned by the Girl Guides' Association.

A little stream flows by the side of the main street in **Waddington** where the houses, each with its pretty garden, are reached by individual bridges. Members of the Waddington family have left their mark around the world, one became Prime Minister of France, and another who helped pioneer the Canadian Pacific Railway has the highest mountain in Canada, Mount Waddington, named after him.

PLACES TO VISIT IN AND AROUND CLITHEROE

Browsholme Hall
Near Bashall Eaves, 6 miles north-west of Clitheroe
Home of the Parker family, keepers of the 'Park' of Bowland since 1507. House has been added to and altered by subsequent generations. Fine oak panelling and a collection of armour and relics of the Forest of Bowland.

Clitheroe Castle Museum
Displays on the theme of life in the nineteenth century. Rose garden.

Museum of Steam
Attached to caraven site, A682, 2 miles south of Gisburn
Largest collection of steam-driven vehicles in the north. Traction engines, showmans' engines and fairground organ, all frequently steamed during the summer. Open at all reasonable times.

Ribchester
On the B6245, 4 miles north of Blackburn
Pleasant riverside village with interesting weavers' cottages lining the street leading to the Roman fort of *Bremetennacum*. Outline of the fort can still be seen; the granary has been excavated as part of the perimeter fort wall now wasted away by changes in the river bank.

Stonyhurst College
Hurst Green, 4 miles from Clitheroe on B6243
Public school founded by the Jesuits in 1593. The house, dating from 1594, retains many interesting architectural features. Open to visitors by appointment.

Whalley Abbey
Off the A59, 4 miles south of Clitheroe
Built between 1330 and 1440. During the Dissolution of the Monasteries in 1537 the property passed into the hands of the Assheton family where it remained until 1923. Now a Blackburn Diocese Conference Centre and a Retreat House. Tranquil ruins and attractive gardens, craft centre and gift shop.

Waddington Old Hall is nineteenth century, but stands on ancient foundations; Henry VI was sheltered here after his defeat at the Battle of Hexham. The church's oldest record is from 1438 and although the foundations are even older, the present structure is mainly nineteenth century.

There is excellent fishing in the Ribble below Waddington and day tickets can be bought from the local angling association, or the Red Pump at Bashall Eaves and the Whitwell Hotel.

The market town of **Clitheroe**, now thankfully bypassed by the A59, manages to retain its agricultural character despite the closeness of nearby limestone quarries. Clitheroe Castle has what is reputed to be the smallest keep in the North and a hole in its south wall is supposed to have been made by Cromwell's cannons during the Civil War in 1649. The castle was built by Roger de Poitou, son of Roger de Montgomery, one of William the Conqueror's commanders at the Battle of Hastings. Most of the castle's layout would still be recognised by the de Lacy's, Clitheroe's major builders. Had it not been for Charles II awarding Clitheroe to General Monk in 1660 for services towards the restoration of the crown, the castle might still be a royal fortress like Lancaster's. Small rose gardens enhance this attractive site with its views of Pendle Hill and the Ribble Valley.

Christianity came early to Clitheroe when St Paulinus' missionaries baptised the locals in a Calder pool, the same pool used for the ordeal testing of witches by King James I's over-zealous 'witch finders'. Clitheroe Church though very much 'Victorianised' is built on Saxon foundations. There is a local legend of a battle when King Stephen of England fought the Scots under William Fitz Duncan at Edisford outside the town in 1138.

The whaleback mass of **Pendle Hill** commands the view southeast from Clitheroe. This is witch country where stories abound, some true and others of folk origin, telling of witches' Sabbaths, strange happenings and broomstick rides by Demdikes and Chattoxes on wild moonless nights. The villages of Newchurch and Barley have made the most of the dreadful wrath meted out to the poor unfortunates in less enlightened times and local curio shops specialise in witchlore. Pendle Hill in a storm can readily conjure thoughts of a witches' Sabbath, but on a fine day the steep pull from Barley by way of Ing Ends to the summit is worth the effort. A long walk (9 miles, 5 hours) can be made by returning across Pendle Moor and Spence Moor to Newchurch or alternatively carry on to the Nick of Pendle and back to Barley by way of a series of tracks which contour around the southern flank of Pendle.

Old ponds attached to now ruined mills from a time when cotton was king in the Pendle area are well stocked with fish, mostly coarse but often brown trout which have been introduced by local angling clubs. Most of the waters are owned by local clubs and permits to fish must be obtained beforehand. A stranger to this area will soon realise why the inhabitants of the nearby cotton towns take such a proprietorial interest in Pendle. All the little nooks and crannies with their remains of old industry cry out to be explored. A small information centre in the car park at Barley will help a first-time visitor find out more. The high road from Barley round the 'big end' of Pendle leads to Lancashire's prettiest village, Downham, and then back into Ribblesdale.

Further up the Ribble, the next stop is **Sawley** with its scanty remains of a larger Cistercian abbey also known as Salley de Monte. Its last abbot was executed for taking part in the Pilgrimage of Grace and many local houses are built of stones taken from the abbey after the Dissolution.

North-west from Sawley a path follows the west side of the river, then off Tosside Beck to **Bolton-by-Bowland**. The village is set in rolling park-like countryside between the Ribble and Tosside Beck, a stream which starts life very near to the Ribble above Long Preston. Bolton-by-Bowland Church fills a slight rise above the village centre and close by are the venerable stocks and even older market cross. Founded in the twelfth century, most of the church's fabric comes from the fifteenth century; note the heavily studded door and the uniquely designed font which was vandalised in the Civil War. Bolton's major family were the Pudsey's, their chantry with its lepers' squint occupies the north side of the nave. Sir Ralph Pudsey whose three wives bore him twenty-five children is buried in an imposing limestone tomb on the south of the chancel. Sir Ralph gave sanctuary to Henry VI after his crushing defeat at Hexham in Northumbria. Holden Clough alpine nurseries are to the west across Tosside Beck.

Lush pastures between Clitheroe and Settle produce some of the region's finest cattle and sheep. This is the southern edge of the Craven district of Yorkshire, with Gisburn, its western gateway and market village on the A59. **Gisburn** has always been a favourite stopping place on the road between Yorkshire and the Lancashire coast, its restaurants and inns have offered refreshment to travellers since the first turnpike road was built. An avenue of beech and lime trees near the village centre leads to Gisburn Hall where there was once a herd of wild cattle similar to that roaming Chillingham Park in Northumberland.

North of Gisburn along the A682 and running parallel to the Ribble is **Hellifield** which provided homes for railway workers on the lines which had their junction a little way beyond the village. The famous Settle to Carlisle line, the most dramatic section of a main railway route from Yorkshire to Scotland, comes through Hellifield although not so busy as formerly — but at least trains still run! The Ribble is to the west of Hellifield where it wanders through flat meadows and at times floods after heavy storms higher up the valley.

Settle is a popular stopping place on the A65, Leeds to Kendal road, both for people moving into the higher dales or beyond and for those who appreciate Settle for its own worth. There has been a market here every Tuesday since a charter was granted in 1249 and the old town hall denotes its importance as an administrative centre for the area. Every March there is a well supported drama festival in Settle, with guest celebrities taking part in what has become a most ambitious series of events. A group of shops known as the Shambles dominates the market square. Prominent on the opposite side is the Ye Olde Naked Man Café which was once an inn. The name and seventeenth-century sign are said to be devised by the innkeeper as a protest against the excessive fashions of his time. Settle is busy and yet at the same time a refreshing town sheltered from the coldest winds by Castlebergh Hill to the east, so that it can be quite the sun trap its gardens proclaim. The town will reward anyone with an observant eye; here is a town of narrow streets and hidden alleys where Georgian and older properties crowd in delightful confusion; carved lintels and old signs are memorials to the people who built these interesting houses. The oldest building is the attractive house known as 'Preston's Folly' built in 1675. It was so named, because its first owner is supposed to have run out of money before it was finished. The old Bridge End Shaw Mill at the junction of the A65 and Stainforth roads, now converted into holiday flats, was operated by a 12ft-diameter waterwheel with internal paddles. You can see the now dormant wheel from the road.

Coaching inns dating from the seventeenth century indicate the early importance of Settle as a link in the chain of communications. It was a handy resting place before the steep climb up Buckhaw Brow on the Keighley to Kendal turnpike road. The railway superceded this more romantic method of travel and the line which goes north from here to Carlisle ranks as one of the most courageous feats of British railway engineering. When it was built in the 1870s the army of navvies who passed across the sleepy acres of Ribblesdale must have appeared to the locals like the hordes of Genghis Khan. Despite

*Preston's Folly,
Settle*

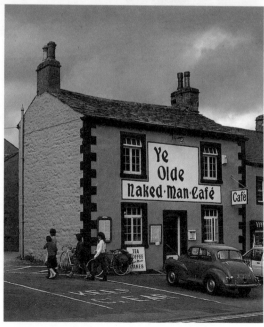

*Ye Olde Naked Man
Café, Settle*

attempts by British Rail to close the line, a recent government statement has reversed this policy and so rewarded the efforts of a long and agonising battle by pressure groups. Not only is the line valuable for its scenic beauty, but it is the sole link with the outside world for many dales' communities. Settle is a popular starting place for train journey's to Carlisle, many of them scheduled as special steam events.

Two small but excellent museums in Settle tell the story of life in bygone days in this part of mid-Craven. These are the Pig Yard Museum on Castle Hill and the Museum of North Craven Life in Victoria Street. The Pig Yard Museum contains the remains of many animals discovered locally, some extinct, but others now found only in Equatorial Africa, an indication that the climate of Britain was once much warmer than now. These relics, the left overs of the meals of our ancient ancestors, were found in Victoria Cave below Attermire Scar. Other exhibits of sophisticated utensils and weapons dating from the Iron Age have led archaeologists to suggest that the cave was used as a refuge when the Romans advanced into Craven in their search for lead.

Langcliffe and Attermire Scars are the visible surface indications of the Mid-Craven Fault, a massive shift in the strata of the earth's crust. This fault is in evidence all the way from Malham to Settle. From Settle north-east to Ingleton it continues as the South Craven Fault and forms the impressive natural boundary of the limestone uplands which is most conspicuous at Giggleswick Scar.

An easy 5-mile walk ($2^1/_2$ hours) from Settle follows a path beneath Langcliffe Scar where there is an opportunity to explore Attermire and Victoria Caves. This walk leaves the town centre by way of Banks Lane (beyond the Shambles and Constitution Hill).

Across the river from Settle, but bypassed by the busy A65 is **Giggleswick** which retains an old and gentle charm. The Norsemen settled here and in the twelfth century St Alkelda founded what is now Giggleswick's parish church. Although founded in the twelfth century, most of the fabric dates from the fifteenth; it has some fine seventeenth-century interior woodwork, especially the pulpit, lectern and communion rails. Colourwashed limestone cottages line Giggleswick's streets and Tems Beck which is crossed by a 12ft-slab of local slate. A market cross and a set of stocks complete the timeless atmosphere of this unspoilt village, but it is perhaps the famous public school founded in 1507 by James Carr, with its green domed chapel, which brings most acclaim to this place.

The South Craven Fault continues as Giggleswick Scar and beneath it the A65 climbs steeply up Buckhaw Brow. About two-thirds of the way up is the Ebbing and Flowing Well. On the rare occasions ❋ that the well functions, it rapidly drains, and then after a pause refills itself. This is due to a unique double chambered cave somewhere behind the well which causes a sudden syphoning effect inside the hole and temporarily cuts off the flow of water.

Giggleswick Scar (4 miles, 2 hours) can be explored from a path 🚶 which begins opposite the turning off the A65 towards Giggleswick, and climbs through Lords Wood to a cairn built by boys from Giggleswick School. The path later contours gently beneath the scar to meet the A65 at the top of Buckhaw Brow.

A sign at Langcliffe marks entry into the Yorkshire Dales National Park. Northwards along Ribblesdale the true limestone country where the Settle to Carlisle railway competes with the B6479 for the available space in the valley bottom is entered. The first Ribblesdale village within the park is **Stackhouse**, a farming community on above the quiet back lane between Giggleswick and Little Stainforth. A footpath a little over 2 miles long (1¹/₂ hours) leads north-east from 🚶 Stackhouse, through aptly named Happy Valley (a popular picnic spot for the locals) to the enigmatic feature known as the Celtic Wall. This is an ancient stone wall almost 70ft in length, 5ft high and 5ft at its base. The purpose of this wall is in doubt, but archaeologists believe that it is over 2,000 years old. Follow the escarpment (4 miles, 2¹/₂ hours) beyond the wall and turn right on the Feizor to link with the Little Stainforth path and eventually back to Stackhouse.

Stainforth was settled before the Norman Conquest and its prettiest features are Catrigg Force high up to the east of the village 🏕 and the pack-horse bridge built by the monks of Sawley Abbey and above a ford once crossed by the drove road from Lancaster to York. Stainforth means 'Stoney Ford', a reference to the attractive scene topped by the pack-horse bridge. The village makes an ideal base for exploring the southern slopes of the Ribblesdale fells. It has several guest houses, a hospitable pub and a Youth Hostel. A short easy walk starting by the tiny green above the village climbs a walled lane for about a mile (³/₄ hour) to reach Catrigg Force, one of the hidden 🚶 beauties of the Dales.

Quarrying intrudes upon the scene near **Helwith Bridge**; limestone, the material of our roads, is taken in ever increasing amounts from the fell-sides and to a lesser extent slate, the bed-rock of the dale is still used for decorative building purposes.

At Helwith Bridge, further up the dale beyond Stainforth, there is the first glimpse of Yorkshire's famous mountain trio. To the right is Penyghent, left is Ingleborough, and beyond but not seen for another few miles is Whernside, Yorkshire's highest point, 2,419ft above sea level. These are the 'Three Peaks' one of the hardest expeditions open to the fell walker and that toughest of all sports — cyclocross. While not wanting to scorn the efforts and energy of fell racers, there is however, a certain distaste in the thought of the fells rapidly becoming places of competition against anything but oneself. The Three Peaks Walk is certainly a fine expedition for the really hardy fell walker. To cross the 24 miles of very rough ground and climb a total of 5,000ft within the hours of daylight will certainly create a sense of achievement, but only those who are fit and have a previous knowledge of the terrain should attempt this walk. Limestone country is full of snags, from outcropping scars to sheer-sided potholes, all lying in wait for the unwary walker. This walk was carried out in 1887 by two school masters from Giggleswick who walked over Inglebor-ough with the intention of having tea at Chapel-le-Dale. Whernside tempted them on and once there, Penyghent completed the chal-lenge. The route has been run in around 4 hours or cyclocrossed in less than 3 hours, but usually needs all the hours of summer daylight.

The Three Peaks Walk 24 miles • 12 to 14 hours

There are few rules controlling the Three Peaks Walk apart from the really important one about doing it in daylight, and the need to complete the circuit in one go. Most people start at the Three Peaks Café in Horton-in-Ribblesdale and walk the route anticlockwise. The café proprietor has installed a factory clocking-in machine and participants are expected to sign 'in' and 'out'. The proprietor expects anyone who drops out for any reason to let him know as the fell rescue services are automatically called out at the end of the day against any incomplete cards. This also applies to anyone who completes the walk, but fails to clock back in again. So if you do the walk, please comply with this very simple but effective scheme. The volunteer rescue service do not take too kindly to being called out on a wild goose chase!

The route of the Three Peaks Walk is very well described in Wainwright's *Walks in Limestone Country* and it is fairly easy to follow

Penyghent

with the aid of the OS map. However the following notes should act as a rough guide.

Starting from **Horton** take the Settle road as far as the bridge beyond the parish church. Turn left over the bridge and past the school to **Brackenbottom Farm**, where a clearly signposted path leads up the hillside to join the Pennine Way path, then steeply through the outcropping crags to the summit of the first peak, **Penyghent**. Cross the summit to a break in its western cliff. Go downhill for about quarter of a mile and fork right in a north-westerly direction (the main path goes back to the Horton via Scar Lane). Walk downhill and aim to the right of the distinct shape of Hull Pot. Note that if you cannot see **Hull Pot** either because it is too dark or misty you should call the whole expedition off and live to try again. Continue along a faint track still north-west through, or better still, around the bog of **Black Dub Moss** and in about a half a mile turn right on to the bridleway from Horton to Langstrothdale. This section again coincides with the Pennine Way, but leaves it at **Old Ing Farm**. Take the farm lane left and about halfway to the neighbouring High Birkwith Farm turn right and follow a drystone wall to **God's Bridge**, a natural bridge of limestone, and **Nether Lodge Farm**. The farm road leads down and across the infant Ribble to the B6479 beyond Ingman Lodge. Turn right along the road and aim towards the Ribblehead viaduct where a cart track by the Ribblehead Inn turns right and then under the viaduct to **Gunnerfleet Farm**. Turn right, walk along the Chapel-le-Dale track to **Winterscales Farm** and then left, beyond the farm buildings to climb steeply up the flank of **Whernside**. After a rest near the summit cairn go left from the summit and aim steeply downhill to **Bruntscar Farm** with its road to Chapel-le-Dale and Hill Inn. Unless the Hill Inn is irresistible, walk north-east up the Ingleton-Ribblehead road to a stile on the right and start to climb again towards a broad col between Ingleborough and Simon Fell, turning right for **Ingleborough's** summit. This section of the walk across the north-west slopes of Ingleborough is dotted with caves and potholes and is worthy of the lengthier exploration in Chapter 2, The Lune Valley.

For the final lap of the Three Peaks Walk it is necessary to walk back along the track from the top of Ingleborough to the lowest point of the col in the direction of **Simon Fell**. Turn right in a south-easterly direction across marshy ground, past **Sulber Nick** and across three walls to a wall above Beecroft Quarry. Follow the wall to the south and at a shooting butt turn left over a stile and follow a cairned path around the quarry to **Beecroft Hall**, eventually over the railway and back to Horton remembering to clock in again at the café.

After all that strenuous exercise perhaps a short gentle digression is called for, and what better way than to comment on the wildlife and history of the area? The most common sound on the high fells is made by the curlew, its haunting call evocative of the windswept rough grass moors which it finds ideal for its nesting sites. Ravens and crows inhabit the high crags and lower down the fells are the haunt of lapwings whose call gives rise to its other name 'pee-wit'. Pied wagtails live in open country near water, but their larger relative, the grey wagtail, will rarely be found away from streams and ponds. Of all the birds of north Ribblesdale the warbling song of the skylark brings home the joy of summer as it climbs higher and higher into the sky.

Plant life abounds. On the high peaty tops can be found bilberry, cloudberry and to a lesser extent heather. Purple saxifrage festoons the limestone crags of Penyghent, along with mountain pansy and bird's eye primrose with the insectivorous plants sundew and butter-wort in boggy places. Ferns such as hart's tongue enjoy the damp recesses of fissures in the limestone pavements. Cotton grass and the purple moor grass together with white mat-grass cover the lower slopes between the acidic high tops and limestone outcrops.

For centuries the sweet grass of limestone country has provided grazing for sheep bred mostly for their fleeces. Monastic wealth came from wool and vast areas of the dales were once owned and farmed by the Cistercians of Fountains and other abbeys. The whole of Upper Ribblesdale was one huge sheepwalk divided amongst the abbeys of Fountains, Furness and Sawley. Ingman Lodge near Ribblehead for example was once a grange for Furness Abbey. Change affects most things in life and improvements in stock breeding brought about specific breeds suited to their environment. The Swaledale and its variant the Dalesbred are particularly favoured now. The Swaledale has a grey nose on a black face and the Dalesbred has white patches on its face. Other breeds are the Rough Fell and Wensleydale, but the Dalesbred is the most common in this area.

The village of **Horton-in-Ribblesdale** is an ideal centre for exploring the woods and caves of Upper Ribblesdale. Unfortunately you must try to ignore the quarries along Moughton fellside to the west. The one above Helwith Bridge quarries Silurian Slate which was once used for paving slabs, the sides of rainwater tanks and even tombstones, but now the stone is only needed for road building and to a lesser extent is still used as a building material. Moughton Whetstone was once used to hone Sheffield razors. Beecroft is a limestone quarry with an attendant smoke plume which regretfully appears necessary with lime and cement production. Despite this nearby industry, Horton is a hospitable place, an obvious stopping place for anyone walking the Pennine Way, exploring the maze of cave formations around the village, or just enjoying the delight of the open spaces around.

The parish church of St Oswald dates from Norman times and is built of local materials from the slabs of its floor to the lead on its roof. Look at its Norman doorway and stained glass windows, especially the west with the ancient fragment showing the mitred head of Thomas à Becket. Do not worry if you get the feeling that the place is leaning because it really is! All the pillars lean to the south and have done so for generations, so there does not seem much danger of the church falling on your head yet! While a number of east windows in dales' churches have a definite slant, nowhere does the whole church interior lean like it does at Horton.

Penyghent Pinnacles

Ingleborough in winter

Penyghent, 2,273ft high (5 miles, 3 hours) is the obvious mecca for most walkers starting from Horton. The majority take the way up and down Horton Scar Lane, but a more enjoyable route is the signposted path which follows the Three Peaks Walk route through Brackenbottom Farm from Horton to Penyghent. From the summit, the route goes beneath an impressive limestone scar with a detached pinnacle to make its way down to Hull Pot before joining the Horton Scar Lane back to the village.

Hidden in tiny ravines amongst this expanse of rolling moorland are the charming survivors of ancient woodlands left over from a time when the climate was much milder than it is today. **Ling Gill** (5 miles, 2 hours) north of Horton, is a National Nature Reserve, easily reached by a short walk from the road end near High Birkwith Farm (if you come by car watch where you leave it, do not block the field gates). Follow the green lane to Old Ing Farm and join the Pennine Way which, in about a mile, passes above Ling Gill ravine. At Ling Gill Bridge, which was built in the sixteenth century, a tablet refers to its repair in 1765 'at the charge of the whole of West Riding'.

A delightful feature of the dales and something of which walkers can make full use are the 'green roads'. These are ancient trackways, often dating from monastic times, which may be traced for miles across open country. They were used originally to connect outlying sheep areas with the parent monasteries and later were used as drove roads when cattle and sheep were walked south from as far away as the Scottish Highlands to the industrial markets of the south. The roads, sometimes unwalled, always follow the easiest gradients and best grazing to feed driven animals, or the pack-horses which carried the commerce of developing industry, before the advent of steam. One such road is the track from Feizor which crosses the Ribble below Stainforth and then climbs out towards Malham before continuing as Mastiles Lane into Wharfedale. Around Horton, Moor Head, Long Lane, Horton Scar Lane, Birkwith Moor Lane and the Sell Gill Lane are all ancient green roads.

From Stainforth to Ribblehead the vast depth of limestone is riddled with water-worn features in the form of potholes and caves. This is the realm of the specialist for whom the excitement and danger of exploring the unknown is ever present. There are no show caves in Upper Ribblesdale, but for those skilled in the arts of cave exploration another world opens up beneath your feet. Even now there are long distance routes being discovered in linked cave systems which only a few years ago were just theories. Nowadays access to the larger cave systems is controlled by a central body, so membership of a recognised club is essential, but most welcome beginners to the sport. Even though potholing is a fascinating sport it is dangerous for the uninitiated. None of the caves and potholes in the area are safe to enter unless you are either proficient or guided by someone suitably qualified, but the following can be admired from the surface: Hull Pot and Hunt Pot on the slopes of Penyghent above Scar Lane and Sell Gill Holes to the side of the Pennine Way path north of Horton.

Of all the potholes in the area, **Alum Pot** is perhaps the most picturesque. The hole is on the lower slopes of Simon Fell to the west of Selside, sheltered amongst trees with Alum Pot Beck falling with a frightening 200ft-plunge into its depths. Another stream enters beneath the surface from Long Churn to the north-west. Water entering Alum Pot does not drain directly into the Ribble but passes beneath it to feed Turn Dub on its far bank. Turn Dub is the tiny pond between the river and the larger Newhouses Tarn above the word 'River' on the OS map. Alum Pot can be reached by an easy path from Selside and Northcote Farm and this walk (a mile, half an hour) can be extended to take in the rest of the cave system connected with Alum Pot. A small charge is made at Northcote Farm for use of the private path.

At **Ribblehead** where the magnificent sweep of its railway viaduct spans the dark moorland, an interesting introduction to the different varieties of caves and limestone crags of the area can be made by wandering along the cart track (4$\frac{1}{2}$ miles, 2 hours) from the Ribblehead Inn. Just before the tracks go under the viaduct, turn right across open moorlands and aim for the limestone pavement above Runscar Scar: here you should pass at least ten assorted caves. There is no right-of-way across the limestone pavement, but it is a well used route.

Thorns Gill to the south-west of Gearstones on the B6255 road is a shallow ravine filled by Gayle Beck, the most northerly feeder for the Ribble where moisture loving semi-alpine plants bloom in profu-sion. Gearstones was once a drover's inn and the road, now partly followed by the B6255 and the Dales' Way footpath was originally Roman.

It is not often that man-made objects can improve the face of nature, but one of the few exceptions is surely the graceful span of twenty-four arches which make up the **Ribblehead Viaduct**. Built in 5 years around 1876 by hundreds of navvies who lived in a primitive camp at Batty Green near the Ribblehead Inn, the viaduct is an important link on the Settle to Carlisle railway. Tales of disease and horrific accidents abound in the making of the viaduct and Blea Moor Tunnel just to its north. The tunnel took 4 years to complete and the work was done by candlelight (the bill for candles alone was £50 per month). No one knows how many men died in making the line for they mostly lie in unmarked graves at Chapel-le-Dale on the Ingleton road. A plaque in Chapel-le-Dale Church commemorates these unknown heroes, but their true memorial is in the Settle to Carlisle line which runs through some of Britain's grandest scenery.

PLACES TO VISIT IN AND AROUND SETTLE AND RIBBLEHEAD

Ebbing and Flowing Well
Buckhaw Brow, on A65 1 mile
north-west of Settle
By the roadside, about half way
up the hill. When working the
well empties itself without
warning and then, just as
mysteriously, refills.

Horton Scar Lane
Horton-in-Ribblesdale
A typical example of green road
and ancient trackway still in
regular use by local farmers and
walkers. Connects Horton-in-
Ribblesdale with Halton Gill in
Littondale.

Penyghent
Dramatic mountain, 2 miles
north-east of Horton-in-Ribblesdale.

Ribblehead Viaduct
6 miles north-east of Ingleton
Opened in 1876 it carries the
Settle to Carlisle railway across
some of the wildest upland
country in England.

Settle
Museum of North Craven Life
Victoria Street
Displays show how man has
made use of the countryside
around Settle since prehistoric
times.

Pig Yard Museum
Castle Hill
Located in a converted eighteenth-century warehouse.
Exhibits of outstanding archaeological items from the Dales,
especially Victoria Cave. Also
remains of hippopotamus, bison,
rhinoceros, hyena and other Ice
Age mammals. Open by ap-
pointment only.

Shambles
Remnants of 'Old Settle', an
interesting cluster of old shops
to one side of the market
square. Ye Olde Naked Man
Café.

Stainforth Bridge and Force
Below Stainforth on B6479
Elegant arched pack-horse
bridge on the ancient highway
between Lancaster and York.
Owned by the National Trust.
Stainforth Force, rushes over
limestone edges into a deep,
black pool and can be reached
by a footpath from the bridge

St Oswald Church
Horton
A delightful dales' church built of
locally-quarried slate and limestone. Lead on its roof was
probably mined locally.

Victoria Cave
2 miles east of Settle on
Attermire Scar
Scene of excavations which
proved that the caves were lived
in from neolithic times to the
Roman occupation.

The Flying Scotsman *on the Settle-Carlisle line near Kirkby Stephen*

A more sedate form of transport: a gipsy caravan en route for Bentham Fair

SELECTED WALKS

Attermire Scar 5 miles • Moderate/Strenuous • $2^3/_4$ hours
The walk starts from Settle, 'capital' of Upper Ribblesdale. Follow the road left of the market place towards Constitution Hill. Bear right along a rough walled lane as far as a stile and turn right. Climb to a clump of trees, turn right along a path signposted to Malham. Cross the grassy hillside, go over two stiles and through a gap in a wall. Turn left to follow a path beneath Attermire Scar and past a series of shallow caves where prehistoric and post-Roman remains were found. Climb up to a metal gate and go left down a well made farm lane. Where the lane is about to join a road, turn left through a small gate to follow a field path along the bottom edge of a mature wood. Go between two sections of woodland and walk down a path into the outskirts of Settle.

Catrigg and Stainforth Force 5 miles • Moderate • $2^1/_4$ hours
Visiting two attractive waterfalls makes this an ideal walk for a hot day. From the roadside car park in Stainforth walk as far as the Craven Heifer Inn, then follow the lane opposite as far as a tiny green surrounding a group of stone cottages. Turn right to climb a walled lane marked 'Unsuitable for Motors'. At a gate marking the top of the lane, climb the stile on the left to go down to Catrigg Force; return to the gate to continue the walk. Cross a stile next to the gate and turn right, uphill across an open field. Cross another stile, turn right as directed by a signpost to Winskill Farm. Do not enter the farmyard, but keep ahead through a gate and downhill on a track signposted to Langcliffe. Climb over a ladder stile on the left and walk downhill through rocky fields, then into a belt of gnarled trees. Go through a small gate and keeping above an old quarry, cross three fields to reach Langcliffe. Bear right at the village green and walk down to the main road. Turn right as far as a railway bridge then turn left down a lane to a group of riverside cottages. Cross the river by a footbridge and turn right, upstream following the riverbank as far as Stainforth Force and its pack-horse bridge. Turn at the bridge and follow the lane to the main road; Stainforth village is $^1/_4$ mile to the right.

A Riverside Walk from Horton-in-Ribblesdale 5 miles • Easy • 2 hours
From the car park, walk to the footbridge and turn right, downstream. Following signposts walk along the riverbank for a little over a mile to a footbridge. Cross the bridge and bear left uphill over a series of fields, crossing boundary walls by their stiles. At the road turn left then right at a barn beside a loop road. Follow the signpost's direction over the fields to Dub Cote Farm. Go down to a minor road and turn right into the outskirts of Horton. Cross the stream by a footbridge on your right

and follow a lane signposted 'Pennine Way' as far as a lane junction. Turn left, downhill into Horton where the car park is to the right, but perhaps more important, the Three Peaks Café is even closer!

A SCENIC CAR DRIVE

The Lower Ribble and Hodder Valleys 50 miles

This pleasant drive is mostly along quiet by-ways and country roads, visiting pretty villages where time stands still in marked contrast to the bustle of nearby industrial Lancashire.

Starting in Whalley at the junction of the A59 and A671 (abbey, restaurants and shops), take the B6246 to Great Mitton and turn left on the B6243 to Longridge. Turn right in the village and climb by a minor road across its fell (scenic view points, picnic places, pub and hang-gliding viewing). Go downhill and turn left at the next cross-roads to drive through Bashall Eaves (Browsholme Hall is on the right) then on to Whitewell (inn). Turn right for Dunsop Bridge (trout farm), where a diversion can be made to the Trough of Bowland and its fells. From Dunsop Bridge take the valley road east to Newton (pub) and join the B6478. Take this road to Slaidburn (interesting church, pub and riverside picnic area); continue across Stephen Moor to a road junction short of Wigglesworth (pub). Turn right for Bolton-by-Bowland (interesting church, cafés) and on to Sawley (ruined abbey, riverside restaurant). Do not join the main A59, but bear right in Sawley for Grindleton and Waddington (pubs, cafés, riverside strolling). At Waddington turn left for Clitheroe (shops, market, castle, etc), then join the A59 for the return to Whalley.

2
THE LUNE VALLEY

Some of the most attractive yet least-known countryside of northern England lies between the Yorkshire Dales and the Lake District. The most popular part of this region is around Ingleton and yet not far away from it is an area of equally rewarding country with quiet villages and secluded side valleys which run through Kirkby Lonsdale and Sedbergh. With the Howgill Fells in the north, this is almost unknown territory.

The Lune Valley separates the Dales from the Lakes, yet its river owes allegiance to neither and has a character of its own. Only around its south-eastern tributaries is limestone found, the result of the North Craven Fault. Northwards, shales and a few gritstones predominate all the way to and including the Howgills. It is these fells which feature strongly in the birth of the Lune. The river starts its life as a number of becks flowing northwards from the north-east flanks of the Howgills. The infant Lune then flows west and south to be joined by the Rawthey below Sedbergh. The river bounds three sides of the Howgills before flowing south-west into Morecambe Bay.

Return momentarily to the Ribblehead Viaduct and look through its arches west towards the B6255 Hawes-Ingleton road. The view on the left is of Ingleborough and to the right the vast bulk of Whernside rears menacingly above Blea Moor. The high country on either side of the road between Ribblehead as far as Chapel-le-Dale is flat, but suddenly the road begins to switch-back and the most distinctive features in the landscape are the tiered limestone cliffs of Raven Scar on the left beneath Ingleborough and on the right, Twistleton Scars buttressing the south-west slopes of Whernside.

The squat little church with its poignant memorial to the men who

The M6 running through part of Lune Gorge

died building the Settle to Carlisle railway gives the scattered hamlet of **Chapel-le-Dale** its name, and was once the 'Chapel of Ease' for nearby Ingleton. Tree shrouded Hurtle Pot in the stream above the church, is supposed to be haunted by a boggart; no doubt a story put about by revellers returning from an evening at the Hill Inn on the nearby Ingleton road.

As you travel down the road towards Ingleton look up to the left where bare bones of the mountain known as scars are still exposed almost as they were after the last Ice Age. Soil build-up on limestone is very sparse and the level strata allows acidic rain water to erode deep fisures and crevices into the flat limestone pavements. Due to the slippery surface of the limestone pavements, especially in wet weather, walking can be a hazardous undertaking to the unwary.

Beneath Raven Scar and close by the road is **White Scar Cave** which is open to the public. Good illumination enhances the beauties of its varied rock formations, stalactites and stalagmites and spectacular waterfalls. Wide footpaths with easy gradients make this cave suitable for wheelchairs.

Ingleton is a busy and popular tourist centre, which originated as a farming community, but grew into an industrial village working local limestone, slate and coal mining. Water from the River Doe powered cotton and woollen mills. Tourism started in 1849 when the railway arrived and crossed the deep ravine of the Greta by a viaduct which still dominates the town. Man has known Ingleton a long time, the B6255 follows part of the Roman road linking their fort of Bainbridge in Wensleydale with the regional headquarters town of Lancaster. The town has been well favoured with roads since the Keighley-Kendal turnpike, now followed by the A65, was built in 1753. Today's tourists bring a good income to the town whether they stay for only a quick cup of tea, or overnight at one of the many bed and breakfast houses, the Youth Hostel or one of the excellent hotels and pubs. Ingleton has a very good open-air heated swimming pool and fine community centre.

Ingleton's narrow winding streets radiate from an ancient market place. Even though the church is a Victorian edition to the town, it was built on much older foundations if the exquisite Norman font is anything to go by. Winding Bell Horse Gate descends in steep twists to the River Greta where the cottages of textile workers once employed in mills powered by the river, fit neatly into the scene. In 1884 influential townspeople formed an 'Improvement Association' to develop Ingleton's tourist potential by building connecting footpaths through the narrow glens of the Doe and Twiss. The 'Falls' Walk' ($4^1/_2$ miles, 3 hours charge and car park) as it is generally known, has become one of Ingleton's best known features.

Before moving northwards to the source of the Lune first explore its southern tributary, the **Wenning**. The river drains the southern slopes of Ingleborough, and west of the A65 flows through almost unknown countryside. Collecting waters from tributaries running north from the Bowland Fells, the Wenning follows a gentle course to its confluence with the Lune near Hornby, giving little hint of its potential strength in times of flood. The old A65 road from Ingleton to Clapham more or less follows the line of the North Craven Fault where limestone sits firmly on top of slate. Water sinks through limestone, but not through slate. Travel slowly along this back road and the division between the two types of rock soon becomes clear; to the north of the road what little surface water there is frequently disappears underground, only to reappear on lower slopes to the south of the old road. Farmer's benefit from this by grazing cattle on the more fertile lower fields and running sheep on the drier open fells.

The distinctively tiered bulk of Ingleborough gives clues to the eye

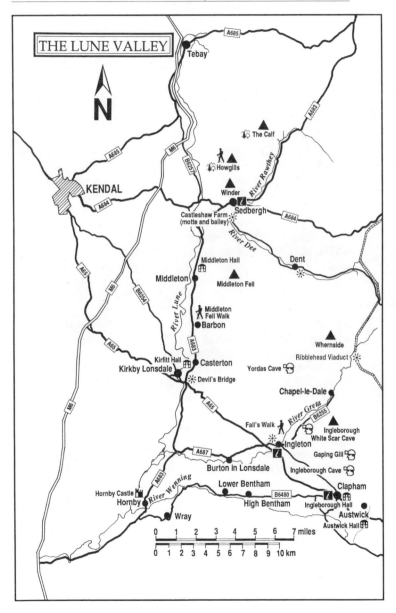

of the trained geologist to whom each layer indicates a separate feature unique in itself. To the observant walker who relates contours and names on a map, the lines of potholes and disappearing streams on a flat band almost encircling Ingleborough near the 1,450ft contour indicate porous rocks, while the complex of streams and the 'moss' north of Clapdale Wood speak of impervious rock layers. The bones of Ingleborough make themselves evident on the line of ascent from Ingleton. The town stands on slate and immediately above it there is a 600ft layer of limestone which provides the easiest walking of the climb with gentle gradients and soft grass underfoot up to about 1,500ft. Above Quaking Pot a 1,000ft band of shales and sandstone which have eroded more easily than the harder limestones lower down the mountain show up by the steepening angle of the path. Later, harder and less eroded shales give way to a final escarpment of millstone grit 100ft thick.

The summit of **Ingleborough** is a fascinating place to the archaeologist, but even an untrained eye will notice the regularly shaped piles of stones scattered around the summit plateau. The first pile seen on the left at the top of the last and steepest part of the climb from Ingleton are the remains of a tower built in 1830 by a local mill owner. Only the curved stones of its base remain to indicate its size. Beyond are two modern features, the triangulation point and a shelter seat built to give protection from all wind directions. A viewpoint indicator sited at the crossing of the shelter walls gives the names of all the major landmarks of the superb panorama visible on a clear day.

Towards the eastern edge of the plateau are the remains of at least six prehistoric hut circles. Beyond them is a ruined wall, said to be Roman, but attributed by others to an ancient tribe known as the Venutians who were besieged here by the Romans. Who built the huts and for what purpose on this waterless but easily defended point, is not known for certain. If the wall is Roman, then quite possibly Ingleborough was used as a signal station, making full use of the fact that it can be seen over a great distance from Cumbria and well down into Lancashire. Beacon fires have blazed on the summit of Ingleborough as warning signals, or in celebration of great occasions in the past.

South from the summit and away down the shales of Little Ingleborough the return to limestone is marked dramatically by the most famous of all potholes — **Gaping Gill**, 360ft deep with a waterfall dropping into a chamber high enough to contain York

PLACES TO VISIT IN AND AROUND INGLETON AND CLAPHAM

Clapham

On A65, 6 miles north-west of Settle

Charming village on the Leeds-Kendal turnpike, now designated as a Conservation Area. Yorkshire Dales National Park Information Centre in centre of village.

Clapdale Wood

$1/_2$ mile north of Clapham

Landscaped wood laid out by the Farrer family of Ingleborough Hall. Many shrubs and plants of Himalayan origin planted by Reginald Farrer (1880-1920), an internationally famous authority on alpine plants. Nature trail within the woods. Small toll charge.

Gaping Gill

3 miles north-west of Clapham

Impressive pothole with a vertical drop of 360ft. Local caving clubs erect a winch-borne chair on spring and August Bank Holidays.

Ingleborough

$3^1/_2$ miles east of Ingleton

A straightforward climb, but only in fine weather. Interesting archaeological remains on the summit. Fine view point.

Ingleborough Cave

$1^1/_2$ miles north of Clapham

Show cave, easily accessible by footpath through Clapdale Wood.

Ingleton

Off A65, 17 miles from M6 junction 34

South-western gateway to the Yorkshire Dales. Popular tourist village with several inns and restaurants. Heated open-air swimming pool.

Norber Boulders

1 mile north-east of Clapham

Erratic Silurian slate boulders left by retreating ice on the 12-15in high pedestals of limestone.

Falls' Walk

A delightful walk through wooded glens follows the River Twiss upstream and Doe downstream, passing waterfalls of breathtaking beauty.

White Scar Cave

1 mile north-east of Ingleton on B6255

Show cave accessible by road. Car parking. Limited wheelchair access.

Minster. The true grandeur is all underground, for at ground level there is just a slippery sided crater surrounded by well worn tracks where Fell Beck disappears. The clue to the subterranean dangers is only given by the flimsy sheep fence around the steepest part of its perimeter. At spring and August Bank Holiday periods caving groups divert the stream and erect a chair and winch which all may use. No charge is usually made for the descent, but the return journey must be paid for! Anyone contemplating the trip must be prepared to get wet and a bit muddy, but otherwise for the really adventurous this can be quite an exhilarating trip. If contemplating a trip down Gaping Gill pothole, make enquiries beforehand in Clapham and try to learn what is entailed. Safety helmets and lamps might be supplied, but to be on the safe side try to provide these for yourself as well as protective equipment which you will not mind getting muddy — in any case take a change of warm dry clothing. It will be cold and wet underground and no matter what the weather is like on the surface, a warm drink will be welcome on your return to daylight!

Cave explorers, including divers, have attempted to open up routes between Gaping Gill and Ingleborough Cave by working in both directions; surveys show that they have reached the line of Trow Gill from both ends, but as yet the few vital yards has eluded all attempts to make the through journey. **Ingleborough Cave** (also known as Clapham Cave) towards the head of Clapdale Wood is open to the public and is one of the oldest show caves in the Pennines still only reached by footpath from Clapham. It was made accessible when a wall of limestone which had held back an underground lake was demolished by use of explosives in 1837.

Downstream from the cave the path enters an area of peaceful woodland; this is **Clapdale Wood**, part of the Ingleborough estate. Although privately owned, the public are allowed to walk along its well maintained footpaths, hence the need to pay a small toll at the end. Little of the woodland is natural, having been improved by successive plantings. Bamboo clumps together with Chinese and Himalayan rhododendrons and azaleas flourish in sheltered dells. Every spring daffodils and other early plants bloom in profusion in sunny spots, making the woodland walk a delightful experience. The stone grotto and lake are additional man-made features.

Ingleborough Hall and its estate, together with much of the village of Clapham, was owned by the Farrer family of whom Reginald Farrer (1880-1920) was probably the best known. Farrer was the father of alpine flower collecting and became a great authority on the subject. He travelled widely in mountainous regions of the Far East in search of flowers and shrubs, some of which can be seen today in Clapdale Wood. The story is told of Farrer returning from expeditions in the Himalayas and refusing to greet his family until he had seen his specimen plants safely potted and tended. The **Reginald Farrer Trail** within the woods as far as Trow Gill is named in his memory. A brochure describing the trail is usually available from the National Park Centre in Clapham and Michael Faraday (1791-1867), pioneer of electricity, also had close links with Clapham as his father was the village blacksmith.

Now that the busy A65 by-passes **Clapham**, the village retains a tranquil atmosphere despite its well deserved popularity. The useful National Park Information Centre next to the car park makes an ideal starting point for a day out in the Clapham area. This is the home of the *Dalesman* magazine, the most widely read regional publication in Britain. St James' Church set amongst trees above Clapham Beck is mostly a Victorian rebuilding on a much older foundation.

Two miles east of Clapham, just off the A65, the village of **Austwick** was settled first by the Norsemen who named it their 'eastern settlement'. It had a market once, but lost it to Clapham; only a restored market cross is left from this time. This is a quiet, gentle village with many attractive old houses, the hall belonging once to the Ingilbys, an important local family.

During the last Ice Age a glacier which filled nearby Crummack Dale above Austwick, deposited a number of large boulders of Silurian rock on the surface limestone. Subsequent weathering of the surrounding softer limestone has left some of these boulders perched on top of small white pedestals. These are the **Norber Boulders**, or erratics to give them their correct geological term. The boulders are above Nappa Scars and can be reached by a sign-posted path (4 miles, 2 hours) starting at a gate close by the crossing of Thwaite Lane and Crummack Lane. The gate is on the Clapham side of the crossroads. This path continues up on to Norber Hill passing the perched boulders on the way. The source of the boulders can be seen on the right, three fields away towards Crummack Farm.

South and west of the A65 marl, a clay made from ground limestone during the Ice Age makes the excellent pasture on either side of the River Wenning. Here it flows through the small towns of **High** and **Lower Bentham** to the Lune (Lonsdale). The twin villages

Clapham village

The village of Austwick (top)

Clapham Church (right)

are more-or-less merged into one, a far cry from the days when this 'home on the common' first held a market. Textile mills were developed in the last century, but now Angus Fire/Armour Limited provide most of the employment in the area. The church of St John the Baptist at Lower Bentham is mentioned in the *Domesday Book*, the only one in the western dales. Built in the Perpendicular style the delicately carved marble and Caen stone reredos is its finest feature. The fells to the south are part of the Forest of Bowland, here crossed by a quiet moorland road which leads to Slaidburn and the Ribble. Several of the short field paths west of Lower Bentham on the south side of the river, can easily be linked up to make a pleasant summer's afternoon walk (2 to 3 miles, 1½ hours) down to Wennington and back.

The village of **Wray** at the junction of the Rivers Hindburn and Roeburn was almost destroyed when a cloudburst high up in Roeburndale caused the river to leave its banks. Wray was once a place of thriving industry with basket weaving and clog making. Silk top hats were also made here at one time. On a rise between the Hindburn and the deepening Lune stands **Hornby** and its castle. Built soon after the Norman Conquest the castle was owned by generations of Neville and Stanley families until 1643, when it was captured by Colonel Ralph Assheton, commander of parliamentary troops in North Lancashire. For some unknown reason the castle was not destroyed or 'slighted' as was normal in such cases and it remained a home for many years. The present building was erected by Edmund Sharpe who was Mayor of Lancaster in 1848.

Leaving the Wenning to return temporarily to the Greta, **Burton in Lonsdale** on the A687 (Morecambe branch of the A65), sits high above the river. It once held a weekly market, with a charter dating from 1274 and was famous for a special kind of black potware and firebricks, but the last kiln cooled in 1930.

The Craven Faults and surface limestone gradually disappear to the north of Ingleton. **Barbon Fell** is to the east of Casterton where the tell-tale signs on the map still show potholes and caves. This is still the territory of the speleologist or cave explorer, but the walker can enjoy Kingsdale and Leck Dale and the intervening fells.

From Thornton in Lonsdale to the north-west of Ingleton a minor road climbs through Kingsdale into Dentdale. Streams flowing into its beck drain the facing slopes of two whaleback mountains; to the east is Whernside, Yorkshire's highest point and a well used feature of the 'Three Peaks Walk', and across the valley is strangely named Gragareth with its rugged cairns known as the 'Three Men of Gragareth'.

On the north-west side of Kingsdale the level moorland above **Keld Heads Scar** offers a whole series of interesting stones, pot-holes and caverns. One, **Yordas Cave**, was once a showplace, now abandoned and hidden from sight inside a small wood (SD705791). If you take a good torch and do not do anything foolhardy, once inside it is possible to explore this cave. The entrance still retains its steps and the best feature of the cave is the Chapter House, a circular chamber with an attractive slender waterfall. The cave floods after heavy rain and can be very muddy afterwards. The best way to get to Yordas Cave and all the other limestone features above Keld Heads Scar is either to walk up from Ingleton (6 miles, 3 hours) or leave a car tidily parked on the Dent-Ingleton road somewhere in the vicinity of Twistleton Lane. Look for an old lime kiln and aim for the OS column above Tow Scar. A hundred yards or so to the right is the Cheese Press Stone — an unusually smooth faced limestone boulder.

Above Keld Heads Scar which overlooks the Kingsdale road there is a delightful grassy track known as Turbary Road; unfortu-nately not a right-of-way. This track was originally made to ease the way for horse drawn sledges bringing peat down from Turbary Pasture.

The next tributary dale flowing into the River Lune is that of **Leck Beck** which in its upper reaches forms the boundary between Lancashire and Cumbria. Leck Beck drains the great sweep of Barbon Fells from Gragareth through Great Coum to Casterton Fell.

The last trace of the limestone before it finally disappears under-ground, shows up dramatically in the lower reaches of **Ease Gill**. Its rock formations and sinks can be explored in a short but interesting walk ($3^1/_2$ miles, 2 hours) south from Bullpot Farm at the end of a 3- mile tarred road from Casterton. While the fell road from Casterton is a public road, parking is limited, so please take care not to block access to farm property if using a car. One word of warning in conclusion — Ease Gill disappears beneath the ground through a system of sinks and in a period of heavy rain they cannot take the huge volume of water flooding down from the cirque of fells above. Once the sinks fill they overflow and the normally dry river bed becomes a torrent, often without warning.

Casterton Fell can be climbed in a short walk (2 miles, an hour) from Fell Road, either by the lane which starts at SD641793 on the

OS map or more or less directly from the other end of the same lane close by Gale Garth Farm. Neither route actually crosses the summit, but it is reached by a short deviation about the 1,300ft contour line.

The village of **Casterton** is an ancient place surrounded by standing stones and circles. Its development as a wool centre in the Middle Ages led to the building of a walk mill where wool cloth was felted, or fulled, by foot in the soft waters of a side stream to the Lune. The Brontë sisters attended a clergy daughter's school here and before that King Henry VIII stayed nearby at Kirfitt Hall when he was courting Catherine Parr of Kendal Castle. The house is supposed to be haunted by the headless Anne Boleyn ever searching for her fickle husband and king.

Kirkby Lonsdale is on the west bank of the Lune below Casterton. The A65 crosses the river on a modern bridge, but upstream is an earlier structure known as the **Devil's Bridge** — a graceful triple arched span of unknown age, but certainly recorded in 1275 when funds were found for its repair. The story which connects it to the Devil is that an old lady wishing to cross the Lune found the ford deep under water. The Devil appeared and offered to build a bridge on condition that the first living creature to cross it would belong to him. She thwarted him by throwing a bun across the bridge and a small dog chased it to become the first across.

Kirkby Lonsdale is 'Cherkaby Lownesdale' in the *Domesday Book* (Kirkby means Church Town). Its church is certainly of Norman origin, but is probably built on earlier foundations. A charter granted

in 1272 to hold fairs and markets was disputed, but a Thursday market has been held regularly since 1335. During the 1715 rising, Jacobite soldiers assembled round the market cross. An afternoon of strolling round Kirkby Lonsdale and the nearby

Stalactites and stalagmites in one of the many potholes on Casterton Fell — the exclusive domain of the well-equipped potholer

The Sedgwick memorial, Dent

river downstream towards Devil's Bridge can make a rewarding experience for both first-time and regular visitors alike. At one time an artificial water course along Market Street worked seven water-wheels, providing power for industries which ranged from bone-crushing to snuff-making.

Steep sided **Barbondale** used by a narrow side road into Dentdale is softened in its lower reaches by woodland which surrounds turreted Barbon Manor. **Barbon** is an old place and comfortably by-passed by the modern A683 from Sedbergh which here follows more or less the line of a Roman road. At High Beckford a little over a mile away to the south-west, the neat symmetrical lines of a pack-horse bridge span **Barbon Beck**. Pleasant waterside paths radiate from Barbon ranging up and down its beck and through surrounding fields, but a greater challenge is the circuit of Middleton Fell, a triangle of rarely visited fells between Barbondale, the Lune Valley and Dentdale. This is also a walk for botanists who will find many rare sub-alpine plants and orchids growing on the open moorland.

The **Middleton Fell Walk** ($2^1/_2$ miles, 4 hours) starts from the centre of Barbon village by the bridge and follows Barbon Beck for about a quarter mile upstream then a left turn through Barbon Manor Park makes for Eskholme Farm. Turn right at the farm and climb steeply up Eskholme Pike, across Thorn Moor to Castle Knott. On to Calf Top (the highest point of the walk at 1,999ft), to Green Maws then swing round across Long Bank where an improving track leads eventually to Fellside Farm and the main road. The Ribble Bus company operate a service along this road and careful planning will help the tired walker to use it for a return to base. Alternatives are to arrange for a co-operative driver to pick you up, or walk back along the field path (5 miles, 2 hours) which visits practically all the farms to the east of the A683. **Middleton Fell** takes its name from a group of farms rather than any particular village. Middleton Hall was never fortified and as a result suffered severe damage during the Civil War when Cromwell's troops broke through the west wall of the courtyard.

Below Sedbergh two northerly and major side rivers join before being in their turn swallowed by the Lune, which joins the Dee and Rawthey at right angles. The more southerly of these twosided dales, the Dee, cuts deep into the confines of the National Park. Limestone has by now completely disappeared beneath the overlying shales and gritstones of the fells — outliers of both the Yorkshire Dales and the Lakes. These fells and their dales have a character all of their own.

Norsemen settled in Dentdale and **Dent** township is a quaint spot with narrow winding streets still paved by ancient cobbles, a feature cleverly repeated in the National Park scenic car park and picnic site at the west end of the village. A few years ago an attempt by the highway authority to tar the cobbled streets of Dent was met with strong opposition from the locals. Its famous son Adam Sedgwick (1785-1873), the father of modern geology, is commemorated by a large granite slab in the main street. During the seventeenth and eighteenth centuries hand-knitting became a major industry in Dent and surrounding villages, the special needles and the dagger-like sheaths used by the knitters have since become treasured antiques. Spinning galleries where yarn for the knitters was spun are important features of many of the colour-washed stone cottages. Their prodigious production once earned the villagers the title 'Terrible Knitters of Dent', a cottage industry which survived well into the nineteenth century. A distinctive sign outside the Sun Inn smiles across the cobbled space to Dent's twelfth-century St Andrew's Church. Jacobean box-pews and brass memorials to local families including the Sedgwicks feature inside, but it is the view from the river bridge of the mound-topped church and the huddled stone cottages of Dent which will make the lasting impression.

An ancient track, the **Old Craven Way**, again links Dent with Ingleton. Climbing out of Dent as a hill road to the east of Deepdale, the track continues across the broad back of Whernside as a well-marked path before dropping down to the Settle to Carlisle line above Blea Moor tunnel. From the railway it swings to the south and makes for Chapel-le-Dale where it joins the B6255, once a Roman road, down to Ingleton.

High up Dentdale, Deeside House Youth Hostel was once a shooting lodge owned by Lord Henry Bentinck. Arten Gill Viaduct above Deeside House has piers which go 50ft into the ground to find solid rock. Black 'Dent Marble' can still be found in this area; once popular in Victorian times, the marble was cut and polished from a dark limestone to show its fossils which stand out clear and white in outline.

Linked to Dentdale by railway and a winding road, **Garsdale** has no village or township, but dotted the length of the dale are farms which originated as Norse settlements, identified in their names; Knudsman Ing, Thursgill, Dandra Garth, Birkrigg and Grisedale are good examples. At the bottom of Garsdale is **Longstone Fell**, an unenclosed area of moorland popular as a picnic spot, which can be reached by a path (2 miles, 1 hour) from Low Branthwaite Farm to the south of the A684. The view of the Howgills opposite is quite superb and worth the effort of the short climb.

Draining the huge mass of the Howgills to the north, the River Rawthey soon becomes a moderately sized stream as it flows away from the National Park to link with the Lune below Brigflatts.

The district surrounding Sedbergh has strong Quaker associations, George Fox the founder of this gentle faith preached throughout the dales. The Society of Friends have their meeting house in the former industrial community of Brigflatts; the tranquil house dating from 1675, still with many of its original furnishings and the oldest meeting house in the north of England, is approached down a signposted side road off the A683 about a mile downstream from Sedbergh.

Sedbergh was named by the Norsemen as 'Setberg' or 'Flat Topped Hill'. The hill or hills are the Howgills towering as a backcloth to this town of 2,500 inhabitants, the largest within the Yorkshire

A view from Crook of Lune to Howgill Fells

Dales National Park. The Howgills, green rounded and smooth sloped, have a unique appeal and reward the traveller who takes the time to explore their quiet solitudes. This is an unspoilt area and except in Sedbergh and nearby villages accommodation is hard to find, but when found, the standard is excellent.

The Howgills and in particular one special hill, Winder, have been well known to generations of boys of Sedbergh School. The school was founded in 1525 by Roger Lupton, originally a chantry school linked to St John's College, Cambridge. In 1552 it became a free grammar school and gradually over the centuries developed into the nationally renowned public school of today.

Sedbergh has been a market town since 1251; nowadays markets are held every Wednesday on the Joss Lane car park and there is also a large weekly livestock market on the Kendal road. Never growing much in size, it was also another centre for hand-knitting, like Dent. Between them the two townships in the heyday of hand-knitting sent over 800 pairs of stockings to market each week. During the eighteenth century some industrial growth came to Sedbergh first through wool and then cotton. Behind the main street are houses some of which have spinning galleries, but all that remains of this industry can be seen in the gallery in Railton's Yard.

Sedbergh can trace its history to Norman times, but all that is left from their occupation of this part of the dales are the mounds of a motte and bailey fortification near Castleshaw Farm to the north-east of the town centre and the parish church which dates from this time.

The **Howgills** and Lune Gorge, offer the most dramatic scenery seen anywhere along the M6 with a broad, inverted triangle in plan, and Sedbergh at the southern apex. Streams radiating from the central point of Brant Fell are tributaries of the Lune. Based on Silurian rock which shows itself only at Black Force and Cautley Crag, the hills have few walls and fewer landmarks. In mist the Howgills can be dangerous as their ridges and high valleys have a nasty habit of merging and turning to mislead the unwary. The hills are the haunt of buzzards and delightful wild ponies. In the deeply cut ravines and secluded valleys many interesting flowers grow in profusion. The Howgills are hills with distant views, to the west is the exciting panorama of the high tops of the Lake District and south-east the rolling moors and hills of the mid-Pennines. Penyghent, Whernside and Ingleborough can be seen from The Calf, the highest point in the Howgills. Man has had little effect on these fells, using them as common land shared by farms around their base to graze sheep and ponies. A drove road came from the north through Bowderdale and crossed the high tops to reach the Rawthey Valley, but otherwise the few fell-crossing paths are comparatively recent. Hill walkers who want to explore the Howgills must plan their routes carefully, for distances are long on these hills. A turning down the wrong valley can result in a long road walk back to base. Careful and accurate map reading is an essential skill on these high fells. Most visitors will probably want to stay in or around Sedbergh and certainly the highest summits can be climbed from there. Anyone wishing to explore the remoter parts must arrange transport at the end of the day if doing a long trek across the high tops. One of the finest expeditions in the Howgills (7 miles, 4 hours) starts at the Cross Keys Hotel on the A683, about 5 miles north-east of Sedbergh. A stream starting its life on The Calf negotiates a band of steep shaley crags in the single leap of Cautley Spout. A signposted path climbs Cautley Beck from the hotel to reach the waterfall, beyond it open fells radiate in all directions from the complex of ridges of Brant Fell. The Cross Keys has a quotation by William Blake over its entrance which describes the atmosphere of these fells:

> 'Great things are done when men and mountains meet.
> These are not done by jostling in the street.'

Moving west from Sedbergh back into the Lune Valley where its narrow gorge is used by the London to Glasgow railway line and also the M6, there are links with travel of much earlier times. Moving back in time, the first item is a dismantled railway which ran from Clapham through the Lune Valley, joining the main line at Lowgill at the southern end of Lune Gorge. Half a mile downstream of this point the Crook of Lune is spanned by a magnificent narrow bridge, once crossed by teams of pack-ponies. North now and further back in time to **Low Borrowbridge** where Romans built a fort to guard the major route north from Ribchester to Penrith. Strategically placed it commanded natural ways south from high country to the north and west.

To complete the examination of the Howgills one must temporarily leave the National Park, which for some strange reason cuts the fells in two, preferring to follow the line of the north-south watershed. The only centre of population on the northern corner of the Howgills is **Tebay**. The village, as distinct from Old Tebay closer to the river, developed with the building of the railway line through the Lune Gap

PLACES TO VISIT IN AND AROUND SEDBERGH

Dent
5 miles south-east of Sedbergh on Hawes road
Small village with narrow winding cobbled streets. Birthplace of Adam Sedgwick, an early geologist.

Howgills
Range of rounded grassy hills to the north of Sedbergh
Excellent walking area for lovers of solitude. Easy walks as far as Cautley Spout Waterfall and Winder Hill. Rest of Howgills range virtually trackless and should only be visited in clear weather.

Kirkby Lonsdale
On A65, 14 miles north-east of M6 junction 34.
Ancient town with many interesting buildings. Artificial water course along Market Street once powered seven waterwheels. Five medieval bridges nearby.

Sedbergh
2 miles east of M6, junction 37
Unspoilt town founded by Norsemen. Mentioned in the *Domesday Book*. Ideal centre for exploring the West Pennine Fells.

Sedgwick Geological Trail
Longstone Common
Lower Garsdale
Meeting point for the geological systems of the Lake District and Pennine Dales. Approx $1\frac{1}{2}$ hours. Leaflet available locally.

and is known locally as 'Railway Town'. The long steep gradient of Shap Fell was too much for most steam locomotives and 'bank' engines were based at Tebay to assist trains over Shap. The site of **Old Tebay** village was at one time the border between England and Scotland. When the Motorway Works Unit was built to serve the M6, it was necessary to remove a huge boulder from Galloper Field. This was the Brandreth Stone and once marked the boundary of two nations. At **Castlehow** there is a motte and bailey, originally defended by wooden palisades in the days of border warfare. The armaments seem to have been sling shot, as a number of iron balls have been found nearby. Old Tebay had its witch, Mary Baines, who predicted horseless carriages!

The north side of the Howgills is the least known part of the whole range of these little-walked fells. Tributaries of the Lune cut deep into its flanks, inviting country for the fell walker who prefers to walk

Cautley Spout Valley, the Howgills

untrodden ground. A long crossing to Sedbergh can be made if transport can be arranged. This walk (11 miles, 6 hours) starts from Bowderdale Farm (NY678046) gains height on West Fell and follows Bowderdale to Bowderdale Head (marked as Hare Shaw on some OS maps). A right turn across The Calf and the path over Calders and Arant How completes the long route to Sedbergh.

Linking the Lune to the Eden Valley, the A685 road from Kendal swings round this northern side of the Howgills, following a low level route as far as possible between Tebay and Kirkby Stephen.

SELECTED WALKS

Ingleton's Waterfalls $4^1/_2$ miles • Moderate/Slippery areas after rain • $2^1/_2$ hours

Probably the most beautiful walk in the Yorkshire Dales, the fact that a small toll is charged does not detract from its interest. Amateur geologists will find evidence of the complex history of the underlying strata of the district; non geologists can follow the short informative guide to the Ingleton Waterfalls Trail produced by the Yorkshire Dales National Park.

From the car park follow the footpath upstream through Swilla Glen, passing Pecca Falls and Thornton Force (snack-bar nearby). Climb out on to the open pasture and cross a footbridge. Turn right along a narrow lane past Twistleton Hall, then by footpath to Beezleys Farm (refreshments). Follow a signposted path downhill into the narrowing valley to pass Beezley and Snow Falls. Where the angle of descent improves a track leads on towards Ingleton Church; the car park is below on the right.

Dentdale 6 miles • Moderate • 4 hours

This walk explores Dentdale upstream from the unspoilt village of Dent. It can be linked to the one-mile Sedgwick Geological Trail, downstream of Danny Bridge. Walk along Dent's cobbled streets, past the church towards Danny Bridge. Do not cross the river, but turn right following a side stream, Dent Beck, as far as a farmhouse. Bear left then right from the farm to reach a gravel path leading up the road at Bridge End. Cross the road and follow a signposted woodland path out to open fields. On sighting a ruined farmhouse, bear left towards the river following stiles marking the way. At a stone barn, go left across a footbridge and walk downstream a little way, then bear right up a leafy lane into a farmyard. Turn right through the yard and along a lane. Turn sharp left at a low stone building and climb a steep bank leading to a stile; cross this and walk towards Rigg End Farm. Cross the access drive and bear left in front of the farm, aiming for a line of trees. Go past the trees, down through open fields and join the lane at a ruined barn. Turn right along the lane then right again at the road. Go past Whernside Manor then left along a footpath signposted to Tommy Bridge; cross the bridge and turn left, downstream. Right at a sign pointing to a shady path, then left on reaching the valley road. Follow the road as far as Danny Bridge to link with the geological trail, otherwise continue uphill into Dent village.

Winder Hill $4^1/_2$ miles • Strenuous • 3 hours

To climb this attractive little hill overlooking Sedbergh, walk along High Street, past the church then turn right into Howgill Lane, following it as far as the 30mph limit. Turn right along a farm lane signposted 'To the Fell'. Go half right through Lockbank farmyard, then left by a grassy path alongside a boundary wall and past a pine wood. Turn right steeply uphill to climb across Winder's summit, go down to a broad col and turn right on a well defined path leading back to Lockbank Farm. Do not enter the farmyard, but turn left away from the farm, following the boundary wall as far as a kissing gate. Turn right and go through the gate and walk downhill beside a shaley gorge. Join a farm lane, following it into the outskirts of Sedbergh; the church and central car park are on the right as you enter the town.

A SCENIC CAR DRIVE

The Lune Valley and its Side Dales 84 miles

From Ingleton take the A65 as far as Kirkby Lonsdale (cafés, shops), then right along the A683 to Sedbergh (pubs, cafés, information centre, market — Wednesday). Follow a narrow unclassified road north-westwards into the Lune Gorge; cross the river by the ancient Crook of Lune Bridge, then right on the A685 through Tebay to Ravenstonedale (inn). Follow a short unclassified road to the right through the dale up to the A683 and turn right again. Follow this road, completing the circuit of the Howgill Fells, into Sedbergh. Left along Dentdale by an unclassified road, Dent village is on the south side of the dale (shops, cafés, pubs, nature trail). Climb out beyond the dale head to join the B6255, turn right continuing ahead at the T-junction near Ribblehead (inn and good views of the viaduct, also the Hill Inn at Chapel-le-Dale). Downhill with good views of Ingleborough on your left, past White Scar Cave (show cave with limited access to wheel-chairs), back to Ingleton (shops, cafés, pubs, nature trail).

3
THE NORTH PENNINES

T he following section is devoted to the headwaters of the South
Tyne, the Allendales, Derwent, Weardale, Teesdale and the
Eden. With the exception of the latter's main valley, all the upper parts
of these dales have been designated as the North Pennines Area of
Outstanding Natural Beauty. Its boundary stretches south from the
Tyne Gap to link with the Yorkshire Dales National Park beyond
Stainmore. Roughly an inverted triangle in shape, the almost totally
wilderness area, interspersed with ancient mining relics extends
from the foot of the Cross Fell watershed in the west, with heather
moors above the Derwent Valley and Weardale as its eastern
boundary. Not quite warranting the status of a National Park, never-
theless this unspoilt, sparsely populated region enjoys many of the
protections given to a National Park. The Eden Valley, although
mainly outside the bounds of this special area, is included in this
section of the guide as a logical progression between the Yorkshire
Dales and those of the North Pennines.

THE UPPER EDEN VALLEY
The group of wild fells east of the Settle to Carlisle railway line, shared
jointly between Yorkshire and Cumbria are the birthplace of three
deep and important dales. One is Garsdale and has already been
mentioned; another is Wensleydale, yet to be described. The third
dale dealt with by this chapter forges its way due north officially
beyond the Yorkshire Dales but linked to them geographically.

The River Eden rises on the high fells of Mallerstang Common
and its upper valley has long been a natural way north and south. Old
drove and pack-horse routes cross the gap beyond the Moor Cock

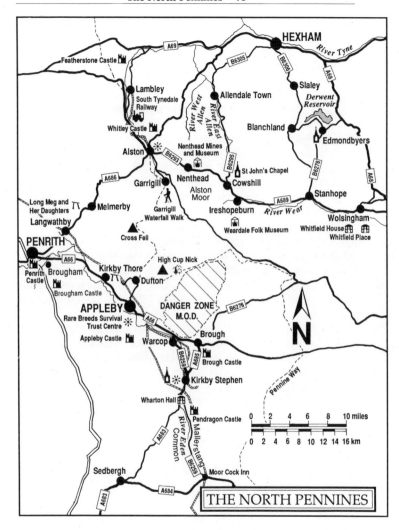

Inn at the junction of the A684 and B6259. Norsemen came this way southwards in their search for land, no doubt following a route used since early man first began to travel through the dales. Trains from Settle climbing over Ribblehead and across the top of Garsdale swoop past Aisgill summit, roar down the steep sides of the Upper

Eden before entering the valley's wider, easier contours as far as Carlisle.

The oldest way into the Eden is by a bridleway known as **The Highway**, which climbs easily with little change in height all the way from Cotter Riggs, in Wensleydale, to enter Westmorland at Hell Gill Bridge, a skilfully contrived arch over a deep limestone ravine. Redoubtable dales traveller Lady Anne Clifford came this way to Pendragon on her way to view her Civil War damaged castles at Brough, Appleby and Brougham.

With the exception of The Highway, the only other defined path in the upper reaches of the Eden crosses the broad col between Little Fell and Wild Boar Fell before dropping down towards Ravenstone-dale. **Wild Boar Fell**, a steep east-facing escarpment is supposed to be where, in the sixteenth century, the last wild boar was killed in England. How true this story is can only be guessed, for there appear to be a number of place names throughout the north of England connected with the wild boar's final demise. The only large wild creatures now are the occasional deer and foxes harried by local farmers. A walk for a clear day (7 miles, 4 hours) would be to follow the path up from Hazel Gill Farm to the col between Little Fell and Wild Boar Fell.

Pendragon Castle sits between the road and the river, well sited to command the way through the Upper Eden, but not much can be recognised now of the sturdy late Norman peel tower. It was burnt by raiding Scots in 1541 and rebuilt to its present but now ruined plan by Lady Anne Clifford in 1660.

Starting from Pendragon an easy walking circuit of lanes ($4^1/_2$ miles, 2 hours) surround nearby Birkett Common, north-west of the castle. These can be taken in any direction, but for the sake of clarity follow the route clockwise towards the railway then over Wharton Fell. At a junction of tracks turn right to eventually recross the railway and then follow a walled lane down to Croop House. Right again along the river back to the start by the castle.

Kirkby Stephen sits at the foot of Mallerstang fells and beyond the Eden meanders north-westwards as a wide fertile valley in marked contrast to its birthplace. Here is the market town for this north-west part of the dales. The church, of almost cathedral-like proportions, has many interesting carvings as well as memorials to the Musgraves and Whartons, owners of Wharton Hall, south of the town. Little remains of the former glories of Wharton, once a fair sized manor house, as most of the original is now in ruins and a farm house occupies the site. If you see parrots flying on a summer's day around Kirkby Stephen, do not be surprised — they are the hobby of a local farmer.

The A66 Scotch Corner to Penrith road across wild Stainmore follows, more or less, the route of a major east-west Roman highway. The importance attached to it can be seen from the number of forts and regularly-spaced signal stations which if not always easy to identify on the ground are clearly marked on the OS map. The wild, high moorland on either side of the road must have been a safe haven for the tribesmen of Cumbria and any Picts who managed to get south of Hadrian's Wall. This was difficult country for military rulers to control and the garrisons must have spent many watchful nights and days on the lookout for fires signalling problems further along the road.

Brough garrisoned the western approaches to Stainmore. The Romans knew it as *Verteræ* and sited their fort to separate the fertile plain of the Eden from the wilderness of the north and east. William Rufus, son of William the Conqueror, built a castle at Brough in 1095 on part of the site of *Verteræ*. It was destroyed by the Scots in 1174 but rebuilt in 1204 and handed to Robert de Vipont, an ancestor of the Cliffords. Eventually their descendant, Lady Anne, came to own it and along with her other northern castles, set about its restoration after the Civil War. The ruined twelfth-century keep and enclosure walls are now maintained by English Heritage.

Unfortunately the Ministry of Defence has an interest in the fells north of Brough and as a result access there presents some problems! Few, if any, public paths enter **Warcop Fell** and the surrounding moors and any exploring must be carried out with an eye open for Range Boundary Warnings. **A red flag signifies that live firing is taking place — on no account should you go beyond a red flag**! The deep gorge of wooded Swindale Beck which flows through Brough cries out for a path, but regrettably there is no public right-of-way alongside its stream. The nearest which one can get to it legally is along the lane through Hillbeck.

Warcop, skirted by the A66, has many old buildings. The hall is Elizabethan and the church is built on even older foundations although somewhat 'improved' during the Victorian craze for restoration. Garlands hanging in the church are relics of a custom of leaving paper flowers in memory of girls who had died unmarried.

Kirkby Stephen

When it was the county town of Westmorland, **Appleby** was the smallest county and assize town in England. In the Middle Ages its population was much greater than today with the town protected by a loop of the Eden on three sides and the castle at its fourth. Appleby developed around a wide high street which rises steeply from the church to a mound topped by a splendid castle. This castle saw many battles in the Middle Ages — captured by the Saxons in 1388 and later sheltering the locals of Appleby from marauding Scots. As with many of the others of this region, Lady Anne Clifford owned Appleby Castle and it was held in the name of King Charles I during the Civil War. In later and more peaceful centuries the castle became a residence and since 1977 has been a centre for the conservation of rare breeds of domestic farm animals. A large collection of wildfowl, pheasants and owls take advantage of the beautiful grounds. A Norman keep, the centre piece of the castle, has a fine display of Roman armour and furniture from medieval times to the seventeenth century. There is also a collection of rare bicycles.

Sleepy for most of the year, Appleby wakes up with a jolt in June with gipsies and travelling people from all over the country gathering for the annual Horse Fair, when semi-wild fell ponies and others are

PLACES TO VISIT IN AND AROUND APPLEBY

Appleby
13 miles south-east of Penrith on A66
Smallest assize and county town in England. Protected by a loop in the River Eden on three sides and a medieval castle on its fourth. In June gipsies gather to attend the Appleby Horse Fair.

Appleby Castle
Rare Breeds Survival Trust Centre
Domestic farm animals together with a large collection of wildfowl, pheasants poultry and owls, some extremely rare. Norman keep. Medieval furniture. Beautifully laid out gardens.

Brough
16 miles north-east of M6, junction 38, at junction of A685 and A66
A town of military importance from Roman times to the Middle Ages, when it guarded the western end of the Stainmore Gap. Brough Castle was built on the site of a Roman fort. The keep is Norman, but was rebuilt several times after attack by the Scots and later by parliamentary troops in the Civil War.

High Cup Valley
5 miles north-east of Appleby
Fine example of a glacial valley. Excellent views west towards Lakeland. Easy walking.

Kirkby Stephen
12 miles north-east of M6 junction 38, on the A685
Pleasant, busy town at the head of the Eden Valley. Ancient market place surrounded by interesting buildings including several fine examples of Georgian architecture. Traces of Norman construction still remain in its parish church.

Long Meg and Her Daughters
2 miles north of Langwathby on A686
Stone group, oval in shape, composed of twenty-seven stones with one outlier known as Long Meg, which has mysterious cup- and-ring markings. Visit during daylight hours.

bought and sold by judges of all grades of horse flesh. Paths up and downstream from Appleby (2 miles, 1 hour) can be followed for a mile or so in either direction, but the return journeys must be along the same track for bridges are few and far between. The main purpose of the paths is to provide anglers with access to the Eden, but they still make for easy and pleasant strolling.

From Appleby Castle the view north and east is of the highest fells of the Pennines. North of High Cup the summits are accessible to the fell walker. The army loses interest immediately before the Pennine Way track from Teesdale to High Cup. North of this point the land east of the high tops forms part of the Moor House Nature Reserve, where free-footed wanderers are not encouraged. Despite all of these annoying restrictions, the huge area of wild fells still left will justify for the hardy fell walker to spend hours of happy wandering.

The Pennine Way comes down to Dufton after crossing some tough country above High Cup Nick and then climbs relentlessly up to its highest point at Cross Fell (2,930ft). Northbound Pennine Wayfarers in Dufton might look despondent, but they can be excused, as they have walked a hard day only to finish south of their starting place of Langdon Beck!

Of all the fell-foot villages nestling beneath the high moors, **Dufton** is by far the prettiest. Its single broad street lined with horse-chestnut trees is at its best in late spring when the trees and cottage gardens are fully awake from their winter's sleep. Nearby Kirkby Thore has a Roman camp (*Bravonicum*), but Dufton on a bright spring or autumn morning beats the lot.

Visitors to Dufton can sample one of the best stretches of the Pennine Way (10 miles, 5 hours) by following the signposted track from Billysbeck Bridge beyond Town Head. This follows a walled lane to open country below Peeping Hill and there is an easy path all the way to High Cup Nick. The Pennine Way continues across the moor to Maize Beck and eventually the Tees, but do not go beyond High Cup this time. The deep 'U' shaped valley beneath High Cup is a classic example of glacial action and the view down the valley, across the vale of Eden and beyond to the Lakeland fells, is just reward for the efforts involved in the climb. The return journey must be by reversing the upward route. On the way down you will notice a slender pillar slightly detached from the main crags of High Cup. This is Nichol's Last where a Dufton cobbler sat and soled and heeled a pair of shoes for a bet. The 80ft high crags lining the edge of High Cup are made of dolerite, a kind of basalt, part of the intrusive Whin Sill which manifests itself throughout the north, from the Tees to Hadrian's Wall and as far east as the Farne Islands.

On the summit of **Dun Fell**, the southern neighbour of Cross Fell, a number of aerials and radomes intrude on an otherwise unspoilt skyline. These are part of a weather and radar station run by the

Ministry of Defence. The service road at 2,780ft is the highest motor road in Britain and can be used by civilian cars to a height of 2,480ft, a factor which could encourage the faint-hearted mountaineer actually to climb a hill! **Cross Fell** itself is the home of a rare British mountain plant, the starry saxifrage — *Saxifraga stellaris* — which flourishes in boggy places around Tees Head. In earlier times Cross Fell was known as Fiends Fell and was believed to be a place of evil. The name Cross Fell comes from the planting of a cross on the summit by St Augustine to drive away those evil forces.

Just outside **Kirkland**, a tiny village beneath Cross Fell, ridges and terraces in fields near Ranbeck Farm are known as the Hanging Walls of Mark Anthony. They are old cultivation terraces probably dating back to the Iron Age. Scars and other hillside features of much later date are the result of man's exploitation of the fells in the search for lead and other minerals.

Lead has attracted man to the Pennine fells and dales since pre-Roman times, through the monastic period when it was much in demand as a roofing material, and for water and gas pipes well into the twentieth century. Its heyday came during the latter part of the last century when the industry became highly organised, especially under the ownership of the London Lead Company, a Quaker led organisation which developed a reputation as an understanding employer. The company realising that lead mining and smelting were unhealthy occupations, encouraged miners to live in smallholdings on the moor edge. Here they had enough land for one or two cattle and a pigsty, as well as grazing rights for a few sheep on the moor. Not only did this part-time open-air activity help keep the miners healthy, but it provided them with an additional income. Miners lived in primitive lodgings known as 'shops', out on the moors for 5 days and went home to their smallholdings at the weekend. Thus the 5-day working week came far earlier than is realised. Leaving home on Monday morning, miners would climb miles out on the moors to their place of work, taking with them enough oatmeal and pork to feed themselves all week. Sleeping communally on straw-filled palliasses, a lead-miners' life was a hard one. The company agent for Westmorland lived at Dufton and for a time it became important as the administrative centre for the area.

Prospecting for lead, as with most other ores, is made by looking at surface deposits, but when these have been worked out it is necessary to go underground. The local method of prospecting was

High Cup Nick on the Pennine Way

simple but violent. A convenient stream would be dammed above the site under investigation and the water let out in one go. This violent rush of water would scour away the surface of the fell, giving the miners a better picture of the underlying rocks. The method was known as 'hushing' and bare hillsides around minor streams are usually the denuded remains of a 'hush' which took place probably during the last century. One example can be seen from the Pennine Way track to Knock Fell, where the unnaturally straight Knock Hush stream flows into Swindale Beck. Several major mines were worked well into the present century and the one below Great Dun Fell warranted a $6^{1}/_{2}$ mile-aerial ropeway to carry ore down to the valley bottom.

Three ancient routes cross the Pennines north of Cross Fell. The first is the Corpse Road between Garrigill and Kirkland. Next in line is the Roman road of Maiden Way, a side road linking major routes in what was then a military zone. The most modern road follows an old drove way across Hartside between Penrith and Alston. It is this road, the A686, which has gained a certain notoriety by being the first road blocked by winter snows.

Beyond the A686 the Eden by-passing **Penrith** with its four-teenth-century castle and prehistoric earthworks, enters its final stage as it flows towards the Solway above Carlisle. The final outliers of the Pennine range are rather featureless rolling hills which continue as far as the Newcastle-Carlisle Gap, but the Eden Valley continues to be an interesting place with ancient megaliths, Roman forts and castles to give a spice to the landscape.

Brougham Castle's impressive remains are at the side of the A66, about $1^{1}/_{2}$ miles south-east of Penrith. Dating from the early thirteenth century, the castle was one of those restored by Lady Anne Clifford after the Civil War. In 1656 she set up the memorial on the roadside half a mile east of the castle. Known as the Countess Pillar, a bronze inscription and a sundial commemorate the parting with her mother 40 years earlier.

A couple of miles north of the A686 and beyond Langwathby and Little Salkeld is the massive stone circle of **Long Meg and Her Daughters**. This is an oval 360ft by 60ft with twenty-seven of a probable sixty stones with an outlier known as 'Long Meg', the tallest stone measuring at a height of 10ft. A number of cup-and-ring carvings adorn Meg, the reason for them is unknown, their significance lost in the mists of time. Half a mile away, to the north-east is

Little Meg, a smaller circle of eleven stones, two of which are again carved with cups-and-rings and also a series of enigmatic spirals.

Using the A686 Penrith to Alston road via Hartside as a logical connection between valleys and also resisting the temptation to venture through Carlisle and Hadrian's Wall you can now turn your attention to the valley of the South Tyne.

THE SOUTH TYNE VALLEY

Cross Fell gives birth to two major northern rivers, the Tees and South Tyne. Although the latter officially starts almost in the shadow of the Tees east of the summit, high above Moor House Nature Reserve, it does have an important tributary, Black Burn, which drains the north slope of Cross Fell. The Pennine Way joins the Garrigill to Kirkland Corpse Road a little way north of Cross Fell, just above an interesting ruined mine. This track is followed all the way to Garrigill past the remains of several mines and is a worthwhile expedition from the latter village. Nature has ravaged the work of the old miners, and their tunnels and shafts are now in a dangerous state, but the spoil heaps and buildings make for interesting exploring. Fluorspar, once discarded as useless but now in demand as a flux for steel-making, is coloured a pretty shade of mauve in this area and many attractive specimens can be picked up along the way.

Garrigill, which means 'Gerrard's Valley' is the starting place for a pleasant short stroll (2½ miles, 1 hour) along the wooded South Tyne as far as a series of beautiful waterfalls. The walk is easy to follow and starts by the George and Dragon Inn, then follows the Tyne Head road for about half a mile beyond the village.

The infant South Tyne flows gently past Garrigill, which was also once the home village of Cross Fell miners, but now much sleepier and smaller than a century ago. Downstream **Alston** developed as the centre of the North Pennine lead mining areas. Alston holds two records, that of being the highest market town in the country and that of being cut off by snow for more days than any other place — not a record to be envied. The market stance is on a sharp corner of the steep main street. Built in the days of more leisurely traffic, this interesting building is rather vulnerable and occasionally gets in the way of heavy lorries. Lead is the reason for Alston's development. The market was created in 1154 for the benefit of the 'king's' miners who had royal protection, but it would also have served the people who lived conveniently in and around the town. Farmers living in the

Alston market place

scattered outlying farms only came to market on special days and relied on pedlars and pack-men for their small-ware needs. During the depression of 1812-31 when lead prices fell, the small-holdings were insufficient to support whole families without their men working in the mines. As a result over 2,000 people moved away from the district in a short space of time. The London Lead Company's philanthropic attitude towards its Alston based workforce is recorded by such items as the Reading Room, built at a time when an artisan's ability to read or write was considered to be rather radical in some quarters. Smeaton's Drainage Level, which drained a complex of mine workings 5 miles away at Nenthead was navigable by boats, underground as far as Alston!

British Rail have abandoned Alston but when the line still linked the main line at Haltwhistle two-coach diesel trains, delightfully named as *Bobby Shaftoe* and *Coffee Johnny*, plied up and down every hour or so. With minimal maintenance the line served a valley community and often during winter storms it was the only link with the outside world. The South Tynedale Railway Preservation Society has since taken over the upper part of the line and laid a narrow gauge track along the South Tyne Valley as far as Lambley Viaduct, running a steam service during the summer months.

The Pennine Way runs more or less parallel to the South Tyne and joins Maiden Way above the extensive ramparts of the Roman fort of **Whitley Castle**. This fort held a garrison on the network of roads inside which Rome tried to contain the subjugated British in the uneasy *Pax Romana*. Maiden Way (6 miles, 3 hours) is clearly defined now by the feet of the Pennine wayfarers and can be followed easily from Slaggyford north to Burnstones Farm.

At **Lambley** the Western Pennines can be said to come to an end. Coal appears at no great depth beside the A689, coal which helped the fortunes of the owners of Featherstone Castle whose grounds are now open to the public.

THE FAR NORTHERN DALES: NENTDALE, WEST AND EAST ALLENDALES AND DERWENTDALE

The whole character of the northern dales differs from those only a few miles to the south. South Tyne, Nent, West and East Allendales and the Derwent are Northumbrian geographically and politically. The air is different, certainly the spoken word sounds closer to 'Geordie' than Yorkshire 'Tyke'. In only a mile or two an invisible border is crossed and the visitor has entered the remains of an ancient kingdom, for that is what Northumbria once was and the fierce native independence still holds true. Now only a fraction of its original size, the kingdom of Northumbria once stretched from the Firth of Forth to Humberside.

The River Nent is short, flowing only a few miles before joining the South Tyne near Alston. **Nenthead** was built as an industrial village by the London Lead Company, mainly in the nineteenth century. Traces of long-finished mining dot the hillsides between Nentdale and the West Allen which, with its sister dale East Allendale, is a quiet and secluded spot with little traffic to worry about. A network of minor roads and pathways gives unlimited opportunity for exploration. Most of the paths were developed during lead mining times and will lead the amateur industrial archaeologist on a voyage of discovery. Abandoned mine workings and processing plant in Nenthead are slowly coming back to life as a visitor centre, with trails and interpretive boards to explain the complex layout of the ore-crushing plant and smelters. About 1$\frac{1}{2}$ miles down the road from Nenthead, a small museum at **Nentsberry** houses a collection of old mining equipment and farming implements, together with a children's play area and a narrow gauge mineral railway.

New Year's Eve is honoured in **Allendale Town** by a strange custom with 'Guizers', dressed in a weird mixture of eastern and medieval clothes parading through the village streets with barrels of blazing tar on their heads. When they reach the market place, they throw the barrels onto a bonfire and after midnight go round local houses 'first footing'. This obviously pagan custom is thought to be linked to a Viking festival brought to the valley by the first settlers.

The last of five dales of the far North Pennines, **Derwentdale**, cuts around Consett, desperately trying to recover from the decline of Britain's steel industry. The Derwent born in the wild moorland of Redburn Common is not far from the source of the Wear. For most of its infancy the Derwent flows through a rocky tree-lined gorge known as the Sweep, before slowing into the artificial lake of Derwent Reservoir. Used as an ammenity the reservoir is available for sailing enthusiasts and is well stocked with trout. **Blanchland**, the first village in the upper valley, is a picture-postcard place. Part of the Crewe estate (the village pub is the Lord Crewe Arms), Blanchland was rebuilt in the eighteenth century to house lead miners on the site of the abbey. Blanchland means 'White Land' after the white Premonstratensian canons who founded the abbey in 1165. After the Dissolution of the Monasteries, the monks were driven away, but the church was spared and remained as the village church. As with many old churches, Blanchland's was renovated in the nineteenth century and little remains of its ancient fabric apart from the tower and north transept.

Edmondbyers to the south of the reservoir has an attractive church which dates from Norman times although much of what is seen now is the result of nineteenth-century restoration. It once had two pubs, but only one retains its licence, the other having been converted into a Youth Hostel.

WEARDALE

South now into Weardale and into the County Palatine of Durham, once a kingdom and still a bishopric. The Wear, a river which like those of the Yorkshire Dales, has created a valley of character but unlike the wholly Yorkshire rivers it flows to the sea in its own right.

Killhope Burn, the Wear's first tributary rises only a mile or so away from Nenthead and in earlier times provided power to drive a massive 40ft-diameter waterwheel at **Killhope**. The wheel and ore-crushing shed of 1840 still stand in splendid isolation on the moor's edge, testimony to the work involved in producing metal from lead ore. The wheel and its attendant buildings has been refurbished to provide an interpretive centre in what was a highly industrialised area. A miners' 'shop', or bunkhouse shows a little of the spartan life of this not so long dead industry and a Dales pony demonstrates its usefulness to lead miners.

The stream runs on purposefully through Weardale Forest. Linking with Burnhope Burn below the village of Cowshill, the Wear loses some of its mountain wildness, later fed by three more major side streams before flowing through an ever widening valley beyond Wolsingham.

The spread of hamlets and smallholdings in Upper Weardale is typical of the way mining communities developed at the height of the lead mining industry. Apart from the refurbished mining complex of Killhope Wheel, there is little to indicate the onetime mining activity.

Cowshill at the junction of the A689 valley road with the B6295 from Allendale Town is typical of the stone-built villages of Upper Weardale. St John's Chapel (its full title is St John Weardale) has a relaxed atmosphere, far removed from the time when it was necessary to form a vigilante group known as 'The Association for the Prosecution of Felons and other Offenders'. This group still survives, but leaving the law in proper hands, devotes itself to an annual get-together. The squat church tower looks out over a village green and a diminutive classical town hall formalises this 'capital' of Upper Weardale. Friendly inns serve the needs of farmers attending the frequent cattle and sheep markets. An agricultural show and a music festival are the highlights of a busy calendar. The tiny nearby hamlet of **Daddry Shield** once hosted cockfights, but is now a law-abiding group of pretty whitewashed cottages.

Beyond Eastgate the obtrusive dust from a cement works rises from a tall chimney and cement dust covers the surrounding walls and hedges, but fortunately the majestic moors rising steeply on all sides rapidly compensate for this intrusion. **Eastgate** was the gatehouse of the Bishop of Durham's Old Park hunting ground, **Westgate** marks the western boundary. Much earlier the whole area around Weardale was popular sporting ground for the Roman upper classes in northern Britain. Edward III had a confrontation with the Scots on the moors above Eastgate in 1327, but fortunately the Scots withdrew before either side drew blood.

Blanchland

Killhope wheel at the Lead Mining Centre

PLACES TO VISIT IN AND AROUND WEARDALE

Alston
On A686, 19 miles north-east of Penrith
Interesting covered market stand in main street. Excellent base for exploring the North Pennines. Voluntary society run a narrow gauge railway nearby. Shops and railway information centre.

Blanchland
B6306, 4 miles west of Edmondbyers
Site of twelfth-century abbey of the White Friars. Now mainly a mid-eighteenth-century estate village.

Derwent Reservoir
B6306, 7 miles north-west of Consett
Fishing, sailing, picnic areas. Pow Hill Country Park and Nature Reserve.

Killhope Wheel Lead Mining Centre
$2\frac{1}{4}$ miles east of Nenthead on B6293 in Upper Weardale
Well preserved iron 'overshot' waterwheel fed by nearby streams. Exhibition on lead mining techniques and lives of lead miners. Restored buildings.

Nenthead Mines and Museum
Nenthead, on B6293
Reconstructed lead mining complex. Trails and interpretive plaques.

Nentsberry Mining and Farming Museum
Mining equipment and farm implements. Narrow gauge railway; play area, picnic site. Pub nearby.

North of England Open-Air Museum
Beamish, off A693, Stanley to Chester-le-Street road
A 200-acre open-air museum of northern life. Includes a 1920s town street with shops, houses, pub, colliery etc. Also a working farm, working replica of early locomotives, tram track, and other exhibits.

Waterfall Walk
Garrigill, 4 miles south of Alston off B6277
Pleasant riverside and gorge walk.

Weardale Folk Museum
High House, Ireshopeburn (A689)
Farming and geology displays. Interesting chapel associated with John Wesley, next door.

Whitley Castle
On B6292, 2 miles north of Alston
Fine example of a well fortified Roman fort on the Maiden Way. No public access, but footpaths from the B6292 pass either side.

Westernhopeburn, on the side road between Eastgate and Westgate, is one of the least altered farmhouses in Weardale. Dated 1601, it is one continuous low stone structure in the medieval style, built to house animals and family under one roof.

A side dale, Rook Hope, joins the Wear at Eastgate and the only access is by a narrow road climbing the valley. It is difficult to imagine that **Rook Hope** was once an industrial village, the centre of a large lead and ironstone mining area. From the now abandoned lead smelter at Lintzgarth a 2- mile long flue climbed to Redburn Common, where poisoned vegetation is still struggling to recover. A railway, now part of the Waskerley Way footpath, climbed high across Stanhope's moors to Consett. Rowley Station near Consett, or Waskerley Station on the moors (NZ052454) are good access points for the Waskerley Way, with plenty of car parking space. Steep gradients were negotiated by inclined planes and hauling cables powered by fixed winding engines.

Rook Hope Dale was the scene of a border battle commemorated in a long and not easily followed song of thirty-seven verses. In the sixteenth century Moss Troopers of North Tyne and Cheviot ranged far and wide in lawless pursuit of other people's cattle and sheep. Thinking Weardale would give them easy pickings a hundred of them came over from Tynedale to drive Weardale cattle and sheep into Rook Hope Dale. A small band of locals pursued them and a fierce battle took place on Nookton Edge where the hundred raiders were defeated by forty locals.

In the Middle Ages the discovery of iron ore in Weardale led to the development of small forges, but with the coming of the Industrial Revolution there was an ever increasing demand for good quality iron. Ore which was mined in the higher valley at Cowshill and Ireshopeburn was transported to a blast furnace built in 1845 at Stanhope. Building the furnace there took advantage not only of nearby ironstone, but limestone, a necessary ingredient in the production of iron. That other essential ingredient was brought in on the rapidly developing railway network from the Durham coalfields further east. As demand for iron increased the Weardale Iron Company was formed, which built a further six blast furnaces at Tow Law lower down the valley. As lead mining declined there was an ever growing concentration on mining ironstone and at one time 1,700 men were employed in the local industry. From those humble beginnings the north-eastern steel industry developed, gradually moving further and more eastwards and culminating with a massive investment at Consett. With the drastic reorganisation of the iron and steel industry, Consett's furnaces no longer stain the night sky red and the complex site has been cleared. Stanhope has also lost its ironstone links, but its limestone industry thrives now producing cement and roadstone.

Stanhope has been called the 'capital of Weardale', a high accolade for a small town, but certainly it marks the transition between encroaching industrial Durham and the wild fells on either side of the upper dale. Prosperity founded on its early lead connections made the ecclesiastical living wealthy and as a result Stanhope has had a long line of eminent rectors, eight of whom became bishops. The church dates from the twelfth century and inside it are two Flemish panel paintings and a Roman altar found on **Bollihope Common** in 1747. As there are no evident Roman remains on Bollihope it is pure conjecture to try and guess how the altar came to be there in the first place, but a possible clue is shown on the OS map. This is the mention of Bollihope Spa a little to the east of Bollihope Carrs (1,773ft) about 5 miles south-west of Stanhope. One can only surmise that maybe there is a Roman bath somewhere around Bollihope Spa, for they had a knack of being able to find suitable springs and Roman baths have been found in less likely places. Who knows there may still be remains waiting to be found up there.

The mock castle at the side of Stanhope's market square is a rather forbidding place, once used as a remand home. Now flats, it was built in 1798 for Cuthbert Rippon, MP for Gateshead. Despite its unattractive appearance from the street, the castle looks much better from the river. The oldest part of the town sits back from the irregular shaped market square and its ancient cross, but far older is the fossilised tree stump built into the church wall.

Two more attractive side dales join the Upper Wear, the first **Bollihope Burn** joins the main river below Frosterley. A special form of limestone speckled by thousands of fossils has been quarried nearby for hundreds of years. Known as Frosterley black marble and much favoured by Victorians, there is a line of it in Durham Cathedral which marks the point beyond which women were once forbidden to pass. The village gained a mention in the *Boldon Beuk*, the 1183 equivalent of the *Domesday Book*.

Tree-lined **Waskerley Beck** flows through **Wolsingham**, a pleasant blend of industry and rural cottages. One or two buildings are of special merit; eighteenth-century Whitfield House has an almost French provincial air. Next to it and in complete contrast is Whitfield Place, a seventeenth-century house with mullioned windows. The church tower is twelfth century, but the rest is in mid-Victorian early English style. Wolsingham holds an annual show the first weekend in September, an ambitious event for such a small place. There is good trout and salmon fishing in the Wear and Tunstall Reservoir above the town is stocked with both brown and rainbow trout. Rod licences and day permits can be bought locally. **Hamsterley Forest** reached along minor roads south of Wolsingham has a short, but pleasant forest drive (toll road), and several interesting walking trails and picnic sites. Downstream from Wolsingham heavy industry makes itself felt, even in this ancient town, founded in the seventh century during an expansion westwards by Angles under King Edwin of Northumbria (AD616-632). Place names ending in 'ham' such as Wolsingham, indicate a homestead or a small farm which was built in a clearing in what would at that time have been dense forest. Wolsingham marks the end of the narrowest part of the dale for beyond this point the Wear begins to meander south-east almost to Bishop Auckland, before turning north past the magnificent cathedral city of Durham, then out through the industrial plain towards Sunderland and the North Sea.

SELECTED WALK

The South Tyne 4¹/₂ miles • Easy • 2 hours
This is an easy walk to follow, down one bank of the South Tyne and up the other! Part of the route uses one of the prettiest sections of the Pennine Way to the north of Garrigill, a charming ex-lead mining village.

From the George and Dragon in Garrigill, follow Pennine Way signs downstream, first along a road then by fieldpath and through a narrow strip of beechwood on the west bank of the river. Ignoring a signposted footbridge taking the Pennine Way across the river continue downstream to the confluence of the South Tyne and Black Burn. Cross the main river at this point and climb up to Bleagate Farm; turn right on a path leading upstream. Go past Sillyhall Farm and into woodland, again ignoring the Pennine Way bridge to walk upstream through the trees and join a minor road by the corner of a cemetery. Turn right and follow this road into Garrigill.

4
TEESDALE

Teesdale is now wholly within County Durham, but it has an ambience which relates it to the Yorkshire Dales. The Tees in its upper reaches is the most boisterous of Pennine rivers, even though man has tried to tame it in its infancy. Cow Green Reservoir was built to serve industry lower downstream, and in so doing altered the face of one of the wildest areas of northern moorland. From its magnificent beginnings in the hills, the Tees eventually becomes the servant of man on industrial Teesside, but it is just not the same river by then. Fortunately this guide is only interested in its Pennine life, and here is ample recompense for the industrial horrors further east.

From Barnard Castle which marks the end of the division between fell and plain, a quiet motor road north-westwards (the B6277) follows the river until they part company above High Force. Beyond this point the road continues to climb to 1,862ft over Harwood Common on its way to Alston and the South Tyne. This road is a delight to motorists in summer when the ever-changing views range from the wooded beauty of the dale above Middleton, to the far-ranging prospect across West Common towards the birthplace of the Tees high on Cross Fell.

Tees Head is in fact a swamp situated at 2,532ft beneath the final 400ft of Cross Fell and is crossed with care by hundreds of walkers who explore the Pennine Way every year. The area of bleak moorland east of Cross Fell through which the infant river threads its course is the National Nature Reserve of Moor House. It is an area of jealously preserved of unspoilt moors and contains a unique collection of the sub-arctic flora which can cope with a growing season of about 165 days. These plants range from the starry saxifrage which blooms in the mossy places around Tees Head to the beautiful spring gentian (*Gentiana verna*) found lower down the valley. So special is this flower to Teesdale that a gentian watch is kept over it by volunteers during the flowering season. To find this startling blue flower is pure delight. **Moor House**, the home and centre of this preserve, is locked in a bend of the Tees above its junction with Trout Beck; courses are run from here and studies funded by the Nature Conservancy. Moor House is in a lonely and secluded spot at the end of the road which follows the South Tyne through Garrigill to its head waters.

Alpine flowers grow well in Upper Teesdale on a soil based on sugar limestone. This stone was made by the action of heat on hard limestone during the time when molten dolerite was flowing between ancient layers of limestone to form the Whin Sill. Sugar limestone crumbles into an alkaline dust which, when mixed naturally with peaty loam, forms an ideal growing medium for delicate plants usually found in mountainous regions.

Downstream from Moor House, the Tees is temporarily arrested by **Cow Green Reservoir**. When the proposal was made to dam this section of the valley the industrialists no doubt thought they had an easy task; to them this was just a piece of wilderness which no one wanted. How wrong they were! The battle to save Cow Green was long and acrimonious. In the end the ranks of Mammon won the day, but they were forced to delay the construction of the dam long enough to allow conservationists time to mount a massive campaign to dig up as many of the rare plants as possible, and transplant them in suitable locations away from the reservoir. Despite the heartache Cow Green was flooded, the man-made lake now makes an attractive foreground to the heights of the Dun Fells and Cross Fell, but even so it is man-made and an intruder in this special place.

Immediately below Cow Green dam the dark coloured dolerite crag of Whin Sill resists the river and makes an impressive foundation to **Cauldron Snout**, but the construction of the dam means that Cauldron Snout can never again be the angry mass of cream and brown foam it once was after heavy rain. However, Cauldron Snout is now accessible by the road to the dam from Langdon Beck. Cars must be parked at Weelhead Syke and the road marked by an interesting nature trail follows the side of the reservoir to the dam; a little way beyond it is Cauldron Snout.

Below Cauldron Snout the Tees is joined by Maize Beck and

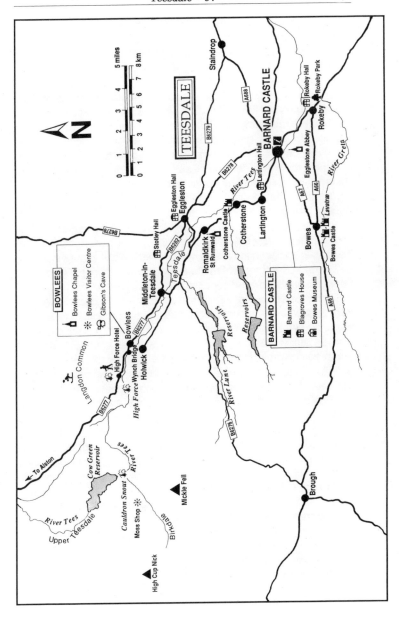

TEESDALE

N

0 1 2 3 4 5 miles
0 1 2 3 4 5 6 7 8 km

BOWLEES
- Bowlees Chapel
- Bowlees Visitor Centre
- Gibson's Cave

BARNARD CASTLE
- Barnard Castle
- Blagroves House
- Bowes Museum

Langdon Common

To Alston

Cow Green Reservoir

River Tees

Upper Teesdale

Cauldron Snout
Moss Shop
High Cup Nick
Mickle Fell
Birkdale

High Force Hotel
Bowlees
Wynch Bridge
High Force
Holwick

Middleton-in-Teesdale

Stotley Hall
Eggleston Hall
Eggleston

B6278

B6282

Teesdale

Romaldkirk
St Romwald
Cotherstone Castle
Cotherstone

River Lune

Reservoirs
Reservoirs

B6276

Lartington Hall
Lartington

River Tees

B6279

Staindrop

A688

BARNARD CASTLE

Eggleston Abbey
Rokeby Hall
Rokeby Park
Rokeby

River Greta

A66

A67

Lavatras

Bowes
Bowes Castle

Brough

about a mile upstream **Birkdale** is probably the most remote farmstead in England. Winters can be so severe and long that the farmer and his wife have had to buy a snow scooter to keep in contact with civilisation and more importantly to check on any sheep trapped under snowdrifts.

The Pennine Way path cuts a corner off Maize Beck on its way over to High Cup Nick and Dufton. Beyond Birkdale and marked on the map is a ruin known as **Moss Shop**, where miners would live for 5 days each week, sleeping on lice infested sacks filled with straw and living on a diet of oatmeal, pork and potatoes. Similar hovels which dot the North Pennine hillsides speak evocatively of the hard life led by miners a century or so ago.

The **Langdon Beck** district is a popular skiing area in winter. Access along the B6277 is usually good in all but the hardest conditions, as the road is kept open throughout the winter. It is the sole link into larger towns for the whole mass of villages in Upper Teesdale, and even the Alston area. The main skiing area is usually on Langdon Common where the even slopes of a dry gully on Three Pikes hill provides good conditions well into spring.

A glance at the OS map will show what intense activity went on here when mining lead was a profitable business. Hushing, to wash away the surface, was practiced here as elsewhere in the dales and scarred gullies can still be seen after at least a century. A whole hotch-potch of field tracks criss-cross the area east of Langdon Beck, usually connecting smallholdings with mines higher on the fell side, the paths being result of miners making their own routes home.

One of the features of Upper Teesdale is the number of whitewashed cottages and farm houses which stand out brightly against an often sombre background. An unusual practice in the Pennines, the custom of white-washing houses in this area, originated from a time when the landowner, Lord Barnard of Raby Castle, was benighted while out shooting. He knocked on the door of a cottage which unfortunately did not belong to one of his tenants. His request for hospitality was refused and he spent an uncomfortable night on the moors as a result. Determined to avoid a recurrence of this problem, he instructed his tenants to paint their houses white so that he could find them in the dark! The custom has remained ever since.

Two miles downstream from the confluence of Langdon Beck with the Tees the valley scenery changes dramatically from bleak, wild, open moorland at first to a wooded valley, but soon to gentle pastures

High Force, Teesdale

below Newbiggin. The transition is dramatically marked by the thundering of **High Force**. Especially after a spate of heavy rain this magnificent fall is one of Britain's wonders — not the highest by a long way, but certainly one of the biggest in volume of water. In dry weather the fall occupies just one 70ft drop, but after rain another fall appears on the right of the dolerite buttress. This is a favourite vantage point and also one where people are caught unawares when a heavy rainfall in the Cross Fell area causes the river to rise in minutes. What was earlier a babbling rivulet can suddenly become an angry torrent. So watch for the signs and never climb onto the island if there is the chance of a storm around.

Most visitors to High Force approach it by way of a path through the grounds opposite High Force Hotel for which, or course, they have to pay. The view is worth every penny, but this way has a disadvantage. Apart from the small area of woodland around the falls, no further exploration is possible. A much more entertaining walk (4 miles, 2 hours) is to cross the Tees below Low Force at Wynch Bridge and walk upstream along the Pennine Way track.

The waterfalls of Teesdale rightly command their full complement of superlatives. All delight the eye of the visitor and it is not surprising to find one hidden in a side valley often missed and neglected other than by those who have discovered its charms. This is the small fall in the valley behind **Bowlees** Visitor Centre where Causeway Syke tumbles over the small shaley outcrop of Gibson's Cave. The fall has cut back the shale so much that it is possible to stand behind a curtain of water and look out on the woodland scene through a fine tracery. The approach to this gem is by the path behind Bowlees Chapel — it will only take a few minutes to climb to the fall and the chances are that while High Force is crowded, you will have this one all to yourself. Causeway Syke Valley is an ideal picnic spot on a warm summer day. The old chapel at Bowlees houses a visitor and information centre devoted to the natural history of Teesdale, where grandparents can show youngsters how to use lead pencils and slates once mined near Cauldron Snout. The little garden outside the centre is planted with a selection of local wild flowers and moorland grasses.

A short fieldpath from Bowlees leads down to the tree shaded river and **Wynch Bridge** where the Tees cascades through the series of dolerite steps known as **Low Force**. The first Wynch Bridge was unique in being the earliest suspension bridge in Europe. It was first built in 1744 and rebuilt in 1828 to give miners living in the east side of the Tees access to the mining areas on the western fells. Probably it was the narrowness of the river at this point and firm rock on both sides which made the bridge builders site it just below Low Force. One thing is certain, the bridge makes an excellent vantage point to admire the spectacular rock formations upstream to Low Force and the tree-lined slopes on either side. The land west of the Tees hereabouts is part of the Teesdale Nature Reserve and as a result is out of bounds to the walker with the exception of one or two long distance public rights-of-way. One of them, the path across **Holwick Fell**, was a drove road where cattle were slowly walked south on their way to market from the Scottish Highlands. Cattle no longer walk to market and **Holwick**, a resting place for drovers on the long trek south, no longer echoes to the lowing of massed beasts. The village is at the end of an unclassified road, 3 miles north-west of Middleton-in-Teesdale, a tiny group of stone cottages and farms fitting snugly beneath the whinstone crags of Holwick Scars. A short walk ($1/_4$ mile, $1/_2$ hour) through Mill Beck Wood, to the south-east of Holwick, leads to a hidden rocky gorge and an attractive waterfall. Known as Fairy Dell, it is on private land, but permission is usually granted to anyone wishing to ramble or picnic there: enquire at the Strathmore Arms in Holwick.

Below Low Force the valley widens a little and meadows appear on either side of the river, meadows which in summer are a mass of wild flowers lasting until haymaking. The Pennine Way path follows the west bank all the way from Middleton-in-Teesdale and with a bit of careful arrangement of transport back, the whole length of the Pennine Way between Langdon Beck and Middleton can be walked by easy-to-follow and well signposted paths. It is 8 miles (4 hours) of the most superb and scenic walking, taking in High Force and Low Force on the way. The walk can be done in either direction, but upstream is probably the best as you do not have to turn around to admire the falls.

Middleton-in-Teesdale grew in importance when the London Lead Company built an estate village around Masterman Place. Making it their local headquarters, they opened an office to control mining interests which were worked on both sides of Teesdale until 1905. The most striking feature of Middleton is its wide, grassy main street with the ornate cast-iron Bainbridge Memorial Fountain at one end. The present church is Victorian, probably built on Norman foundations. Town End Chapel to the east is a magnificent piece of

Low Force, Teesdale

Middleton-in-Teesdale

Victorian architecture. **Stotley Hall** is about $1^1/_2$ miles away, along the Barnard Castle road, an attractive example of a prosperous seventeenth-century farmhouse. Regular cattle auctions, quaint shops and coaching inns complete the rural scene of Middleton-in-Teesdale.

It is hard to say exactly when lead mining ceased as a commercially viable enterprise in the dales as some small scale mining went on intermittently until the 1920s, but it is generally reckoned that cheap imports of lead from America, Australia and Spain killed off the dales' industry from the mid-1880s onwards. The Middleton area mines were about the last of the major sites to close.

A short car ride round the narrow lane which climbs north out of Middleton around Hudeshope Beck to Coldberry Moor will take you past some of the old mines — do not go in them. Some fine examples of hushing can be found above the sharp bends on either side of the crossing of Hudeshope Beck. This is where the hillside has been washed away and traces of exposed ore-bearing rock can still be found.

The Pennine Way reaches Teesdale by cutting north-east across the corner of a long ridge running down from Lune Moor. Between the

Pennine Way path and the B6276 Brough road through Lunedale can be seen a conspicuous round hill with a plantation of trees on its summit. This is **Kirkcarrion** and is said to be haunted. How true the story is can only be guessed, but the mound has some ancient significance being the site of a massive tumulus.

Below Kirkcarrion is the **Lune Valley** — not the Lancashire River Lune but a much shorter stream and one which enters the Tees from the west. This river flows from the southerly end of the Cross Fell, Dufton Fell and Murton Fell range and in its upper reaches drains an area of wilderness uncrossed by any path and claimed by the military as a practice area. Traces of old mining activity can be found above 1,400ft. The valley's lower reaches have been dammed to make Selset and Grassholme reservoirs, both of which are stocked with fish. Apart from the Pennine Way path there is little to attract the walker into Lunedale, but the motor road B6276 from Middleton to Brough is a delightful high level motor route on a fine day.

Downstream from where the Lune joins the Tees the valley bottom is flat and gradually widens with ever improving lush grazing, and so sets the pattern which is continued until industrial Teesside is reached. A line of stone cottages that are **Mickleton** occupy a sunny rise about a mile south of the confluence of the Lune and the Tees. Neolithic burials have been found nearby.

At the height of their fortunes the London Lead Company built a crushing mill at **Eggleston**. With this they attempted to extract the maximum amount of ore from mines higher up the main and side valleys. Eggleston, surrounded by a complex of 'B' roads to the west of the Tees, was more important in the past than it is today; since prehistoric times in fact. There was a stone circle nearby, but regrettably it disappeared when the stones were broken up for road building. A drove road came south from Hexham through Eggleston and divided one section going eastwards along the Tees while the other crossed Romaldkirk Moor to join the one south to Stainmore. The bridge across the Tees below Eggleston Hall was built in the seventeenth century, probably before then stock and people had to cross the river by a ford which could be hazardous when the river was in spate. There is also a delightful pack-horse bridge of similar date which crosses the village stream near the church. This church is Victorian and replaced one of earlier date; its ruins are in the private grounds of Eggleston Hall to the south. The hall is nineteenth century and a fine example of a Victorian country gentleman's house.

On the other side of Eggleston Bridge the road climbs gently to the beautifully situated village of **Romaldkirk**. The twelfth-century church of St Rumwald, son of a king of Northumberland, is set at the end of a narrow alley which leads off the large village green. It is frequently referred to as 'Cathedral of the Dales', and was completed about 1290. Houses built through the centuries add charm and character to the place. Southwards across Baldersdale which the waterboard is determined to drown (there are now three reservoirs), is **Cotherstone** once home of the Fitzhughs and where the castle has provided convenient building materials for the villagers from time to time; as witness several cottages which are made from worked stones of higher quality than would have normally been used. The Tees on either side of Barnard Castle is tree-lined and conveniently placed bridges north of Cotherstone make it possible to link up paths which follow both banks. **Lartington**, on the B6277 into Barnard Castle, shelters behind a wood and serves the needs of its hall and park built in the reign of Charles I. Lartington Hall is the venue for the annual Teesdale Country Fair.

The first time visitor to **Barnard Castle**, on approaching the town from the south-east may think he has been transported to France. This misunderstanding can be excused because the massive building which stands on rising ground east of the town and resembles a French *château* was in fact designed by a French architect Jules Pellachet. The **Bowes Museum** was originally built for George Bowes, illegitimate son of the tenth Earl of Strathmore and from whom he inherited vast Durham estates and collieries. The foundation stone was laid in 1869 but George Bowes and his wife with whom he shared the idea of a vast museum of antiquities and art, died before it was completed in 1892. Over the years the building became something of a white elephant until it was taken over by Durham County Council in 1952 and is now run efficiently as the county musuem covering diverse subjects from local Roman relics to the great masters and is regarded as one of the finest art collections outside London. Galleries are devoted to period French furniture. Pride of place in the main entrance is given to a life size working model of a silver swan which catches tiny fishes! The museum and surrounding gardens are open all the year except Christmas and New Year.

Barnard Castle is a venerable town full of delightfully interesting corners. Its castle was built to command an important river crossing

PLACES TO VISIT IN UPPER TEESDALE

Bowlees Visitor Centre
B6277, 3 miles north-west of Middleton-in-Teesdale
The natural history of Upper Teesdale visually explained in an easy to follow, yet well documented manner. Picnic site nearby.

Cauldron Snout Waterfall
Cow Green access by track from Wheelhead Syke Car Park Spectacular falls below dam of Cow Green Reservoir.

Gibson's Cave
Bowlees
Small water worn cave. Access by footpath and nature trail from Bowlees Visitor Centre.

High Force
B6277, 5 miles north-west of Middleton-in-Teesdale
The River Tees drops 70ft in a dramatic spectacle of rock and water. Easy access by footpath below High Force Hotel, small fee.

Middleton-in-Teesdale
A small, purpose-built early nineteenth-century town added by the London Lead Company to an existing, much older village. Used by the company as one of their northern mining headquarters.

Wheelhead Syke Nature Trail
Cow Green Reservoir, approached from Langdon Beck off B6277
Scenic car park above reservoir. Nature trail leads from car park across moorland. Opportunity to see spring gentians flowering.

and is named after Barnard (Bernard) son of Guy Balliol who was granted land here by William II in 1093. The river crossing on this important north-south route is still marked by a venerable bridge dating from 1569. The castle was extended and strengthened several times over the years and at one time was the property of Warwick the Kingmaker through whom it passed to Richard III. It is his emblem, the wild boar, which can be seen on the wall of the Great Chamber. The castle is now maintained by English Heritage and opens at their standard advertised times.

The ancient street names of Barnard Castle speak of the time when the town was a secure place against Scottish raiders and it was safer to live near a castle for protection. Streets with names like Newgate, Bridgegate and Thorngate radiate from the castle.

The market cross in Barnard Castle

Bowes Museum, Barnard Castle

Thorngate, lined for part of its length by eighteenth-century town houses, descends to the river past an old mill and then leads on the The Bank. Above it all stands the solidly built octagonal market cross which dominated local trade when the only source of fresh meat and vegetables was that brought in from outside farms. Built in 1747, the colonnaded shelter is crowned by a cupola and weathervane. The town hall, lit by elegant Venetian windows, fills the upper storey. Further down the street, sixteenth-century Blagroves House, now a restaurant, is three storeys high beneath a gabled roof. Charles Dickens stayed at the King's Head Hotel in Horsemarket when he was collecting material for *Nicholas Nickleby*. In Newgate a plaque marks the site of a shop owned by the man who was the inspiration for Dicken's *Master Humphrey's Clock*, intended as a frame for both *Barnaby Rudge* and *The Old Curiosity Shop*. Opposite Blagroves House a shop specialising in high quality dolls' houses, both in kit form and the finished product, offers an interesting diversion.

From Barnard Castle a field path leads downstream through East Lendings to a view of the most northerly of the dales' abbeys, **Egglestone Abbey**. Founded in the twelfth century by Premonstratensian canons, this elegant abbey is the very epitome of holiness as it sits in quiet splendour above the tree-lined Tees. After the Dissolution, part of the abbey was converted into a farmhouse and several additions were made in later years, especially in the seventeenth century. Much of the cruciform, aisleless church still survives, especially the nave and chancel. The windows are early English although the matching east window is thought to be seventeenth century. Beautifully carved medieval grave slabs dot the green outside.

Downstream again a path follows the course of the river into **Rokeby Park** and its hall (open to the public). **Rokeby Hall** was built in the Palladian style in 1735 by Sir Thomas Robinson, at one time Governor of Barbados, and he was known locally as 'Long Sir Tom' from his build and angular gait. Rokeby is the true home of Velazquez's *Rokeby Venus* which now hangs in the National Gallery in London, but many other paintings and a unique collection of needlework by Anne Marritt (1726-97) are on display in the compact main buildings. On the eastern edge of the park is Mortham Tower, a fourteenth-century peel tower, the fortified home of the Rokeby family for generations until it was bought by Sir Thomas Robinson who altered and extended the wings which had been added in Tudor times.

The river separating Rokeby Park from Mortham Tower is the Greta. Water flowing down it has drained from the wilds of Stainmore across which runs the A66, an important trans-Pennine highway since Roman times. A drove road south crossed the Greta to the west on a natural limestone bridge known as God's Bridge, and from there the route wandered south into Swaledale. Rokeby Park is bounded by the A66 which still follows the line of the Roman road to this day. The road by Rokeby takes a sharp swing to the south-east away from the Tees and aims for the A1 at Scotch Corner. Hard by **Greta Bridge** are the earth bank remains of a fort and beyond is one of the best features of the southern part of Teesdale — the wooded ravine of **Brignall Banks**, through which the Greta flows its last few miles before joining the main river. Here is another of those delightful walks where you can be certain of being able to wander quietly and hardly see another sole all day.

Whorlton, 4 miles downstream of Barnard Castle is a picturesque grouping of terraced cottages and attractive gardens on the north bank of the Tees. A steep road descends to a suspension bridge (built in 1829) and nearby on the south bank is a riverside lido and picnic site.

The romantic ruin of St Mary's Church above the eastern side of the valley, is over a quarter of a mile from Brignall and one cannot but puzzle over why it was built there rather than in the village. No doubt people tired of walking through damp woodland to and from church and in 1833 they built one in a more convenient place, although burials continued in the old churchyard for another 50 years.

Just under 2 miles south of the A66 and in a wild and desolate spot on Scargill Moor stands the site of a series of Roman shrines. The site is about a mile west-north-west of Spanham Farm (NZ016101) and towards Eller Beck; the altar stones are in Bowes Museum.

Bowes is a quieter place now that the A66 by-passes it to the north on an embankment. It has stood here since the Romans built their fort of *Lavatræ* to command the approaches to Stainmore. Likewise the Normans following the Conquest built a castle here in 1171, but it was never more than a fortified tower. Little remains of *Lavatræ*, most of the stones having been used to build the castle and later the village church, but the ditches and some of the ramparts of *Lavatræ* can be seen. The fort covered an area of about 3 acres and from excavations it appears that the fort was occupied from the second to fourth centuries AD. Water for the fort was brought by

The River Tees near Barnard Castle

Egglestone Abbey near Barnard Castle

Falcon Clints in Upper Teesdale

Tan Hill Inn

aqueduct from Levy (or Laver) Pool about 2 miles away to the north. *Lavatræ* was strategically sited at the junction of two roads, one running north-east to *Vinovia* (Binchester) to join Dere Street on its way north to Hadrian's Wall. The other road runs south-east for 25 miles to *Cataractonium* (modern Catterick) a garrison town even to this day.

On the edge of Bowes is Dotheboys Hall, featured in Charles Dickens' *Nicholas Nickleby*. Dotheboys Hall was a private school run by the sadistic and greedy Wackford Squeers who thought nothing of starving and beating his charges and whose education was his least thought. The character of Wackford Squeers was built on a real person who unfortunately was typical of his type before legislation came about following protests from such radical thinkers as Dickens.

An arm of the Pennine Way passes through Bowes before moving north again to Baldersdale. The Greta flows roughly parallel to the A66 and at one time was followed by a railway line, one of the most difficult lines in the country. Trains travelling on the steep west to east gradient had to have an extra engine, and the story is that contrary to the rules which demanded that the train be stopped for an extra engine to be coupled. To save time the second locomotive would chase the train, and without being coupled would push from the rear. Dangerous but effective.

The main Pennine Way route follows Sleightholme Beck all the way from England's highest pub, the **Tan Hill Inn**. This pub has served well throughout the years, helping travellers of all kinds from gipsies and cattle drovers to Pennine Way walkers, and more importantly the miners who dug coal from shallow pits which still dot the moorland with their open and unfenced shafts. The annual show of the Swaledale Sheep-breeders Association is held at Tan Hill on the last Thursday in May.

SELECTED WALKS

Cauldron Snout $9^1/_2$ miles • Fairly Strenuous • 5 hours
The walk to this dramatic waterfall is from Langdon Beck Youth Hostel
on the B6277 road through Teesdale. Follow Pennine Way signs
opposite the hostel and along a farm lane to Saur Hill Farm. Continue
by footpath down to the Tees and follow it, upstream. At Falcon Clints
the going is quite rocky, leading to the dramatic spectacle of Cauldron
Snout. Climb the rocks at the side of the waterfall with care, especially
after rain when they can be exceptionally slippery. Follow the access
road to your right of Cow Green Reservoir and across Widdybank Fell
(look out for gentians in spring, but do not pick any). Continue along
the road until you reach a road bridge over Harwood Beck; do not
cross the bridge, but turn right downstream to Saur Hill and go left
over the bridge to reach the Youth Hostel.

Low Force and High Force 4 miles • Easy • $1^3/_4$ hours
Visiting two contrasting waterfalls, the walk follows part of the
Teesdale section of the Pennine Way. Interesting features along the
walk have been created by the dolerite extrusions of the Great Whin
Sill which extends across much of northern England. The scent of
juniper berries near High Force on a summer's day can be almost
over-powering.
    From Bowlees Visitor Centre go down to the river and cross
Wynch Bridge. Turn right, upstream past Low Force. Continue along
the riverbank to High Force then retrace your steps back to Holwick
Head Bridge. Cross the bridge, climb up to the B6277 and turn right
for about a quarter of a mile then left on a side road to Dirt Pit. Turn
right and follow a farm track back to the visitor centre.

A SCENIC CAR DRIVE

Through the Northern Dales 84 miles
The drive starts and finishes in historic Barnard Castle. Follow the
A67 to Bowes (castle and Roman remains), then via the A66 across
wild Stainmore to Brough (interesting market town, cafés, shops,
pubs) and on to Appleby (shops, cafés, pubs, castle and Rare Breeds
Conservation Centre). Using side roads, go through Dufton and
Skirwith to Melmerby and turn right along the A686 across Hartside
Pass (café). In Alston (cafés, pubs, interesting market cross, narrow
gauge railway), follow the A689 through Nenthead (lead mining trail)
into Weardale, calling at the Killhope Wheel Lead Mining Centre along
the way. Turn right at St John's Chapel and climb across Langdon
Common into Teesdale. Divert to Cow Green Reservoir (viewpoint,
nature trail), then follow the B6277, calling at High Force (waterfall,

PLACES TO VISIT IN AND AROUND BARNARD CASTLE

Barnard Castle
Castle
A67 Darlington to Bowes road.
Castle built by Barnard, son of
Guy Balliol in 1093 on land
granted by William II. Easy
access from town centre.
Maintained by English Heritage.

Town
An interesting collection of
venerable buildings lining old
streets which once were
entered through gateways in a
fortified wall. Covered market
cross and Blagroves House of
particular interest.

Bowes Castle
On A66, 4 miles south-west of
Barnard Castle
Massive twelfth-century stone
keep overlooking the River
Greta. Built on the site of a
Roman fort which commanded
the eastern side of Stainmore.
Admission free.
At the western end of Bowes
village is Dotheboys Hall, once
a notorious boys' school, now a
private house.

Bowes Museum
Outskirts of Barnard Castle on
the Whorlton road
French-style *château* housing a
collection of national importance
including paintings by El Greco
and Goya. Displays of furniture
and fashions.

Egglestone Abbey
1 mile south of Barnard Castle
Ruins of small abbey on a hill
overlooking the Tees. Thirt-
eenth- to fourteenth-century
nave survives.

God's Bridge
(NY957 127), $1/_4$ mile south of
Pasture End Farm, 2 miles west
of Bowes on A66
Natural limestone bridge
spanning the River Greta. Once
carried a drove road, now used
by Pennine Wayfarers.

inn) and Bowlees (visitor centre, Low Force, pub). On through Middleton-in-Teesdale (interesting ex-lead mining village, cafés, shops,
pubs). Continue down the valley by way of Eggleston (interesting old
village) to Barnard Castle (castle, Bowes Museum, shops, cafés,
restaurants, hotels).

5
SWALEDALE

Narrow, sinuous and always grand, Swaledale is the most northerly of Yorkshire's major dales. Its river, the Swale, is born among peat hags and heather 2,000ft up on Birkdale Common, near the boundary with Cumbria. For its first few miles it is a frisky moorland beck, becoming youthfully exuberant above Keld, lively and increasingly mature in the next 10 miles to Reeth, and never losing its unique Pennine character until its leaves Richmond behind and enters the Vale of York.

The enclosing fells of Upper Swaledale are mostly acid moorland on sandstones and shales. Plant life is limited, grazing meagre. Lower down, limestone outcrops as crags and scars around Keld and mingles with alluvial soils in the valleys to support a richer flora. Stock find good pasture on hillsides and in valley meadows where lush grasses ripen sufficiently in the short summer to yield a vital hay crop by July. No other crops are grown in Swaledale; its farming is wholly pastoral — sheep on the fells, cattle, both dairy and beef in the valleys, with the occasional suckler herds on the higher slopes.

All buildings are made of stone — farms, barns, villages. These together with the enclosing dry-stone walls built patiently by craftsmen of yesteryear, developed much of the character of the dale. Above Reeth, Swaledale was very much an area of Norse settlement l,000 years ago. Until the turn of this century some dales farmers practiced a method of husbandry still common in parts of Norway and the Alps. A subsidiary house further up the dale was occupied during the summer, with sheep and cattle grazing pastures on the high fells, while valley fields produced the hay essential for winter feed.

It was for this hay that barns, or laithes were built. Nowhere in Britain is the pattern of dispersed barns shown so well as in Swaledale. The area of high dale's pasture west of Gunnerside is a fine example of this still practised method of farming husbandry. Utterly functional, and placed exactly where they were needed, the stone barns were for storing hay in the upper storey, and housing cattle below, usually from November to May. An average barn would store hay gathered from one or two fields, and accommodate four cattle, a small centre for foddering, milking, and 'mucking-out' during the long winter months. With changing methods of farming, some dales' barns have become redundant and in order to preserve their unique character, many are being put to other uses such as Camping Barns.

Swaledale experienced relative prosperity during the height of the lead mining industry. Men of Swaledale were renowned for their skills below ground, skills which were developed long before the Roman occupation, and continued into the present century. Not only did they mine lead but a little silver was found, though never enough to be commercially viable. Coal was also mined extensively beneath the moors around Tan Hill, providing fuel not only for domestic use, but mostly for lead smelting. Ownership of the lead mines had a long and complex history since the days when the Romans used it for waterpipes and roof cover. Monasteries owning vast areas of the North until the Dissolution were keen to exploit the underground riches to help cover the huge roof areas of their churches. Northern lead was used on cathedrals all over the country and a thriving trade started in medieval times transporting pigs (or ingots) of lead.

The highest village in the dale is Keld and it separates two faces of Swaledale. To the west the uplands are bleak and boggy, but eastwards the narrow valley is a delight, with its villages spaced almost equidistantly down the dale. These villages still serve as focal points for the hardy hill farms with their land on the steep valley sides, and common grazing on the open moors. In spring the moors are alive with the cry of the curlew, a call evocative of the vast open spaces of the High Pennines. Above is the sound of the wind soughing through the coarse grasses of the fells.

A multitude of small streams which drain Mallerstang Edge flow through the soggy mass of Birkdale Common and join west of Keld

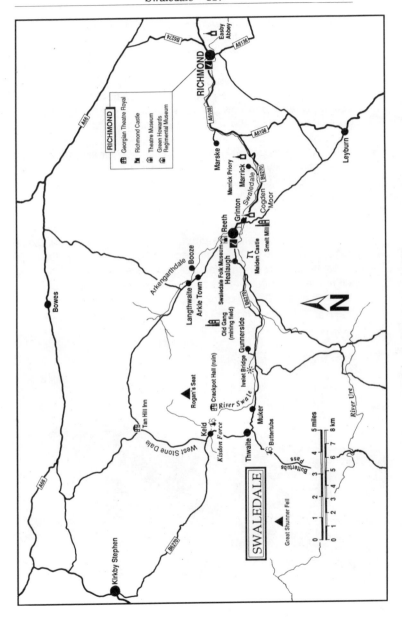

to form the River Swale proper. Pennine Wayfarers usually use Keld as a stopping place. **Keld**, which means a 'place by the river' was first settled by the Norsemen but the village today owes much of its appearance to the lead mining days of last century. The dour village still echoing its non-conformist traditions, huddles around a tiny square, away from the lonely road from Swaledale to Kirkby Stephen. Scattered relics of a now dead lead industry dot the nearby fells; ruined Crackpot Hall above wooded Swinnergill is the result of mining too close beneath it.

An ancient track, known as The Corpse Way, from the days when Swaledale's only church was over 10 miles away at Grinton, runs east across the airy side of Kisdon Hill from Keld. Still recognisable for much of it's length it can be followed either as the valley road, or by footpaths along the dale.

As though to recompense for the bleak heights in the upper limits of the dale, the river scenery around Keld is a delight. Here the Swale has cut through to the hard limestone beds which appear in dramatic steps, creating lively waterfalls. Of these, Kisdon Force is the best, set in a deep wooded gorge with wild flowers massing above it on Kisdon Hill. The hill separates the river's course from that of the road between Keld and Thwaite.

The village of Thwaite

Swaledale, near Keld

From Keld follow the Pennine Way route south-east, as far as the gate at the end of Keld Lane, then turn left away from the route down into the valley to Kisdon Force. Retrace your steps and rejoin the Pennine Way to follow it on a flat limestone shelf which gradually gives way to a path through high meadows all the way to Kisdon Farm. Leave the Pennine Way here and at the farm turn sharp right up the hill on a path across Kisdon Hill and back to Keld. This short walk ($4^1/_2$ miles, $2^1/_2$ hours) travels through a wonderland and the view down Swaledale from above Kisdon Farm is breathtaking.

Thwaite is a little huddle of stone houses and farms which seem to crouch together in mutual protection against winter storms. Here again is a village founded by Norsemen, for Thwaite means 'a clearing in woodland'. There are not many trees now, but if the valley below Keld is anything to go by then this sheltered part of the dale would once have been densely wooded. The trees were felled to create farmland and never given the opportunity to regenerate.

Swaledale's most famous sons of modern times were Richard and Cherry Kearton who were born at Thwaite and went to school in Muker, the next village down the dale. A lintel decorated with wildlife indicates the house where they were born and their name lives on at the friendly Kearton Guest House in Thwaite. Towards the end of the last century these two did more than anyone to popularise natural history when the subject was considered to be far too academic for the masses. Richard was a lecturer and Cherry became the first freelance wildlife photographer, filming big game in Africa and travelling all over the world in search of material. Photographing birds and animals in the days before sophisticated telephoto lenses and fast film was extremely difficult. To overcome their many problems, not the least being the need to get close to their subject, the Keartons employed many ingenious methods. These included the use, as a hide, of a stuffed cow, which often blew over in a high wind, or received the inquisitive attentions of live ones! Other methods were to hide in artificial tree trunks or boulders. They often stood on each other's shoulders or hung over precipices to obtain the shots they wanted.

High up on the eastern side of Shunner Fell and almost at the summit of the Muker-Hawes road are the **Buttertubs**, a series of deep holes easily accessible from the road. They are deep enough to break the bones of anyone foolish enough to wander carelessly on their brink and fall, but shallow enough to see the shade-loving hartstongue and other ferns which live in them. The technical term for the Buttertubs is 'swallow hole' and perhaps this is an apt description of them as they have been formed by the action of water dissolving parts of the limestone strata. Frost action, followed by more water, has created what is seen today.

Muker, meaning 'a cultivated enclosure', is another Norse settlement, but built on earlier foundations, as indicated by the number of Neolithic artefacts which have been unearthed from time to time around the village. The church is sixteenth century and corpses were brought to its burial ground from most of the upper dale. Prior to 1580 when it was built, all burials were at Grinton. Most of the original character of Muker Church was lost by eighteenth- and nineteenth-century alterations, but it did not lose any of its charm and is still the focal point of the village.

Muker is especially proud of its band which was formed in 1879. Brass bands seem to have been a feature of the old lead mining villages and were encouraged by the lead companies, especially the London Lead Company who set their employees' welfare high in their priorities.

Downstream from Muker short tributary valleys branch off at almost regular intervals north and south. Some are traversed by roads, others by paths, but all are of interest and worth exploring. This is where the true unspoilt character of the dales is still to be found. **Oxnop** entering Swaledale from the south below the Askrigg road, is such a valley, a ghyll dale where mountain ash, scrub birch, hawthorn, holly and willow fill the sheltered ravine echoing a time before man began to dominate the landscape. The wood was a favourite hunting ground for the Keartons in their search for wildlife subjects. A path skirts the boundary of the woodland and starts from the roadside close to the junction of the B6270, valley road and the side lane to Gunnerside.

Opposite Oxnop Ghyll and Kearton's Wood, the Swale is spanned by Ivelet Bridge, an excellent example of a pack-horse bridge which carries an ancient track across to **Gunnerside** village. This name again comes from old Norse and means 'Gunner's Pasture'. Above the village to the north Old Gang mines were one of the most famous of all the lead mining complexes in the dales.

Gunnerside is at the foot of Gunnerside Gill which rises beneath Rogan's Seat about 6 miles away. Gunnerside Gill is a living museum of lead mining and two moorland tracks which follow its edges served

Surrender Bridge, Hard Level Gill

Old Gang smelt mill,
Hard Level Gill

The village of Muker

the complex almost self-supporting industry. The valley sides are scarred with the results of repeated hushings which have left alluvial fans of debris at the foot of the slope. Two smelt mills, Lownathwaite and Blakethwaite were worked well into the late nineteenth century. Spoil heaps and the remains of various buildings associated with mining activity can readily be seen.

There is an excellent traverse of the top of Gunnerside Gill's ravine. This walk (8 miles, 4 hours) which starts from Gunnerside village and visits many of the ruined mine buildings, spoil heaps and hushes, is covered by an informative trail leaflet produced by the Yorkshire Dales National Park Authority.

A high level path joins Gunnerside to Low Row and Feetham, linking villages further down the dale which have almost merged, but which still keep their individual character. Thomas Armstrong, the Yorkshire novelist, lived hereabouts, and his book, *Adam Brunskill*, is based on lead mining in this part of Swaledale during the second half of last century.

Healaugh at the foot of Barney Beck, was originally a Saxon dwelling place in a forest clearing. The village serves as a suitable base for exploring the upper reaches of Barney Beck, in the area known as Hard Level Gill. This is where the remains of one of the most famous and productive mining complexes can be seen. Known as the Old Gang mining field, it is possible to get within a mile or so of it from a car parked near Surrender Bridge on the moorland road north from Feetham to Arkengarthdale, where a beck-side track leads upstream to the mining complex at the dale head. Even though all is now ruins, it is easy to pick out the various buildings from their foundations. The mines were owned by a variety of persons and companies through more than 150 years. Lead ore dug out of the Old Gang mines was processed entirely within the confines of Hard Level Gill before being carried out of the dale by pack-horse trains. **Do not attempt to enter any of the old mines — they are all in dangerous condition**.

One of the attractive qualities of Upper Swaledale is its ability to allow the pedestrian to walk all the way from Keld to Grinton by riverside footpaths. Except where the road touches the river bank, a public footpath exists all the way down the valley. From Keld to Muker paths exist on both sides of the south-flowing river, but from Muker onwards the path keeps mainly to the north bank.

Early man left his mark with a giant earthwork at **Maiden Castle** and its attendant tumuli and dikes high on the fell side opposite Healaugh and Reeth. Theories abound, but no real answer can be offered about its original purpose. Reached by footpaths west of Grinton, one can only stand in awe at the tremendous labours involved in such huge earth moving schemes.

An impression of Swaledale life in the heyday of lead mining is displayed in the Swaledale Folk Museum at Reeth. The museum not only covers the history of lead mining in the locality, but also highlights social conditions of bygone days from the point of view of a farming community as well as mining.

In Saxon times **Reeth** was only a settlement on the forest edge, but by the time of the Norman Conquest it had grown sufficently in importance to be noted in the *Domesday Book*. Later it became a centre for hand-knitting and the local lead industry was controlled from here, but it was always a market town for the local farming community. Its eighteenth-century houses and hotels clustered around the triangular village green make it one of the honeypots of the dales. Down the ages, Reeth has been a bustling place, in the middle of the nineteenth century there were seven fairs and a weekly market. Now the streets around the green can be packed with cars on a fine summer day. In early autumn an annual show and sheep sales are held on the meadows below the town.

Reeth fills a sheltered position above the meeting of Arkle Beck and the Swale. **Arkengarthdale**, the side dale climbing north-west from Reeth, had one of the first turnpike roads to be built in the area. It was originally part of a drove road which came south from Teesdale to Tan Hill then down Arkengarthdale as far as Langthwaite before climbing over Reeth Moor to Feetham. From here the drove road continued south to Askrigg in Wensleydale and on to the Roman road across Cam Fell into Ribblesdale. The reason for improving this section of the drove road in Arkengarthdale in 1741 was to help move coal mined around Tan Hill down to the lower part of Arkengarthdale. Here it was used to fuel the smelting furnaces around Langthwaite.

If there is one dale where the whole story of lead mining can be seen from mine to smelt mill then Arkengarthdale is it. The museum at Reeth tells everything in graphic form, but the true museum is to be found above and beneath the dale. Hushes scar the hillsides; levels where mines were driven either horizontally or at an angle from the middle slopes. Deep shafts open dangerously on the upper fells and ruined crushing mills and smelting mills dot the valley floor. All this was activity fuelled by the coal of Tan Hill. Most of the mines were owned by Charles Bathurst and his descendants who operated as the CB Company. The only surviving roofed building from this complex is the powder house in a field by the road junction west of the CB Hotel. The building dates from about 1807.

The townships of Arkengarthdale were founded before mining came to dominate the dale. **Arkle Town** was a Norse settlement which gave its name to the dale, but the main village is **Langthwaite**, whose church, however, is one of the Commissioners' churches built soon after Waterloo. Above it is the delightful Georgian-styled CB Hotel. Devotees of the TV programme about a Dales' vet's life, *All Creatures Great and Small*, will instantly recognise the hump-backed bridge and attractive group of cottages just off the main road at Langthwaite. For many episodes the bridge was used in the opening scene. The watersplash, used in another of the series, is not far away on the moorland road to Feetham.

In a side valley and reached by a side road from Langthwaite, is the hamlet of **Booze**. There is no pub, and the name means 'the house by the curve' — there are no connections with inns or drunkenness!

There are old miners' tracks on both sides of the upper valley

Arkengarthdale from Great Pinseat

A Dales' farmhouse above Langthwaite, Arkengarthdale

High Seat, Mallerstang Edge

which will give the walker ample scope especially when used to explore the mining remains, but the road from Reeth to Tan Hill is probably the best way of exploring Arkengarthdale.

Rich deposits of lead were worked on the opposite side of the Swale from Arkengarthdale. These are mostly centred on a broad swathe above Grinton where the inevitable scars left by hushing and other mining debris cover the fell sides. In early times **Grinton** was the centre of Swaledale, with the only consecrated ground in the dale. Corpses brought to it from the upper dale were carried in wicker baskets by relays of men from each village through which it passed. The custom continued until 1586 when the Muker burial ground was consecrated. Grinton Church, which has often been referred to as the 'Cathedral of the Dales', was originally Norman but was added to in the thirteenth and fourteenth centuries. Of its many interesting features, perhaps the best is the 'Leper's Squint' where people with this dreadful affliction were able to watch the service without actually coming into contact with the rest of the congregation. The village inn sits at the junction of the valley road with the one over to Wensleydale, and a turreted shooting lodge on the moors above Grinton now serves as a very well appointed Youth Hostel.

Man has lived a long time around Grinton. The many tumuli and earthworks surrounding the village indicate a great involvement with some force either political or religious, but none have had as much effort put into them as the huge and complex earthwork which appears to have been a barrier between Grinton Gill and the enigmatic earthwork of Maiden Castle. Roman remains found hereabouts give rise to the thought of battles between the invaders and local tribes.

On **Cogden Moor** and just off the Leyburn road above Grinton stands the remains of a smelt mill built by the London Lead Company in about 1840 and after recent conservation one of the best examples in the Dales. The best way to reach these interesting ruins is by a path which follows the course of Cogden Beck from the sharp hairpin bend half a mile above Grinton Lodge. The whole of this valley is scarred with the remains of hushing and an hour or so may be spent picking over the stones to find samples of lead ore, fluorspar and other minerals. From the mill continue up onto the moor to an area of spoil heaps, before swinging round to the left to rejoin the road beyond the old Wellington Vein mine.

After all the wanderings in and around Swaledale's mining past a complete change of environment comes with the south-west facing villages of Fremington and Marrick on the north side of the dale below Reeth. Their history is almost as old as man in the dale. Below **Marrick** and reached by a long flight of steps, is Marrick Priory a twelfth-century Benedictine nunnery, whose chapel is now used as a Field Study Centre. Further downstream is Ellerton Abbey founded by the nuns of the Cistercian order in the fourteenth century. Little remains of this nunnery except a tower and parts of the nave walls.

The main road from Grinton (the B6270) accompanies the river to Richmond with good valley scenery all the way. In contrast to Richmond, the old road which climbs high above Marrick has more open views to offer of these lower reaches of the Pennine section of Swaledale.

Marske-in-Swaledale, although strictly in the side dale of Marske Beck, is idyllic, purely agricultural and surrounded by wooded hills beneath wild moors. The hall was home and birthplace of the Hutton family who provided two Archbishops of York, one of whom, Matthew, became Archbishop of Canterbury in 1757. Marske's church has Norman origins, with additions in the thirteenth and seventeenth centuries.

On a high rocky crag above the Swale stands a memorial stone erected in 1606 by Robert Willance. It commemorates his survival after his horse fell from the crag in fog. Willance broke a leg and only saved himself by cutting open the dead horse's belly and thrusting his leg inside to keep it warm. The old road descends to Richmond, past Beacon Hill which, on a clear day, is an excellent view point and from which the spires of York Minster can be seen far to the south.

Swaledale's capital, **Richmond** with its cobbled ways and attractive town houses, is the northern gateway to the Dales. The castle commanded all access in and out of Swaledale manned by troops whose twentieth-century counterparts train at nearby Catterick. Earl Alan Rufus built his massive castle soon after the Norman Conquest and roofed it with Swaledale lead. Later the upkeep of the town walls was paid for by lead coming out of the dale, on a toll of two old pence a mule load. Richmond became a stronghold in an area often under attack by Scottish invaders. Fragments of the old walls can still be seen in Friar's Wynd and at the bar on Cornforth Hill. Legends link Richmond Castle with King Arthur and his Knights of the Round Table; a local worthy is reputed to have stumbled upon their treasure in a hidden cavern beneath the castle, but fled on seeing the

Grinton Smelt Mill

A view of Richmond from the castle

PLACES TO VISIT AROUND UPPER SWALEDALE

Arkengarthdale
Above Reeth on B6270
Remains of mining activity with ruined smelt mills, flues, hushes, powder house. Pleasant short walks take in most of these features.

Buttertubs
$2^1/_2$ miles south of Thwaite on Hawes road, below top of the pass
Shallow potholes on hillside on both sides of the road. Car parking and explanatory plaque.

Grinton
Church which is often claimed to be the 'Cathedral of the Dales' and was originally Norman.

Kisdon Force
$^1/_2$ mile east of Keld on B6270
Waterfall in wooded gorge. Approached by an easy footpath from Keld.

Marrick Priory
Reached by a stone causeway from Marrick village $^1/_2$ mile to the north-east

Ruins set by a wooded stretch of the Swale.

Reeth
A once important lead mining centre. Attractive houses and inns surround a pleasant village green. Swaledale Folk Museum at Reeth Green depicts life in Swaledale in bygone days, including lead mining, farming, and village life.

Richmond
Ancient market town and guardian of the northern dales. Castle was built in 1071 by Alan Rufus. The keep is one of the tallest in England.
Green Howards Regimental Museum, Trinity Church Square Richmondshire Museum, working Georgian Theatre Royal and Theatre Museum, on Victoria Road.

Thwaite
At junction of Hawes and B6270 roads, in Upper Swaledale Typical dales village of Norse origin.

assembled warriors. Unfortunately he could not find the cave again and so King Arthur and his Knights still sleep awaiting the call in England's hour of need.

As Richmond grew in importance it became the focal point for the commercial and agricultural interests of the dale and also the surrounding area; there has been a market since 1155. The town incidentally is far older than its Surrey namesake. Tradesmen settled in the town and formed their guilds, some of which have existed in Richmond for over 400 years. Nowadays the guilds are only interesting anachronisms which meet twice yearly for dinners, their only function to appoint a new 'freeman' to their numbers. At one time the office of freeman carried a number of useful privileges not the least being the freedom from road, bridges and market tolls anywhere in England!

The local regiment is the Green Howards who along with the Royal Corps of Signals and RAF Catterick, can march through Richmond with bands playing and bayonets fixed. The Green Howards Regimental Museum is housed in Trinity Church Square opposite the Kings Head. The *Lass of Richmond Hill*, Frances l'Anson, lived at Hill House and was immortalised by Leonard McNally who wrote the song and married her in 1787. Richmond is home to the fine Georgian Theatre Royal close to the market place, built in 1788 by Samuel Butler and faithfully restored in 1963 by a local society. The theatre with its tiny authentic Georgian stage, to which one must add the crowded Georgian intimacy of its auditorium, gives a varied repertoire of plays and concerts throughout the season.

Reached by road, or by a short riverside path through woods below Richmond, is **Easby Abbey**. This Premonstratensian abbey was founded in 1152 by Roaldus, Constable of Richmond. When Henry VIII was carrying out his Dissolution of the Monasteries the canons supported the Pilgrimage of Grace. Joining other northern religious houses in 1596, they started out for London to petition the king. On the king's orders the Duke of Norfolk attacked the protestors at Skipworth Moor, and many of those captured were later executed on Tower Hill.

Beyond Richmond the Swale meanders on through rich agricultural land of the northern part of the Vale of York, before joining the Ure on its way to York, and eventually into the Humber and the North Sea.

SELECTED WALKS

Kisdon Hill 4$^1/_2$ miles • Moderate • 2$^1/_2$ hours
This walk follows part of the Swaledale 'corpse road' from Keld and returns along the Pennine Way around the graceful contours of Kisdon Hill.

From Keld follow the B6270 downhill to a footpath sign on the left marked 'Muker'. Take the rough track, across a stream then bear right towards the hillside. Continue along an elevated track until you reach a signpost indicating the Pennine Way and turn left. Follow a level path across the limestone outcrop (caution; slippery when wet). Look across the valley on the right. Ruined Crackpot Hall is opposite and later Kisdon Force can be reached by a short detour. Go through natural woodland, then uphill along a narrow lane into Keld.

Thwaite and Muker 3 miles • Easy • 1$^1/_2$ hours
This walk could be linked to the one previous by joining it at the Pennine Way sign near Kisdon Farm above Thwaite, to make a figure-of-eight route. It visits two of the most attractive and unspoilt villages in Swaledale.

Follow Pennine Way signs north-east through a complex of fields from Thwaite, then climb above Doctor Wood. Keep left of Kisdon Farm then right at the signpost (left if linking to the Kisdon Hill walk, returning to this point later). Go down a farm track into Muker (pub nearby). Do not go as far as the main road, but turn right along a narrow back street to reach open fields. Use stiles and walk in single file along the grassy path. On reaching the road turn right as far as the bridge, but do not cross. Keep ahead on a field path into Thwaite.

Marrick Priory 5$^1/_2$ miles • Moderate/Easy • 2$^3/_4$ hours
Here is a walk which can be linked with a visit to Reeth. It quickly leaves the crowds behind, calling at a tranquil priory along the way.

Walk down to Reeth Bridge and turn left on to a field path. Climb up to High Fremington Farm and keep to the rear of the farm buildings. Follow a path across a series of fields as far as a narrow lane and turn left, uphill (watch out for traffic). At a sharp left hand bend at the top of the hill, go right at a footpath sign and cross three fields. Follow the path as far as a stone stile giving access into a lane and turn right for Marrick. Take the first right into the village, then right again following a sign to 'Marrick Priory'. Cross a field then go down a flight of stone steps at the side of a wood. Walk past farm buildings and the priory to their access road. Turn left on to the road, go through an iron gate and immediately right into a field. There is no path, but the right-of-way can be followed diagonally left by lining up stiles and gates across a series of fields. Go down to the road and turn left for about 70yd then right over a stile. Follow the riverbank, upstream to the road bridge. Cross the road and go through a stile, bear right on a footpath to Reeth.

A SCENIC CAR DRIVE

Through Swaledale 42 miles

At a first glance it might not seem possible to follow a circuit around Swaledale without using the same road continuously, but with the exception of a short stretch of the B6270 near Reeth and by using unclassified side roads, the dale's varied beauties can be explored without seeing the same place twice.

The drive starts in Richmond; take the minor road north-west from the town centre, out on to Richmond Moor above Whitcliffe Scar (view point accessible only by footpath) and go steeply down into Marske. Continue via Fremington into Reeth (folk museum, village green, cafés, pubs) and turn right for Arkengarthdale. Drive along the dale, through Langthwaite (pubs) and across the moors to the Tan Hill Inn (view point). Left at the T-junction and down West Stones Dale to the B6270; turn left along the dale road, through Keld, Thwaite (restaurant), Muker (pub) and Gunnerside (pubs, cafés, art gallery, shop and Gunnerside Beck walking trail). Continue to follow the valley bottom road, through Feetham, Healaugh and Reeth. Bear right to cross the river and still following the B6270, left through Grinton (pub) and then joining the A6108 along an increasingly wooded stretch of the Swale back to Richmond (castle, shops, cafés, pubs, museum).

Richmond Castle from the River Tees

Easby Abbey near Richmond

6
WENSLEYDALE

In sharp contrast to its northerly sisters, Wensleydale shows a more gentle face even in its upper reaches. Where Swaledale is narrow, Wensleydale soon broadens into lush pasture. Its mining activity was confined to working an extension of the Grinton ores, and through the centuries Wensleydale evolved a distinctive pastoral character which makes it a particular favourite for many visitors.

The name Wensleydale derives not from a river but from a village. Indeed, were it called by its ancient river name the valley should really be Yoredale, but today the river is known as the Ure, which rises among the lonely mosses and sedge-grasses of Abbotside Common, on the eastern edge of Mallerstang. Its furthest point starts south of Hell Gill Bridge, close to the county boundaries of Cumbria and North Yorkshire, a line also used by the National Park. After a short southwards flow its waters, quickly augmented by other becks draining from the high fells, swing eastwards by the Moorcock Inn near Garsdale Head, and continue in this direction out beyond Leyburn and Jervaulx Abbey, where the flat lands of the Vale of York draws it southwards towards the Ouse.

Wensley village, several miles down the dale, was, during the thirteenth century, the only market in the valley, and it is perhaps this medieval importance which led to its giving the valley the name by which it is now known. Today, Leyburn, near Wensley, and Hawes, in the upper dale, are the market towns, busy centres both agriculturally and as focal points for an increasing number of visitors.

Several of the river's high tributaries, notably from Widdale near Hawes, together with its tributary Snaizeholme Beck, contributes a greater volume of water, but a logical continuation upstream from the

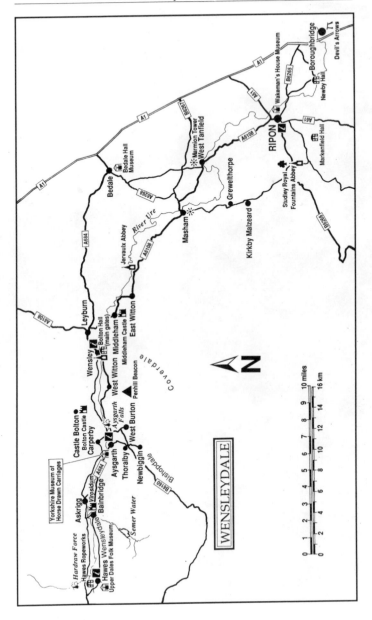

WENSLEYDALE

Yorkshire Museum of Horse Drawn Carriages

Hardraw Force
Hawes Ropeworks
Hawes
Wensleydale
Upper Dales Folk Museum
Askrigg
Yorebridge
Bainbridge
Semer Water
Carperby
Castle Bolton
Bolton Castle
Aysgarth
Aysgarth Falls
Thoralby
West Burton
Newbiggin
Bishopdale
Wensley
Bolton Hall (main gates)
Leyburn
West Witton
Middleham
Middleham Castle
East Witton
Penhill Beacon
Coverdale
Jervaulx Abbey
River Ure
Bedale
Bedale Hall Museum
Masham
Kirkby Malzeard
Grewelthorpe
Marmion Tower
West Tanfield
RIPON
Wakeman's House Museum
Markenfield Hall
Studley Royal
Fountains Abbey
Boroughbridge
Devil's Arrows
Newby Hall

A1
A684
A6108
A6108
A684
B6160
A6108
A6268
B6267
A1
A61
A6108
A61
B6265
B6267

N

miles 0 1 2 3 4 5 6 7 8 9 10 miles
km   0 2 4 6 8 10 12 14 16 km

Lead mining display at the Upper Dales Folk Museum, Hawes

Crocketts Hotel, Hawes

The River Ure, near Hawes

main dale leads to Garsdale Common where the Moorcock Inn at 1,063ft above sea level is on the watershed with Garsdale. Side valleys are an important feature of Wensleydale, each in itself worthy of separate exploration. Widdale has been mentioned and with the exception of Apedale near Castle Bolton, all the central tributaries flow north into Wensleydale. Sleddale has a short run through Hawes, next comes Raydale with mysterious Semer Water, one of the Dales' few lakes, then Bishopdale with its own tributary of Walden Beck, Coverdale where they breed champion racehorses, and finally Colsterdale which joins the Ure near Masham and is probably the least known of all the minor dales.

Lady Anne Clifford came this way when she visited her northern estates. Many ancient footpaths and bridleways link Wensleydale to dales north and south. It is possible to walk the length of Wensleydale from the Moorcock Inn to Middleham using public footpaths and quiet side roads.

Appersett, at the mouth of Widdale and the first village in Upper Swaledale, is one of a group of hamlets near Hawes whose name includes a legacy from the days of Norse settlement and farming. A 'sett', or *sætr*, was a place for the summer pasturing of stock. Other examples further down the dale, are Burtersett, Countersett and Marsett.

Widdale links across to Ribblesdale and forms a natural route for the B6255, with Widdale Fell to the north-west and Cam Pasture and Dodd Fell to the south and east. Widdale has its own tributary, Snaizeholme, and although there is no footpath out of the dale head, it is possible to follow Snaizeholme Beck all the way from the B6255 to Stone Gill Foot by right-of-way (4 miles, 2 hours).

The Pennine Way passes through Hawes using a complex system of ancient roads and tracks on its route from Ribblesdale. This is part drove road and part Roman road across Cam Pasture and then a long sweeping run down from Dodd Fell by way of Sleddale Pasture on a delightful green road. It is these green roads which feature so much in the Pennine dales at Yorkshire. They are often walled for most of their length and are therefore safe and easy to follow stretching for mile after mile in solitude over the high fells of the Pennines. Invariably they follow the high ground over the shortest route between centres of agricultural population. Modern transport tends to shun their more exposed passage and has left the green roads well alone.

Hawes has rightly been called 'the capital of Upper Wensley-dale'. Its name comes from the Anglo-Saxon *haus*, meaning a mountain pass, such as Honister Hause in the Lake District, a major pass between Borrowdale and the Buttermere valley. Hawes is one of the highest market towns in England. Having held a market charter only since 1700, Hawes is a comparative newcomer but today it is a thriving little place linked by good roads to neighbouring dales, all easily accessible from the A684. Its growth increased when the railway came through the dale in 1878 and made it possible for Victorian tourists to 'discover' Upper Wensleydale. Since the decline of branch lines and the closure of what was scenically a most attractive line, Hawes Station has been put to use as an information centre, and also housing the Upper Dales Folk Museum where a comprehensive display of farm implements and mementoes of life in the dales is on view. The bulk of the collection was made by two women who have done much to record the past in these parts, Marie Hartley and Joan Ingilby. Industry in Hawes, apart from farming, has been specialised. At one time it was an important centre for hand-knitted hosiery and for 200 years has been noted for rope making, a craft which is carried on in a long shed close to the station car park. Hawes Ropeworks has become a popular tourist attraction where you can watch the production and maybe buy from a wide range of rope articles, including tethers for cows and horses.

Hawes is very busy during the tourist season, with a weekly livestock market at its most active during sheep and lamb sales from August to October in the market at the east end of the town. Each year over 100,000 sheep and lambs change hands together with over 12,000 head of cattle. Although its roots go back to the fifteenth century, few old buildings remain, seventeenth-century dates and initials indicate their first owners. Walkers following the Pennine Way reach Hawes along a quaint stone flagged passage which enters the main street beneath an often flower decked archway.

Adjacent to and dominated by Hawes, the hamlet of **Gayle** is a much older place and is thought to be built on the foundations of a Celtic settlement. Visitors to Gayle will be difficult to please if they are not entranced by the gentle hypnotism of the series of waterfalls where Duerley Beck crosses the limestone beds and ledges above the bridge. Gayle Force is immediately above the bridge and Aisgill Force, some 30ft high, can be reached by a footpath to the south- west of the village. Wensleydale cheese, once produced from ewes'

Pack-horse bridge at
Sedbusk near Hawes

Hardraw Force

Sheep pen at Hardraw — sheep are a vital part of the Dales' economy

Carved detail over a doorway in Askrigg

143

milk in farmhouses throughout the dale, is now made in the Hawes Creamery between Hawes and Gayle.

Pennine Way walkers leave Hawes by the Muker road and once over the river turn left to Hardraw where the Green Dragon Inn extracts a small toll to view the spectacle of **Hardraw Force** — England's highest waterfall above ground (Gaping Gill and other pothole falls are greater, but below ground). At Hardraw, the soft Yoredale shales have been worn back by the force of water and it is now possible to walk behind the fall. The natural auditorium is frequently used in summer for brass band concerts.

Visitors looking for an exhilarating walk (12 miles, 6 to 7 hours) can follow the Pennine Way to the summit of Great Shunner Fell and on a clear day this makes an excellent view point. To the south are Whernside, Ingleborough and Penyghent, but the best views of all are those to the Lakeland fells on the western horizon. The walk up Shunner Fell leaves Hardraw and turns right along the walled lane beyond the Green Dragon.

Wensleydale, like Swaledale, has an old and a new road, but where the Swaledale roads keep swapping sides, the old and the new in Wensleydale keep mostly to their appointed courses. The old in this case being the one on the north side avoiding a river crossing all the way east from Appersett. While traffic hurtles along on the A684 life is more relaxed along the line of the old road. **Askrigg** is typical of the villages north of the Ure, a tightly-knit village of seventeenth- and eighteenth-century houses at the foot of its common land. Two roads from Swaledale join at Askrigg on their sweep descent from Askrigg Common. Askrigg was old before the Normans came and a market was held there until Hawes superceded it. As was the case in other villages around, hand-knitting was a flourishing industry before mechanisation came along. This is 'Herriot' country; a sturdy cobble-fronted house opposite the ancient church has been used so often as Skeldale House in the *All Creatures Great and Small* TV series, that the name has stuck! Two waterfalls nearby are Mill Gill Force and Whitfield Force and the easy stroll to Mill Gill Force (1 mile, 1 hour) would make a pleasant saunter after lunch in Askrigg. To reach it take the lane behind the church to its end and then cross the beck by a signposted path and on through a pretty wood. Follow the stream as far as the waterfall.

Across the dale and on a tight double bend on the A684 is **Bainbridge**. The present day village is mostly on the west bank of the

River Bain, and leaves the relics of Roman Bainbridge for some future archaeologists to uncover. Roman *Virosidum*, on a high mound above the village once held a cohort of 500 men. As the fort is on private land, permission must be sought before entering the site. What little is known of the fort indicates that it was an important outpost guarding Wensleydale. The fort was connected by a direct road to *Isurium*, modern Aldborough near Boroughbridge in the east, and another road led south-west over Cam Fell towards Ribblehead, then to Lancaster or Ribchester. Most of the Roman road can still be traced as the green lane across Cam Fell, then as a metalled road to Ribblehead and beyond.

After the Norman Conquest, Bainbridge was the headquarters of the forest wardens of the Forest of Wensleydale who were charged with its protection for the king. The forest in this case was the woodland variety but gradually clearances provided farm land for an ever increasing population. The only link with the ancient forest is the custom of blowing the horn at 9pm every night from late September to Shrovetide, to warn travellers still out in the forest.

To the south of Bainbridge, a quiet road through Countersett, a village with long standing Quaker traditions, leads into Raydale and to a natural lake — a rarity in the dales. **Semer Water** was formed during the last Ice Age when a retreating glacier left a moraine, or pile of debris, which acted as a dam. So say the geologists but local lore has a much more romantic legend. This says that there is a drowned village beneath Semer Water. A poor traveller tried to get shelter one wild and stormy night, but was refused by all except a shepherd and his wife whose house stood beyond the village. The next morning the traveller laid the following curse:

> *Semerwater rise — Semerwater sink,*
> *And swallow all the town,*
> *Save yon little house*
> *Where they gave me food and drink.*

Immediately a tremendous deluge started and drowned all the village and its inhabitants except the kind shepherd and his wife. True or false, the strange twist to this tale is that in 1937 when the level of the lake was being lowered in a land reclamation scheme, a Bronze Age village was found beneath the waters. Another story concerns the conspicuous boulder near the lake's outflow. Known as the 'Carlin Stone', it is said to have been thrown there by the Devil, but is part of the moraine dam.

Limestone beds which feature so prominently in the western part of the dales dip below ground to the east and north-east, but in lower Wensleydale they are visible as the river bed, and what an effect it makes.

Below Aysgarth the river tumbles over three broad steps in the limestone to create the famous **Aysgarth Falls**, one of the most popular picnic spots in the dales. Careful screening of the National Park car park on the site of the old railway station north of the river,

Bainbridge

ensures that cars do not detract visually from the scenic value of the falls. Paths to the falls are signposted and there is an excellent information centre by the old station and a nature trail through the surrounding woodlands. The obvious power of the river was used to drive the mill, which now houses the Yorkshire Museum of Horse Drawn Carriages. The mill has had a mixed career; a woollen mill, later a flour mill, and once supplied material for 7,000 red flannel shirts for Italian soldiers of Garibaldi's army. A viewing platform recently added to the museum gives the best views of Aysgarth's Upper Falls, but the Middle and Lower Falls are the most impressive.

Aysgarth village in the *Domesday Book* is recorded as 'Eshescard' meaning 'an open space marked by oaks'. Its church, though built on ancient foundations, is mainly nineteenth century and con-

The Upper Falls, Aysgarth in drought conditions

tains medieval woodwork removed from Jervaulx Abbey after the Dissolution. In particular a fifteenth-century screen, regarded as the finest piece of Cistercian woodwork in North Yorkshire, and a finely carved reading desk almost identical to the choir stalls at Wensley is here.

Bishopdale, another of the tributaries of the Ure, is quiet and little known despite having the road from Wharfedale down its length. Few motorists who drive over from Buckden take the trouble to stop and explore its hidden byways, but those who do will be well rewarded. The three Bishopdale villages, **West Burton**, **Thoralby** and **Newbiggin** are clusters of interesting houses, most of them around 200 years old. Both West Burton and Thoralby have pretty waterfalls nearby and a complex of interlinked footpaths weaves in and out of the farmsteads on the dale's side. West Burton is built medieval fashion around a wide green, but despite its apparent age does not have a church or a market cross. The stepped obelisk at the head of the village green only dates from 1820. A fieldpath north from West Burton towards the A684, passes two strange looking towers on private land close to Edgley Farm. Even though they may look like follies, they once served a useful purpose as smoke houses for curing bacon. The track which climbs from Newbiggin above Bishopdale to Wasset Fell was originally used by the miners who worked the sparse veins on the fells between Bishopdale and Walden Beck.

In late August **West Witton**, straggling for a mile along the A684, has a traditional bonfire ceremony. The true origin is probably pagan and lost in antiquity, but is known locally as the 'Burning of Owd Bartle' or St Bartholomew, and takes place on the saint's feast day. West Witton was mentioned in the *Domesday Book* as 'Wittone', a 'stone village'. Penhill to the south of the village is an ancient beacon site, a point for both warning and celebratory fires. A three-quarters of a mile climb from the Melmerby road leads to this vantage point with its views of Wensleydale. A little over a mile west of West Witton and reached by a footpath leaving the A684 at Swinithwaite Templar's Chapel, the scant remains of the Knights Templar, withold the story of why this enigmatic semi-military order held their devotions in such a remote, but beautiful spot.

Across the shoulder of Penhill is **Coverdale**, the last of the Ure's southern feeders, another of the often ignored places of solitude. The long valley road through its scattered communities offers many rewards to the motorist, but great care must be taken on its descent into Wharfedale down steep Park Rash. This road was once a pack-horse way and the village of Horsehouse in the middle of the dale was a principal resting place before the long haul across the moors to Kettlewell. Pack-horse trains would have crossed the river by the beautiful bridge below the church.

Footpaths which in the old days were made to provide the shortest passage between two places can be used for pleasure today. Two which linked Coverdale to Bishopdale (with careful planning and the use of the OS map) offer an enjoyable day's walk of about 10 miles across Carlton Moor.

Returning to the main dale and travelling north along the road from Aysgarth, the village of **Carperby** proudly boasts the fact that it has twice won the best kept village competition organised by the Yorkshire Rural Community Council. There was once a market here centred on the seven-stepped cross which was raised in 1674. Nearby in the fields north of the road can be seen examples of lynchets — horizontal strips ploughed along a hillside in medieval days to provide more arable land. James Herriot and his bride spent their honeymoon at the cosy Wheatsheaf Inn at Carperby. Followers of his stories will recall that while there, he also had to carry out a series of tuberculosis tests on a nearby herd of cattle.

The first road to be built through Wensleydale kept well above the north bank of the river and wound up and down steep hillsides in a manner which would be unacceptable for motorised traffic. As a result the villages on this side have remained unspoilt with very little development over the years.

Castle Bolton village saw excitement for over a year during the Civil War and it is nice to think that little has happened to it since then. Bolton Castle dominates the western end of this unspoilt village. It was built in 1379 at a cost of £12,000 for the first Lord Scrope, a Chancellor of England. The ill fated Mary, Queen of Scots was lodged here from July 1567 to January 1569 on her slow journey south and eventual execution. Colonel Chaytor held the castle for the Crown against the troops of Oliver Cromwell until forced by starvation to surrender in 1645. The castle remained unoccupied until recently when work was commenced to preserve this fine building. A licenced restaurant occupies the restored section of the castle.

Across Apedale Beck **Redmire** housed miners who worked the veins of the south side of the Grinton ore field. In 1861 the population was 420 but now it is about half that number. Redmire takes its name

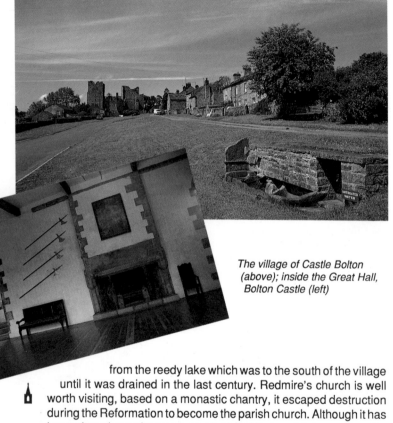

The village of Castle Bolton (above); inside the Great Hall, Bolton Castle (left)

from the reedy lake which was to the south of the village until it was drained in the last century. Redmire's church is well worth visiting, based on a monastic chantry, it escaped destruction during the Reformation to become the parish church. Although it has been altered over the years, much of the Norman fabric remains, the doorway being the best example. Marked on the OS map as 'Old Flue' above Preston-under-Scar, the longest flue in England ran underground from the smelt mill at Keld Heads to Cobscar over half a mile away on the moors to the north. Some of the richest lead veins in Wensleydale were worked around here. Not shown on any OS map are the prehistoric dwellings discovered a little to the east of Preston-under-Scar. The road from Catterick across the scar has the surprise view of Wensleydale from Scarth Nick. Below Redmire, Apedale

PLACES TO VISIT IN WENSLEYDALE

Aysgarth Falls
$\frac{1}{4}$ mile east of Aysgarth
A series of limestone steps create the Upper and Lower Falls. Information centre, nature trail and car parking.

Bedale Hall Museum
Junction of A684 and A6268
Hall dates from seventeenth century. Georgian ballroom with fine Italian plaster ceiling and rare floor. Museum displays local arts and crafts, tradesmen's tools, clocks, coins, weights etc.

Castle Bolton
Village and castle 4$\frac{1}{2}$ miles north-east of Aysgarth on Reeth road
Attractive village made up of houses ranging in two rows away from the castle. Castle built by Richard Scrope in the fourteenth century. Mary Queen of Scots kept prisoner here. Held out against Cromwell during the Civil War. The Great Hall and adjacent rooms have been restored and are laid out with kitchen and household implements of older times. Licensed restaurant.

Hardraw Force
1 mile north of Hawes. Behind the Green Dragon Inn, Hardraw
Highest above-ground waterfall in England. Natural ampitheatre occasionally holds band concerts. Small charge for admission.

Hawes
Upper Dales Folk Museum
Station Yard
Exhibits of life on dales farms based on the Marie Hartley and Joan Ingilby Collection.

Yorkshire Dales National Park Information Centre
Station Yard
Provides details of current events in the area along with displays to help understand the environment of the National Park.

Jervaulx Abbey
5 miles south-east of Leyburn
The ruins show a fascinating ground floor plan of this once great Cistercian abbey. Several ancient gravestones and the remains of the fifteenth-century kitchen can be seen.

Middleham Castle
On A6018, 2 miles south-east of Leyburn
Ruins dating from 1170. One of the largest keeps in England.

Semer Water
1 mile south of Bainbridge. Access from A684
Natural lake made by a clay dam left by the retreating Ice Age.

Beck feeds in to the Ure near Redmire Force, the last of the limestone-step waterfalls of Wensleydale.

The dale takes its name from **Wensley**. The village sits astride the A684, an important market until the plague of 1563 wiped out its inhabitants. It is now overshadowed in commercial importance by Hawes, but Wensley is a far prettier place surrounding its ancient village green. The partly restored mill below the bridge near the waterfall and now used as a pottery, was operated by an over-shot waterwheel. The church is one of the most beautiful in the Dales and the most interesting. It escaped the Victorian rebuilding that afflicted many churches in the area and most of what is seen was built in the thirteenth and fifteenth centuries, the date of much of its fine wood-work. The beautifully carved screen, which came from Easby Abbey, stands behind the imposing Bolton box pew, while near the church door is a reliquary, also from Easby Abbey and said to be the only one of its kind in England. It may have held the remains of St Agatha, their patron saint. The finely carved choir stalls were made in 1527 by the same carvers who worked on Ripon Cathedral. Peter Goldsmith, who was the surgeon on board HMS *Victory* and in whose arms Lord Nelson died at Trafalgar came from Wensley and is buried in the churchyard.

Bolton Hall, home of Lord Bolton has its main gates in the centre of Wensley and there are public footpaths through the beautiful parkland of the hall, though the hall itself is not open. The hall was built in 1678 to replace Bolton Castle after it became untenable following the Civil War. It was first owned by Charles Powlett who later became the Duke of Bolton, and was partially rebuilt early this century after a serious fire.

The substantial village of **Leyburn**, recorded in the *Domesday Book* as 'le Borne' or 'the stream by the clearing' sits well above and to the north of the Ure. It had its market charter granted by Charles II and in 1686 market day was changed from Tuesday to Friday. Five busy roads meeting at Leyburn have contributed to its development. From the west end of the market place a footpath leads to the wooded crag of Leyburn Shawl. Remains of ancient earthworks surround the crag and prehistoric implements have been found nearby. A spot known as 'Queen's Gap' on the Shawl, is supposed to be where Mary, Queen of Scots was recaptured after only 2 hours freedom during her imprisonment in Bolton Castle.

Middleham is linked to Leyburn by an iron girder bridge built by public subscription in 1850, replacing an earlier suspension bridge which collapsed in 1831 after only 2 years use. The impressive ruins of Middleham Castle date from 1170, and three centuries later became home for the future Richard III. Much maligned by Shakespeare, King Richard became the owner of Middleham Castle in 1471, through his marriage to Anne, daughter of Richard Neville, Earl of Warwick, the 'Kingmaker'. It is a pleasant thought to see King Richard resting at Middleham between phases of the power struggle that became known as the 'Wars of the Roses'. His son Edward was born at Middleham, but died aged 12; his room can still be seen in the castle ruins. The keep is original and despite it being made untenable after Richard's defeat on Bosworth Field in 1485, the castle ruins are a fine state of preservation, a true memorial to the medieval stone-masons who built it. King Richard's crest was a white boar one of which, very much worn with age, still decorates the Swine Cross in the market place. Another feature of the town is St Alkelda's Well, the martyred Saxon princess who died at the hands of the Danes rather than renounce her Christian beliefs. Middleham is also a racehorse training town with a dozen trainers handling several hundred horses, often to be seen at exercise on Middleham Moor to the west.

Across Coverdale, tree-lined **East Witton** is built on a crossroads of two minor roads, with the A6108, formerly the coach road from York to Kendal taking a right-angled bend through the village. Sleepy now, but it has had a market charter since 1306 and the Poll Tax of 1379 shows 220 tax paying inhabitants.

A minor road leaves the A6108 about half a mile north of East Witton, to cross the Ure into **Spennithorne**. This village has changed little in size since Ralph Fitz Randolph built a castle there in 1194. Only a few stones remain, but from them it is possible to conjure the impression of a fair sized fortress. The village churchyard boasts a Russian cross from Sebastopol, erected by a member of the local Van Straubenzee family, who fought at Sebastopol in the Crimean War.

Below Middleham the valley widens and its character becomes more wooded. The ruins of **Jervaulx Abbey** are about 3 miles from Middleham along the Masham road. It was built in the twelfth century by Cistercian monks originally from Fors in France, who moved there from the then inhospitable area around Askrigg. The monks made a special cheese, a forerunner to Wensleydale cheese, from ewes' milk. The scant ruins of Jervaulx Abbey remain in mute testimony to

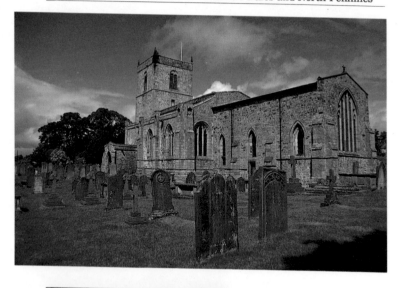

Wensley Church

Carved wooden screen,
originally from Jervaulx
Abbey, in Wensley Church

The Boar Cross in Middleham

Henry VIII's determination to crush the power of the monasteries. In 1536 the Pilgrimage of Grace started from here, led unwillingly by the abbot, Adam Sedburgh. The pilgrims hoped to persuade the king away from his policy of destroying the monasteries, but he tricked them by offering a pardon. As soon as they made to return to their dales he took revenge. Adam Sedburgh was imprisoned in the Tower of London, where his name can still be seen scratched on a wall. He was executed at Tyburn in 1537 and Jervaulx was destroyed. All that is left of this once extensive religious house are a few graceful arches and stone pillars still peacefully mouldering into tranquil antiquity.

Fortunately for **Bedale** the A1, the Great North Road, is well to the ✳ east and as a result traffic noise has no effect on this quiet market town. Featured in the *Domesday Book*, it has held a Tuesday market around its slender stepped cross since 1251. Sited on gently rising land between the lower reaches of Swaledale and Wensleydale, the town was once an important commercial centre, connecting the central dales with east coast ports. An imaginative scheme which came to nothing, planned to canalise Bedale Beck and so connect the town to the navigable Swale. All that is left are incongruent mooring rings and the grandiose title of The Harbour given to an area around

Bedale Mill. Water still powers this mill, the last in Bedale.

St Gregory's, Bedale's parish church, has a mixture of styles but the largest of its bells hung in Jervaulx Abbey over 400 years ago. The bell tower was used as a lookout against raiding Scots in the fourteenth century. Nearby Bedale Hall is Georgian, a fine setting for the local government officials to work in. Three miles south of Bedale, the tiny village of **Snape** has an almost park-like aspect. An avenue of trees planted in 1701 lead into this village whose roots go back to the twelfth century. Fitz Randulph of Middleham Castle built another of his fortresses here and through various marriages it became the property of Catherine Parr, the last of Henry VIII's wives and whom she survived. Snape's prosperity was based on woolcombing, but with the centralising of the Yorkshire wool trade on industrial towns of the West Riding, the village declined. A survey of 1811 shows Snape having four inns, a poorhouse and a lock-up known as the Black Hole! Thorpe Perrow, home of the Danbys, is close by and its famous Arboretum is open from mid-March to the end of October.

The Bedale Hunt use the broad acres between the A1 and Wensleydale. Parkland and ancestral homes dot this prosperous landscape; many of the houses open their gardens throughout the summer, but it is best to check the details locally.

A minor road south of Thorpe Perrow to the B6267, makes a curious dog-leg through a pretty village called **Well**. The unusual name refers to St Michael's Well, which has been a site of veneration since pagan times, part of a complex of henges and tumuli in the surrounding area. A prosperous Roman built a luxurious villa near the well and decorated it with the tessellated pavement now on display in the parish church. At the time of the Domesday survey the church was only a wooden structure and the present building has Norman foundations. Little remains from that era apart from the dog-tooth working around the doorway, following Scottish raids around 1318. The font cover dates from 1352, one of the oldest in England and was the gift of Ralph Neville, Lord of Middleham who was responsible for rebuilding the church. A row of alms houses near the church which were built in 1758 are linked with a charity originally endowed by Ralph Neville.

Devotees of 'real ale' make the pilgrimage to **Masham**, for this is the home of one of the oldest and truest brews, Theakston's 'Old Peculier'; the spelling is correct, a 'peculier' was a kind of medieval weights and measures official. Masham guards a crossing of the Ure on its southerly course into the Vale of York. Its church contains some Norman work but has been Victorianised; its best features are the octagonal fifteenth-century lantern and tall spire topping a Norman tower and the inside has many unspoilt features dating as far back as the eleventh century. A venerable stone column decorated with the twelve apostles and the Adoration of the Magi standing in the churchyard is probably seventh century. A market has been held at Masham since 1250, and the huge market place gives an air of spaciousness to the town. The imposing market cross once incorporated a bull ring and a set of stocks. Masham's big annual event is a traction engine rally and steam fair which is held on a nearby meadow.

Colsterdale enters the Ure just below the town, one of the least known and yet arguably one of the prettiest of Wensleydale's tributary dales. Its river, the Burn, starts its life to the west high on Great Haw and near to where the monks of Jervaulx Abbey mined coal and ironstone, smelting the metal lower down the dale. Swinton Castle, known locally as the 'Tea Caddy Castle' and now used as a college, stands within attractive parkland above the south bank of the Burn.

Grewelthorpe and Kirkby Malzeard are two villages in the middle of a 'cat's cradle' of by-ways south of the main dale. The former, **Grewelthorpe** has a pretty village pond which is probably a flooded gravel pit; 'grewel' is an old word for gravel. Four hundred years ago, the women of this village, losing patience at their menfolk's delay over disputed coal mining rights, fought a bloody battle with their neighbours from Kirkby Malzeard. The resulting settlement still allows both lots of villagers to gather coal beneath Grewelthorpe Moor, but few if any, still bother.

Kirkby Malzeard was recorded in the *Domesday Book* as the 'church in the forest clearing'. The forest is long gone, but the village retains its quiet charm despite twentieth-century pressures. The parish church was once known as the 'Queen of the Moors', but most of the present structure is the result of rebuilding following a disastrous fire in 1908. Mowbray Castle was to the east of the church, but as the stone cross in the churchyard explains, it was destroyed by order of Henry II in 1173. Edward I granted a charter to hold a weekly market, but it is a long time since one was held. The market cross is a replica, the original being destroyed by a local worthy in 1866. He considered it an eyesore, a sentiment not accepted by the rest of the

Jervaulx Abbey

village who promptly set about building the present cross!

Moving downstream again, the A6108 crosses the river by an ancient bridge to enter **West Tanfield**, a village to delight the eye. Marmion Tower dominates the scene, the gatehouse of a vanished ancestral home. Sir Walter Scott based his novel *Marmion* on the family, but there is no record of any Marmion being at the Battle of Flodden.

Ripon can claim to be one of England's oldest boroughs with a history closely linked to its church for thirteen centuries. Alfred the Great granted the town its charter in 886. In 650, St Wilfrid became bishop and built its first church soon afterwards. The crypt of this still survives and can be visited beneath the present central tower. Today's minster, raised to cathedral status in 1836, contains some fine ecclesiastical woodwork together with one of the greatest of our early English west fronts.

As a religious centre in its own right, as well as being close to Fountains Abbey's monastic influence, conveniently placed between the pastoral countryside of Wensleydale, Nidderdale and the rich arable lands of the Vale of York, Ripon soon acquired charters for markets and fairs. It developed round the twin centres of minster and

PLACES TO VISIT IN AND AROUND RIPON

Fountains Abbey and Studley Royal

3 miles south-west of Ripon off the B6265 to Pateley Bridge
The largest monastic ruin in Britain; founded by Cistercian monks in 1132; landscape gardens laid out 1720-40 with lake, formal watergarden and temples. Deer park, St Mary's Church, Jacobean mansion house and small museum.

Lightwater Valley Country Park

3 miles north of Ripon on A6108
Visitor centre, adventure playground, miniature railway, fruit farm, craft centre, old time fair, boating, gift shops, restaurants, fruit picking.

Newby Hall

4 miles south-west of Ripon off Boroughbridge old road
Built in 1690s for Sir Edward Blackett, then redesigned in the eighteenth century by Robert Adam. Works of art, sculptures and valuable furnishings fill the hall. House and landscaped gardens open to the public. Children's adventure playground, miniature steam railway.

Norton Conyers

$3^1/_2$ miles north of Ripon off A61
Fine Jacobean manor house belonging to the Grahams, who still live there, since 1624. Exhibition of pictures, furniture and wedding dresses. Walled garden.

Ripon

Cathedral dates from 672. Rich ecclesiastical treasure displayed in the Saxon crypt.

Wakeman's House Museum
Market square, Ripon
Building dating from the fourteenth century. Residence of the 'wakeman' or nightwatchman in medieval times. Office still marked by the sounding of a nightly horn and ringing a curfew bell at 9pm. Now houses an information centre and museum of local crafts and history.

market place, the two parts of the town most attractive to visitors. The medieval street pattern is still based on these areas, but most of Ripon's attractive buildings are the result of Georgian and Victorian growth. In the centre of the market place is an impressive obelisk of 1781, and on the south side the elegant town hall of 1801 almost overshadows a surviving half-timbered building, the sixteenth-century Wakeman's House, formerly the home of Hugh Ripley, who died in 1637 — the last wakeman and Ripon's first mayor. One of the wakeman's duties was that of horn blower, a custom still continued each evening at 9pm, when he blows a horn at each corner of the market place, and outside the house of the current mayor wherever he or she resides. The Ure is navigable as far as Ripon, the town being connected to the main river by canal, and a busy marina makes an attractive foreground to the town. There is a racetrack on water-meadows between the canal and the river where meets are held throughout the year.

Fountains Abbey is 3 miles south-west of Ripon. Founded in 1132 on what was then a wild site by the little River Skell, it became one of the richest of all Cistercian monasteries. Today, in their setting of an eighteenth-century landscaped park, its ruins are probably the most beautiful and certainly the most extensive, of any Cistercian foundation in Britain. Tranquil and serene it may be today, but Fountains had its share of troubles. The thirteen monks from the Benedictine abbey of St Mary's in York found their chosen site (a thorn filled barren wilderness), and at first lived under an elm tree, and amongst the surrounding rocks. After 15 years work, in 1147 some-one maliciously set fire to the abbey and with the exception of the church everything had to be rebuilt. By 1478 records show that the church was in a bad state of repair and work began on the great tower. The worst time for Fountains history was during the reign of Henry VIII. In 1536, Abbot William Thirsk was executed for taking part in the Pilgrimage of Grace and his successor, Marmaduke Bradley no doubt a king's man, meekly surrendered the abbey to its ultimate fate on 26 November 1539.

The riverside below Fountains Abbey opens out into ornamental gardens and ponds full of exotic geese and visiting water birds. This is **Studley Royal** park created in the 1720s by John Aislabie as a deer park near his house, of which only the stable block remains. The park is part of an estate sold to Sir Richard Gresham in 1540 following the dissolution of Fountains Abbey. Studley Royal is now administered as a country park by North Yorkshire County Council. A short stroll (1$\frac{1}{2}$ hours, 2 miles) which takes in the glories of the abbey and the beauty of Studley starts at the abbey car park and follows the Skell past Fountains Hall to the abbey. It continues down stream past Half Moon Pound and through the ornamental gardens of the park to follow the canal to the lake with its numerous geese and ducks both wild and tame. Take plenty of time over this stroll, maybe combining it with a riverside picnic. In the late summer and early autumn, the abbey ruins are floodlit.

Reached by a turning off the A61 Harrogate road (about 2 miles south of Ripon), **Markenfield Hall** is over 400 years old, the finest example of a moated farmhouse in the North. The last Markenfield had to flee the country in 1569 after taking part in the abortive 'Rising of the North'. Fortunately kept in good repair by subsequent owners it remains, 'the most complete example of a country gentleman's home in Plantagenet days'.

Newby Hall is at the end of a rural lane off the B6265 Borough-bridge road, about 4 miles south-west of Ripon. The exquisite Queen Anne mansion enriched by the designer Robert Adam is open to the public and the house contains a priceless collection of works of art, tapestries and artistic furnishings set out in oppulent, yet homely surroundings.

The final place in Wensleydale before the Ure joins the Swale is **Boroughbridge**, once a busy staging post on the Great North Road and even now scarsely by-passed by roaring traffic on the A1. Three huge stones standing beside the A1 are the sole survivors of seven. Known locally as the 'Devil's Arrows', they show that man has lived here since prehistoric times. Roman conquerors built *Isurium* here on Dere Street, their forerunner of the A1. The site of the fort including an ampitheatre, covers an area of about 60 acres and from the number of artifacts found on site, it obviously had great strategic importance. Many of these together with several finely decorated pavements, can be seen in the small museum on the site.

The cloisters,
Fountains Abbey

Newby Hall

SELECTED WALKS

Cam Road and the Pennine Way 6 miles • Moderate • 3 hours
The walk is from the National Park Information Centre in Hawes. Turn right into the main street and walk as far as the public toilets. Turn left through a small car park and cross two fields in the direction of the Wensleydale Creameries. Cross the road by the creamery to follow a narrow path across a series of small fields, using stiles to keep on course. On reaching the main road, turn left for about 150yd then left again, uphill on a broad unpaved track; this is Cam Road. Follow the track for a couple of miles, pausing only to admire the all-round views. Pass the upper limits of a pine plantation and at Ten End look out for a cairn on your left, marked faintly with the letters P/W; this is the Pennine Way. Turn sharp left along the grassy path over gently rising ground, then downhill with good views of Upper Wensleydale. On reaching a farm lane, turn right as far as a road, then right again for about 100yd. Climb over a stile on your left and follow a profusion of Pennine Way signs through Gayle village. Keep to the left of Hawes Church and enter the village beneath an archway, the car park and information centre are along the street on the right.

Semer Water 4 miles • Easy • 2 hours
Follow the cul-de-sac road south from the village green, past Dame's School Cottage, then along a private drive marked with a footpath sign. Bear right from the house, out into open fields. Follow signs to the right of a large house and across more fields, aiming for an old barn. Go through a stile on its right; turn left along the road past Semerdale Hall and through Countersett. In Countersett, turn left, downhill to Semer Water. Cross the triple-arched road bridge, then left through a narrow stile and follow a signposted path along the riverbank. Cross a ladder stile and climb, to the right away from the river by following waymark posts. At the side road, turn left as far as the main road and left again into Bainbridge.

Aysgarth and West Burton 5 miles • Easy • 2 to 3 hours
This walk visits unspoilt West Burton and enjoys quiet views of Aysgarth's Middle and Lower Falls from the less frequented south bank of the Ure. From the car park cross the river and climb the steps to Aysgarth Church, then go towards and across the main road. Using stiles cross a series of fields until you reach Eshington Bridge. Cross the bridge and turn right on a path signposted to West Burton. On reaching the village, bear left then right as far as the wide village green. Follow a lane from the lower end of the green down to the waterfall. Cross a narrow stone bridge, then left and right on a path past Barrack Wood. Left along a farm lane and right on a footpath

signposted 'Edgley'; waymarked stiles and gates indicate the route. Turn right at the road for about 130yd, then diagonally left across a field as far as the main road. Left over Hestholme Bridge and right on a waymarked path on its far side. Follow the riverbank, above the falls back to Aysgarth.

A SCENIC CAR DRIVE

Around Wensleydale 93 miles

From Ripon follow the B6265 for 3 miles, maybe detouring left to visit Studley Park and Fountains Abbey. Right from the B6265 on to unclassified roads through Kirkby Malzeard and Grewelthorpe to Masham (pubs and cafés). Left on the A6108 through Middleham (ancient castle, pubs, cafés, shops) and over the suspension bridge to Leyburn (pubs, cafés, shops). Left along the A684, through West Witton (Knights Templar's Chapel) and Aysgarth (scenic waterfalls, museum, cafés, car park and National Park Information Centre); through Bainbridge (possible diversion left to Semer Water) and Hawes (car parking, National Park Information Centre, museum, ropeworks, market, shops, pubs, restaurants, cafés). Right by minor road to Hardraw (pub, scenic waterfall), then along the north side of the dale through Sedbusk to Askrigg (James Herriot connections, pubs, cafés). Through Carperby (Wheatsheaf Hotel) to Castle Bolton (historic castle, restaurant) and via Redmire to Leyburn. Left along the A684 as far as Bedale (pubs, shops, etc). Right for the B6268 (possible diversion to Thorpe Perrow Arboretum). Right again at the junction with the B6267 and left along the A6108 back to Ripon.

7
NIDDERDALE
AND WHARFEDALE

Nidderdale

A short step across the moor from Skell Dale and Fountains Abbey, the character changes yet again in this, the shortest of the main dales. Nidderdale packs a great deal of interest into its length and also provides drinking water for the densely populated regions to its south. Strangely, even though its beauty compares favourably with the main dales, Nidderdale is excluded from the Yorkshire Dales National Park. As a result it is often ignored by visitors and so can be less crowded during the more popular holiday periods.

Approach the dale by the back road from Masham in Wensleydale, past Leighton Reservoir, then over Ouster Bank and steeply down to Lofthouse. The road continues as a narrow toll road to Scar House and Angram reservoirs almost at the dale head. Cars must be left at the first reservoir as Angram may only be visited on foot.

Middlesmoor is reached by a steep winding road from Lofthouse. This high airy settlement has existed at least since Saxon times, as shown by the ancient font in the village church. Across the valley is the spectacular How Stean Gorge which has been developed as a visitor centre. Footbridges on different levels allow access across the deep chasm and there is a childrens' play area nearby. Tom Taylor's Chamber, a nearby cave, is named after a local rogue who once took refuge in it, and is where in the last century a hoard of Roman coins was found.

The moors on either side of Nidderdale are mostly privately

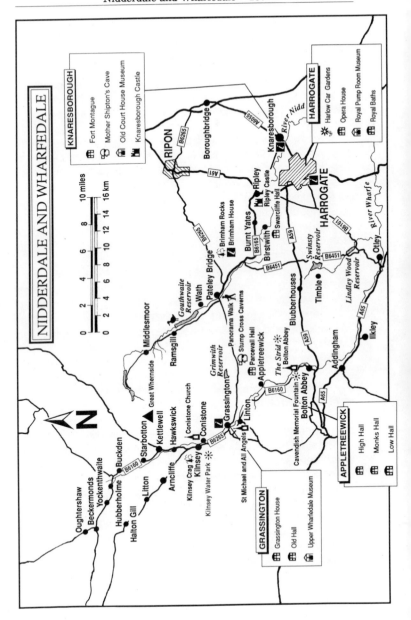

NIDDERDALE AND WHARFEDALE

KNARESBOROUGH
- Fort Montague
- Mother Shipton's Cave
- Old Court House Museum
- Knaresborough Castle

HARROGATE
- Harlow Car Gardens
- Opera House
- Royal Pump Room Museum
- Royal Baths

GRASSINGTON
- Grassington House
- Old Hall
- Upper Wharfedale Museum

APPLETREEWICK
- High Hall
- Monks Hall
- Low Hall

owned and as a result have very restricted public access. There is, however, an excellent ancient high level way which climbs out of the dale above the top reservoirs and crosses the northern flank of Great Whernside before descending to Starbotton in Wharfedale.

Down the valley, **Ramsgill** at the northern end of Gouthwaite Reservoir, has a church, once an outlying chapel of Byland Abbey where the heathen dale dwellers of early times were converted to Christianity.

After the Ice Age, debris left by the retreating glaciers in Nidderdale blocked the flow of the river and for a time there was a natural lake until erosion released its waters. When Bradford Corporation decided to build Gouthwaite Reservoir the story was brought full circle with the second flooding of what should rightly be Gouthwaite Lake. Not only does the water add to the attractive scenery of the dale, but wild birds and waterfowl have colonised the shores and the area has been designated a nature reserve run by the Yorkshire Naturalist's Trust.

When the reservoirs were being built in Upper Nidderdale, access was difficult along the narrow winding lanes of the dale, so a light railway was built as far as the dale head to ease the movement of stores and building materials. When the reservoirs were finished, the line was operated by Bradford Corporation as the Nidd Valley Light Railway, carrying goods and passengers. Regretfully, this only recorded instance of a municipally-run railway was closed in 1929 and the line dismantled by 1936.

Quiet **Wath** enjoys a secluded position below Gouthwaite Reservoir, its hotel a perfect base from which to explore Upper Nidderdale. Foster Beck Mill on the opposite side of the valley is now an inn, but still retains its huge cast-iron waterwheel in full working order.

Pateley Bridge occupies a sheltered situation facing south-west, which makes it an ideal suntrap, so it is small wonder that it has become such a popular spot for caravanners and picnickers. It is also a convenient centre for the south-east dales. The small town is old, it was granted a market charter in the fourteenth century and although the street market was abandoned some time ago, there are still fortnightly sheep sales and an annual agricultural show. There is a signpost marked 'Panorama Walk' (2 miles, 1 hour) in Pateley Bridge; follow it uphill above the town to link up with an easy and level path which commands the extensive view of Nidderdale and the moors beyond.

Lead ore was mined in the dale, mostly around **Greenhow Hill**, south of the B6265 road where the 9-mile long Bycliffe vein was worked. Smelting was carried out on the opposite side of the dale below Brimham Rocks at a place now recognised only by the name of Smelthouses. The local ore had a comparatively high silver content and was much prized by the Romans who mined in this area. A pig (ingot) of Greenhow lead from the first century AD is now at Ripley Castle and another in the British Museum.

The busy but pleasant B6265 was built as a turnpike road between Knaresborough and Grassington to help move fuel and stores in and lead out of the area. In 1858 a party of lead miners discovered a natural cavern which has since been developed as a show cave known as the **Stump Cross Caverns**. The system is over 3 miles long, but only the show cave is open to the public. This is floodlit to highlight the marvellous formations of stalagmites and stalactites and other rock formations.

Back across the dale below Pateley Bridge and a little to the south-east of the B6265 are the rock formations of **Brimham Rocks**. These are a series of peculiarly shaped Millstone Grit outcrops sculptured into fantastic shapes by the erosion of softer layers topped by harder rocks. Most have names, some are fanciful but others are more easily identifiable such as the 'Dancing Bear' and the precariously perched 'Idol Rock' which, although weighing several tons, is perched on a pedestal about a foot in diameter. The best way to see Brimham Rocks is on foot after parking in one of the well placed car parks (SE209644) off the road between the B6265 and Summer Bridge. The National Trust who own the area, have erected large scale maps showing the positions and names of the various rocks. The best way is to follow their suggested itinerary and walk round the strange formations in a clockwise direction. There is an information centre at Brimham House in the centre of the rocks and a refreshment hut nearby.

The B6165 makes a wide sweep above the dale, keeping roughly parallel with the river. At its highest point, the name **Burnt Yates** is intriguing; probably a contraction of 'Boundary Gates', for the village once marked the boundary of the lands of Fountains Abbey and the Forest of Knaresborough. The tiny village school was founded in 1750. Endowments of the time allowed for thirty poor boys to be taught the Three R's and thirty poor girls to be instructed in needlework and spinning.

Ripley across the moors and at the junction of the B6165 with the A61, is an ancient village and was mentioned in the *Domesday Book*. Fortunately it is now spared the heavy traffic of the A61 since a by-pass was built. Oliver Cromwell stayed here after the battle of Marston Moor. The village seen today has a French look about it, and no wonder, for it was modelled on one in Alsace-Lorraine for Sir William Amcotts Ingilby in 1827. The French similarity is complete right down to the *hôtel de ville*, or town hall, which was added in 1854. The money to rebuild the village was raised from the sale of an outlying farm now the town centre of Harrogate. No longer in any danger from through traffic, visitors can wander round Ripley's cobbled market square with its cross and venerable stocks.

The Ingilby family have been associated with Ripley since the fourteenth century. Their home, Ripley Castle, is open to the public and is at the lower end of the village beyond the fourteenth-century church with its 'Weeping Cross'. Apparently the name comes from the action of penitents who confessed their sins at its base.

Two more Nidderdale villages are worthy of a mention. **Birstwith**, now popular with Harrogate commuters is where Charlotte Brontë spent an unhappy holiday at Swarcliffe Hall when she was a governess. **Hampsthwaite** has a charter granted by Edward I and was an important river crossing from Roman times — a pack-horse bridge still spans the river.

The spa town of **Harrogate** flourished until the nineteenth century and then fell into a decline after World War I. By adopting its present role as a dormitory to the commercial cities of Yorkshire, as well as developing its own identity and modern character, the town still retains an unrivalled popularity as a health and pleasure resort. Over the years Harrogate has developed important conference facilities and also attracted many high class shops to its elegant Victorian high street. Remnants of the spa can still be seen in places such as the Opera House and Royal Baths. The Royal Pump Room with its Sulphur Well has been preserved as a museum of life in a spa as it would have been during the Victorian hey-day of the town. A legacy of the more gentle days of Harrogate lies in the number of parks and open spaces such as the Stray, a 200-acre open space almost surrounding the town centre and jealously preserved by the inhabitants. On the western edge of Harrogate are the famous Harlow Car Gardens, owned by the Northern Horticultural Society. A never ending display of colour flourishes throughout the year, ranging from

PLACES TO VISIT AROUND NIDDERDALE

Brimham Rocks
2 miles south-east of Pateley Bridge
Natural rock sculptures. National Trust land. Guide leaflet and information available at Brimham House in the centre of the land form. Refreshments. Car parking on perimeter, access to spectacular rock formations on foot only, 500yd.

Gouthwaite Reservoir Nature Reserve
4 miles north-west of Pateley Bridge on the Nidderdale road
Reservoir and bird sanctuary and wildfowl, etc. View from road side.

Harrogate
Museum, art gallery, Harlow Car Gardens. Stray, Rudding Park.

How Stean Gorge
10 miles north-west of Pateley Bridge on the Nidderdale road
Narrow gorge with public access by a series of footbridges. Children's play area, car park. Open all the year.

Knaresborough
Old Court House Museum
Fourteenth-century building, now housing a reconstructed court room scene of 1602.

Fort Montague
Eighteenth-century house carved from solid rock overlooking the River Nidd.

Mother Shipton's Cave
Reputed home of a fifteenth-century witch who prophesied many modern inventions.

Dropping Well
Petrifying well alongside Mother Shipton's Cave.

Knaresborough Castle
Norman construction dating from the twelfth century.

Boating
Rowing boats available for hire from the promenade.

Ripley
On A61, $3\frac{1}{2}$ miles north of Harrogate
Attractive 'squire's' village with architectural curiosities. Fourteenth-century Ripley Castle open to the public.

Stump Cross Caverns
5 miles west of Pateley Bridge on B6265
Show caves open to the public, access from road, car parking. Visitor centre, café, gift shop.

spring flowers to rhododendrons, alpines and then roses, for which Harlow Car is particularly famous; all vying in colourful competition with displays of exotic flowers and herbaceous borders. Harlow Car also has a more serious purpose, being used as a trial ground for new fruit and vegetable plants suited to northern weather conditions.

To the north-east and almost totally on the north bank of the River Nidd, is the old town of **Knaresborough**. The Romans are thought to have built a fort here, but it grew mainly in Anglo Saxon times with the development of a castle to protect against Viking raids. The ruins that are seen today are a twelfth-century castle left more or less as it was after Cromwell made it useless during the Civil War. Knaresborough has many interesting buildings and features, such as the oldest chemist's shop in England, along with the Old Court House Museum and a house Fort Montague, carved out of the solid rock overlooking the Nidd. Visit Mother Shipton's Cave where Mother Shipton, in the fifteenth century, prophesied the coming of aeroplanes, iron ships, motor cars, men walking under water and many other inventions and events such as world wars. She was born in this cave near the Dropping Well on the banks of the Nidd. In the Dropping Well inanimate articles are coated with limestone from limeladen water dropping from the roof of the crag and appear to be turned to stone. Rowing boats can be hired to enjoy the tranquil stretch of the Nidd beneath the shadow of Knaresborough Castle, or for the less energetic a simple stroll by the river completes the pleasures of Nidderdale.

Turning west and back to the more central dales, the A59 Harrogate to Skipton road crosses short Washburn Dale, now mostly flooded to provide drinking water for Leeds and Bradford and with quaintly named Blubberhouses as its only village. Minor roads crisscross the dale and the B6451, Dangerous Corner to Otley road, crosses the neck of Lindley Wood Reservoir, but to really explore this almost lost valley, it will be necessary to follow the many rights-of-way on foot. One possibility is to use public footpaths radiating from the remote village of Timble to reach Swinsty Reservoir and maybe continue further down the dale to Lindley Wood. **Timble** is about a mile east of the minor road from Blubberhouses to Otley. The village has one pub and limited parking should be easy to find.

Wharfedale

Glacial action in the Ice Age carved a deep gorge through the easily worn limestone, widening and deepening a course for the River Wharfe. Left to its own devices, the river prefers a less energetic life and meanders gently along the dale bottom for most of the year. This gentleness is something of a sham, for in spate after rapidly melting snow or a cloudburst, the Wharfe can become a dangerous river.

The Dales Way Walk

The long distance Dales Way Walk follows Wharfedale for a good third of its length. The route starts at Ilkley and follows the dale all the way through Grassington, Kettlewell and Buckden before meeting the Pennine Way for a short distance above Ribblehead. After a sharp dog-leg on Cam Fell the path continues through Dent and Sedbergh into the Lune Valley and across the M6 by the Crook of Lune. The last lap is through the Lakeland foothills around the Kent and finally to Bowness on Windermere. As a walk it does not have half the rigours of the Pennine Way and its length of 73 miles is often scoffed at by long distance walkers, but for scenery there can be no finer walk especially if taken in short easy stages. It can be easily split up over many separate days or taken over a short holiday week. Time on a walk like this should be of no consequence. Apart from the 15 miles from Sedbergh to Burnside accommodation and refreshment stops are relatively easy to find and should not cause any problems to anyone who prefers to walk without too many prior arrangements and bookings.

The River Wharfe starts its life in Langstrothdale high up on the moors of Cam Pasture and shares its birthplace with the Ribble. Quickly flowing south, the river flows past settlements which, within the memory of men not long dead, were still used as summer farms in the Scandinavian method of farming. The first hamlet in the ancient Forest of Langstroth is **Oughtershaw** where its hall was built centuries ago by the woods. Next at the foot of forested Greenfield Beck is **Beckermonds** (or Beggarmuns as the locals call it). The river flows through Yockenthwaite, a Norse-Irish name for the 'clearing of Eogan', and near to where Bronze Age people built a mysterious cairned circle. Ever widening, it runs on past Deepdale to **Hubberholme**, named after 'Hubba' the Viking chief who once controlled this part of Wharfedale. Hubberholme is one of those tiny places often ignored, but with its own inimitable appeal. The pride and joy of the village is the beautiful Norman church of St Michael, once a chapel of ease to the main church at Arncliffe. Inside is a rare medieval rood loft painted in red, black and gold. Other woodwork is mostly modern and is the work of Robert Thompson of Kilburn whose trade mark is the carved mouse which you will find hidden in out-of-the-way corners. The George Inn across the valley was once owned by the church and every New Year's Day the vicar would officiate over a kind of parliament when the 'poor pasture' was let for the benefit of the local poor. This 1,000-year-old custom still operates, but is now in the hands of a local auctioneer.

The river makes a sharp turn southwards between Hubberholme and Buckden and the widening valley bottom gives a sheltered site for the first of Wharfedale's picture postcard villages, **Buckden**. Like most of the dales villages, Buckden was settled by the Norsemen, but they only developed a more sophisticated husbandry on the land already partly settled by earlier man. In the twelfth century, Buckden became the residence of officials controlling the Forest of Langstroth. In later years the village developed as the social centre of the upper dale, a tradition which continues to this day. At one time

A cyclist enjoying typical Dales' scenery near Oughtershaw

Hubberholme Church

the inn doubled as a wool sale room and is where some of the old weighing equipment survives.

That intrepid seventeenth-century traveller, Lady Anne Clifford, came this way on a journey of inspection of her northern estates. She climbed from Buckden across Buckden Raikes going steeply above the village and then across Stake Moss to Bainbridge. She, not unnaturally, felt that this was one of the most dangerous places she had ever visited. The road she followed is now superceded by the B6160, but the original builders of this track were Roman. On an airy ledge below the point where the old and new roads join, the upland community of **Cray** clusters around the welcoming sight of the White

Lion Inn. The climb from Buckden to Cray is still steep, but the modern road especially in summer, holds none of the terrors Lady Anne Clifford experienced.

Starbotton was developed by the Angles, but grew with the discovery of lead on Cam Head Moor above a curious boundary ditch built in prehistoric times. The village is recorded in the *Domesday Book*, but in 1686 the worst recorded flood in Wharfedale's history wiped out practically the whole village. Only a handful of houses prior to this date remain.

There is a short but steep climb ($3^1/_2$ miles, 2 hours) to the eastern fells above Starbotton. The view down Wharfedale will make the effort seem little. The path follows a route straight up the side of Cam Gill Beck across the curiously named Knuckle Bone Pasture to Starbotton Fell. Here the track divides, and one must follow the right hand path over Starbotton Out Moor to join the walled access lane from Cam Head Beck back to Starbotton.

The road from Wharfedale to Coverdale which starts in Kettlewell was used to test the climbing ability of cars up the notorious Park Rash, parts of which have a gradient of 1 in 4. For a short while it was on the coach route between London and Richmond via Skipton, but was found to be so difficult that it was abandoned. The valley road skirts Kettlewell and crosses the Wharfe by a lovely old bridge where the masons who built it left a wealth of their coded marks.

Kettlewell is Norse for 'bubbling spring' and makes a handy base for a weekend's exploration along a whole series of footpaths and tracks radiating from either side of the village. Some were old routes to other villages, gave access to high pasture, or were lead miners' tracks. Others which appear to end abruptly, were sledge roads used for bringing peat down from the high tops in the days when this valuable and accessible fuel was used extensively throughout the dales.

Narrow terraced fields around Kettlewell and other dale's villages are known as 'lynchets' and were created as ploughable strips as far back as the Middle Ages. The parish church is built on Norman foundations, although the present structure is early Victorian. Stand at the roadside, a little way beyond the 'Kettlewell' sign at the Starbotton end of the village, and wait for a lull in the traffic. On a calm day there is a remarkable echo from this point.

The long moorland ridge of Old Cote Moor west of Kettlewell, divides Wharfedale from its tributary Littondale. Its river the Skirfare drains the northern slopes of Fountains Fell and Penyghent. Although very similar in character to the main dale, Littondale is almost a hidden gem with the main village of Arncliffe and its satellites Hawkswick, Litton and Halton Gill spaced at regular intervals on either side of it along the dale bottom.

The valley road continues with a struggle over the steep sides of Penyghent to Stainforth in Ribblesdale and a branch road from Arncliffe provides an even greater challenge of steep switchbacks below Fountains Fell before timid motorists can thankfully arrive in Malham and safety.

Pack-horse trains once used the green lane from Halton Gill to Horton-in-Ribblesdale, but now it makes a quiet path across the northern shoulder of Penyghent. Halton Gill would have been a much busier place during the hey-day of pack-horse trains; the road from Stainforth was originally one of their trails and another, now a footpath, climbed from Yockenthwaite in nearby Wharfedale by way of the 1,000ft high pass across Horse Head Moor.

Halton Gill is not the most isolated dwelling place in the dales, the lonely farmstead of Cosh House, 2 miles above Foxup at the confluence of the two streams which make the Skirfare, has the rare privilege of being the remotest house in this part of Yorkshire. The seventeenth-century chapel in Halton Gill is combined with the schoolhouse.

The concave eastern slopes of Darnbrook Fell, Fountains Fell's eastern outlier, dominate **Litton**. This pleasantly sited village which gives its name to the dale was part of the lands of Fountains Abbey. Litton marked the western boundary of their wealth-generating sheep walk. Coal was mined on the summit of Fountains Fell from shallow bell shaped pits. They can still be traced as shallow depressions and nearby is the sturdy stone structure which was used as a coke oven.

Arncliffe, the name is old Norse and is said to relate to eagles nesting on the local scars, is mostly built around its attractive village green. The church was first built in the twelfth century, although the building today has stood since 1796. The names of Littondale men who fought the Scots at Flodden Field in 1513 are recorded inside the church; names on the list will which still bring a response from their descendants who live in the dale. Charles Kingsley wrote part of his novel, *The Water Babies* while on holiday at Arncliffe.

Walkers can enjoy the beauty of Littondale and its river by

Kettlewell

Painting by the River Wharfe in Kettlewell

Hikers in Kilnsey

following the path from Litton as far as Arncliffe and then on to Hawkswick on the south bank. Paths link Halton Gill with Hubberholme, Litton with Buckden and Arncliffe with Starbotton; all the second named villages being in Wharfedale. A combination of any two paths can be used to make a really good round trip walk.

Hawkswick, the lowest village of Littondale, can claim to have been occupied by man since at least the Iron Age. A number of their sites have been found around the village and Dowkabottom high to the south-west was inhabited until the fourth century. Hawkswick Cote along with Arncliffe Cote, were formally grange farms belonging to Fountains Abbey. Wild Littondale joins Wharfedale, the waters of the Skirfare mingling with the main river at Amerdale Dub, a favourite hiding place for trout.

Motorists travelling down Wharfedale from its junction with Littondale soon see the remarkable 170ft high **Kilnsey Crag**. Overhanging 40ft, its receding lower part was carved by glacial action during the last Ice Age. The crag overshadows the annual Kilnsey Show at the end of August. **Kilnsey** is at the eastern end of Mastiles Lane, a green road over the limestone moors to Malham, fortunately still resisting proposals to upgrade it to a motor road. Once owned by Fountains Abbey which had a grange here, it has seen busier times; once there were corn and textile mills. Now, limestone is quarried behind the crag and a trout farm has been established down the road from the crag. Known as Kilnsey Water Park, not only is it operated as a commercial trout farm, but there is also an extensive aquarium, water garden centre, angling areas and landscaped ponds where visitors can feed the energetic trout and other fishes.

Across the dale from Kilnsey, is **Conistone**, a village which can trace its history back to Saxon times. Conistone's church is probably the oldest in Wharfedale, certainly the least 'improved' by our Victorian forebears. Behind the village is the narrow and impressive limestone gorge of Gurling Trough.

The large area of woodland south of Conistone is all that remains of the forest which once filled Wharfedale. Grass Wood together with the adjacent Bastow Wood is a nature reserve. Fascinating plant life abounds in the reserve, an unspoilt relic of our ancient woodland. Just inside the south-east corner of Grass Wood, a series of mounds are all that is left of a medieval village obliterated by the Black Death. Even though a public right-of-way passes through Grass Wood and visitors are welcomed, it is on the strict understanding that no flowers are taken or trees damaged. Dogs must be on a lead and on no account should any fires be started.

Man's exploitation of the fells above Grassington has its greatest impact west of the B6265. A huge limestone quarry based on Cracoe defaces the landscape in answer to the insatiable demands for better roads. The men of Cracoe who died in both world wars are remembered by a stone column high on a fell to the south. On the scarred fells to the north-east all is now silent, but lead was mined in quantity under **Grassington Moor** until the late nineteenth century. Levels were driven for great distances beneath the moor, the last of which attempted to link the Pateley Bridge workings to those above Grassington and was about 2,610yd long. The remains of the crushing plant can still be seen on Grassington Moor and are accessible on foot from the end of the road beyond Spring House Farm SE019658. Water to drive the plant was scarce and a network of channels which can still be identified across the hillside, brought water over 6 miles from a series of small reservoirs. There is also a remarkable complex of smelt mill flues crossing the moor just below the surface, with a restored terminal stack at the north end.

Grassington is mostly Georgian in appearance and character, although its foundations are considerably older. The present town grew with the fortunes of nearby lead mining. Amongst its old houses is a fruit shop (once a smithy) which housed the notorious Tom Lee who murdered a local doctor and threw the body into the Wharfe. Lee was caught and hanged at York in 1766 and his body afterwards was left on a gibbet near Grass Wood. Sudden and horrible death features prominently in Grassington's history: it suffered during the Scottish raids of the fourteenth century and worse by far was the visitation by the Black Death in 1349 which killed a quarter of the inhabitants of the surrounding area. Many villages were wiped out and never recovered; all that is left of once crowded habitations are poignant mounds such as those in Grass Wood, or on the nearby moors. The Upper Wharfedale Museum of farming and industry together with a fine collection of local minerals is housed in The Square. Quaint and narrow streets lead off The Square, all lined with interesting buildings. Grassington House is Georgian and the Old Hall, down a side street, has foundations older than are indicated by its venerable facade. Salt Pie Hill opposite the post office, is where the village stock of salt was kept in the days when salt was the only method of preserving food. Grassington is also the administrative centre for the

Grassington Moor

The Upper Wharfedale Museum, Grassington

The old pack-horse bridge and ford, Linton

A view over the River Wharfe towards Linton Church

Yorkshire Dales National Park, the office is on Hebden Road, the B6265.

Footpaths on either bank of the Wharfe above and below Grassington can be linked to give 2 or 3 hours pleasant stroll. A short distance upstream from the road bridge, is Ghaistrill's Strid not quite as dramatic as the one in Bolton Woods downstream, but pretty enough to provide a quiet picnic spot.

Although smaller than its neighbour across the valley, **Linton** has the major church in the area. St Michael and All Angels was built in the fourteenth century and serves the communities of Threshfield, Hebden and Grassington. Linton marks the eastern boundary of the Craven district and certainly the character is Craven, with none of the mountainous feel of the dales, but here a pastoral calm becomes evident with the widening of Craven's broad acres. Linton village, some distance from the church, has a clear stream, a tree-blessed green, a Vanbrughian hosptial (almshouse), endowed in 1721 by Richard Fountaine for 'indigent women', and fine houses and cottages built in the seventeenth and eighteenth centuries. In a very short distance, Linton Beck is crossed by a clapper bridge, packhorse bridge, modern road bridge, stepping stones and also a ford, an indication of the once greater importance of this village.

Besom-brooms were once made at **Threshfield**, an industry which was supposed to have been brought to this compact little village by a cattle raiding moss-trooper who became separated from the rest of his gang. Threshfield School is in an attractive Elizabethan building on the Grassington road; Old Pam, a fairy ghost, is supposed to haunt a room above the porch.

Hebden, about 2 miles downstream from Grassington is mostly built around an ancient stone bridge which was superseded by a larger one built to carry the turnpike, now the B6265 Pateley Bridge road. Hebden village sports are held every August Bank Holiday Monday, fell racing and other atheletic events being the main features. A local beauty spot is Scala Force the approach to which is by a road on the left bank of the stream, leading to the moors.

Above Hebden and along an access road to the north of the B6265, **Grimwith Reservoir** belies its unattractive name. A concessionary footpath from the scenic car park above the dam wall, circles the reservoir where wildfowl, especially Canada geese, have made their nesting grounds.

The glory of **Burnsall** lies in its riverside position and its attractive bridge completes the picture. Built in 1612, it is still strong enough to stand frequent batterings by the Wharfe when in spate. Until this one was built, many bridges had failed the test. The present one is the gift of William Craven, a local boy who made good and became, like Dick Whittington, a Lord Mayor of London. Burnsall is famous for its feast sports which are held on the complicated calendar formulation of the first Saturday after the first Sunday after 12 August. Burnsall's primary school was once an endowed grammar school and was built in 1610. Adjoining it is a church with Anglo Danish crosses and tombs and a Norse font. Outside are the combined lychgate and village stocks beside the tree-lined village green.

Above Appletreewick and by the deeply carved gorge of **Trollers Ghyll** where there is an eerie echo, is **Parcevall Hall**. The ghyll, or gill is a smaller version of Goredale Scar near Malham. Legend has it that this is where trolls once lived and it is said to be haunted by a phantom dog called Barguest. The beautiful Elizabethan house once sheltered a notorious highwayman by the name of William Nevison who terrorised travellers on nearby roads. The house is now used as a Bradford Diocesan Retreat and Conference Centre. The hall and its beautifully landscaped gardens stocked with many rare plants and shrubs are open to the public on most days throughout the year.

Appletreewick, the locals pronounce it 'Ap'trick', has several fine houses at least 4-500 years old, noteably High Hall, Monks Hall and Low Hall. High Hall was the home of William Craven. The village was once classed as a township and gained a charter in 1311 to hold a fair which became known as the 'Onion Fair'. This was abandoned years ago, but Onion Lane is a reminder of that strangely named festival.

The Dales Way follows the river bank all the way down to Bolton Abbey from Grassinton. By using the Parklink-Wharfedale bus a full day can be spent walking along what is undoubtedly the finest stretch of the Wharfe.

Almost all the local moors are part of the Duke of Devonshire's Chatsworth estates. Access is permitted to **Barden Fell** and Barden Moor outside the grouse shooting season and advantage can be taken of this privilege by using access points above Howgill village to get on to Barden Fell. No dogs are allowed and access is withdrawn during times of high fire risk. If you are in any doubt about the possibility of shooting going on, or any other problem, it is advisable to contact either the Chatsworth Estate Office (☎ Bolton Abbey 227), or get in contact with the Yorkshire Dales National Park Information

Hebden

Centre (☎ Grassington 752748).

Beyond the gently curving right-angled bend opposite Howgill, the Wharfe flows between beech wooded banks almost as far as Bolton Abbey, and for many this is the most beautiful part of the river. Artists ranging from masters such as Turner to the most amature have gained inspiration from its ever changing views.

At Barden Bridge, seventeenth-century **Barden Tower** fits delightfully into the scene. Now an artist's studio and guest house, the tower was first built by Lord Henry Clifford, the 'Shepherd Lord'; he was known by this title from being brought up by a shepherd's family while a fugitive during the Wars of the Roses. It was he who led the men of Craven at the Battle of Flodden in 1513; the halberd he carried in that battle is still owned by the Clifford family.

Lady Anne Clifford lived most of her younger days at Barden Tower which, like her other properties, was damaged in the Civil War. She was a remarkable lady, for not only did she devote her energies to building and rebuilding but she also did a tremendous amount of philanthropic work in the area. Good works featured not only in Lady Anne Clifford's life; she obviously followed her mother's example who built a hospital at Beamsley, near Bolton Bridge in 1593. The site of the building is away from the village by the side of the A59 and can be recognised from an archway leading into a private garden, but there is now only a circular building remaining of this once extensive structure.

With the exception of the two reservoirs in Barden Beck, **Barden Moor** to the west of Barden Bridge has been granted concessionary access by the Chatsworth estates. Entry points are marked on OS maps and there are the same restrictions as apply to Barden Fell and Simon Seat on the opposite side of the dale.

Below Barden the Wharfe flows through a rocky cleft known as **The Strid**. This deep narrow channel has been worn through softer rock by water action, which has also left strange formations and basins. The Strid means 'stride' but only the foolish attempt to jump the gap. Strategically placed lifebelts should be enough warning, but The Strid has claimed many lives of those who did not heed the sensible advice. Legend has it that a white horse appears whenever someone is about to be drowned in The Strid — so beware if you see one!

Sheepshaw Beck flows down from Hazlewood Moor and through the Valley of Desolation, so named by a topographer who visited the site after a disasterous storm. Woodland again fills the valley where

Burnsall

a concessionary footpath leads towards the open moors.

Footpaths follow both banks of the Wharfe into **Bolton Woods**. Those on the west bank were established between 1789 and 1843 by the vicar of Bolton Priory church, the Reverend William Carr. He began a tradition of public access which has continued to the present time. The first visitors came from mill towns of the West Riding, by train to the now abandoned Bolton Abbey Station and then by wagonette to the priory and Strid Wood. For people who normally worked a 50 to 60 hour week this place would be like heaven. The woods are part of the Chatsworth estates and a small charge is made towards the upkeep of the paths. This is payable at the Strid Cottage entrance or the Cavendish Pavilion. Five nature trails are laid out in the woods and an explanatory booklet is on sale.

The soaring ruined arch of **Bolton Abbey's** east window which dominates the wide sweep of the River Wharfe, is the result of the Dissolution by Henry VIII in 1540. Until then it had been home for a small community of Augustinian canons since 1154. Obeying a life of chastity and poverty, the monks, or more correctly Black Canons, came to this delightful spot after living for 34 years at nearby Embsay. Each wore a black cassock and a sleeved surplice with a hooded cloak fastened only at the neck; a black square cap covered their heads. Even though the order prospered from extensive lead mining and wool interests, the monks spent most of their days in prayer, or looking after the needs of the local people. Life, however was not always tranquil: in 1318 and 1320 Black Douglas, the Scottish border raider, twice attacked Bolton Abbey during his forays into Craven.

Strictly it is not an abbey but a priory, however Bolton Abbey is the most commonly used title, which has also been given to the nearby village. Richard Moon, the last prior, tried to save the abbey from dissolution by a bribe of £10 sent to Thomas Cromwell, Henry VIII's lieutenant, but this had no affect and the monks were driven out into the world on 29 January 1540. The abbey soon fell into ruins, its stones used in local buildings, but the nave was spared and became the parish church.

Standing on a high wooded promontory above the abbey, the ornate six-sided Cavendish Memorial Fountain was built in memory of Lord Frederick Charles Cavendish, second son of the seventh Duke of Devonshire, who was assassinated in Phoenix Park, Dublin, in 1882.

Crossing the busy A59 at Bolton Bridge and moving downstream by the B6160, one enters ever increasing urbanisation, but the towns of mid-Wharfedale still retain their dales' character. **Addingham**, once a double line of cottages along what became the A65, dates from Anglian times and is named after a local chieftain 'Adda'. The church still embodies many of its original Norman features, especially a number of its arches. The town developed during the eighteenth century around five water mills. Four of them were textile mills and no longer function, but the fifth a timber mill, still operates. One of the textile mills was attacked by Luddites during unrest in the early part of the Industrial Revolution.

Ilkley, the start of the Dales Way, was *Olicana* to the Romans who built a fort here, but little remains except that the site is known and their two Roman altars have been built into the basement of the church tower. Ilkley parish church has foundations which go back to the dawn of Christianity in the dales; three Runic crosses stand in the churchyard and in the wall of the south aisle the recumbent cross-legged statue of Sir Adam de Myddleton has lain there since his death in 1315. Adjacent to the church is the Elizabethan manor house, now a museum, which was built on the site of the fort's west gate. Modern Ilkley developed first with pretentions of being a spa town and later along with neighbouring Otley it became a dormitory for the commercial kings of Leeds and Bradford. With its back to Rombalds Moor (known throughout the country as Ilkley Moor) and the setting of Yorkshire's 'national anthem' — *On Ilkla Moor Baht'at* — Ilkley is a fine place to live. Few towns of its size can boast so much open country opening from the top of their High Street.

Visitors to Ilkley can hardly avoid seeing the distinctive mass of the Cow and Calf rocks. Behind them the moor is rich in the carved stones of our prehistoric ancestors who have left not only their cairns and circles but enigmatically carved 'cup-and-ring' stones and the famous Swastika Stone above Heber's Ghyll, supposedly the symbol of fire worship and the only one of three in the world, the others being in Greece and Sweden. Below the outcrop of Ilkley Crags a solitary building marks the site of 'White Wells' an eighteenth-century bath house built by a local benefactor. A walk from the Cow and Calf along the edge of the moor will take in all these features. Another popular Ilkley Moor walk is across to the famous Dick Hudson's pub above Shipley.

The Wharfe flows eastwards away from the dales, but fortunately misses the industrial heartland of Yorkshire. Beyond Ilkley the river

Bolton Abbey

passes its sister town of Otley which was granted a market charter in 1222. The river continues, round the northern boundary of Yorkshire's major house, Harewood, to skirt the racecourse town of Wetherby and on into the Vale of York, past Samuel Smith's brewery at Tadcaster to join the Ouse and eventually the sea.

SELECTED WALKS (Nidderdale)

Lofthouse and Gouthwaite Reservoir 5 miles • Easy • 2$^1/_2$ hours
From Lofthouse follow the road across both the Nidd and How Stean Beck, then turn left and left again along farm lanes on the west side of the dale as far as Ramsgill. Left in the village to Bouthwaite and its views along the reservoir, then left again to follow a series of paths and then the valley road back to Lofthouse.

Pateley Bridge and the Panorama Walk 3$^1/_2$ miles • Easy/Moderate • 2 hours
This signposted walk climbs past the village cemetery towards the ruin of the first church built in Pateley Bridge, then swings left along the Panorama Walk to join a minor road leading left to Wath. Go down to the river and turn left along its left bank as far as Pateley Bridge.

Brimham Rocks 1 to 3 miles • Easy 1$^1/_2$ hours
A complex of footpaths between the B6265 Ripon road, and Summer Bridge on the B6165 can, with the aid of the OS map, be used to enjoy a number of walks, all leading to the strange formations of Brimham Rocks. (Café and information centre).

SELECTED WALKS (Wharfedale)

Buckden and Upper Wharfedale 5 miles • Moderate • 2$^1/_2$-3 hours
Park in the official car park above Buckden's village green and take an upward slanting track, signposted 'To Buckden Pike and Cray'. Pausing only to admire the views of Upper Wharfedale, climb out on to a grassy terrace. Ignore any paths to the right and walk on until you see a steep path to the left, down to Cray. Follow this over a stream and cross the road, then go behind the White Lion Inn to find a level path beyond the last building. Follow this path, above a limestone crag cut only by narrow gulleys, as far as a turning left to Scar House. Go through the farmyard and down its access track into the dale bottom. At Hubberholme, call at the church then cross the bridge to turn left past the George Inn. Follow the road for about $^1/_2$ mile then

turn left, through a gate on to a fieldpath signposted to Buckden Bridge. Turn left over the bridge into Buckden.

Conistone's Pastures 5 miles • Easy/Moderate • 3 hours
From the centre of Conistone, walk along the Grassington road for about 100yd, past the Methodist chapel and turn left at the side of a cottage. Follow a cart track signposted 'Grassington', uphill and then ahead on a grassy path, following the direction of fingerposts. Go over a stone stile then around the upper limits of a rocky gorge. Climb a ladder stile then gradually bear right across the rocky pathless upland pastures. Keep well to the left of the woodland boundary as far as a boundary wall in sight of Grassington and at right-angles to your route. Do not cross this wall, but turn sharp left, away from it on to a grassy path across a series of upland pastures; cross field boundaries by their stiles or gates. Cross a stile and go left as indicated by a signpost, towards Conistone. Go down into a narrow dry valley and follow it all the way to Conistone.

Bolton Abbey and Strid Wood 6$^1/_2$ miles • Easy • 4 hours
From Bolton Abbey village follow the road as far as the Cavendish Memorial and turn right then left, down a flight of steps towards the riverside meadows. Walk upstream to the Cavendish Pavilion, pay the small entry fee, pick up a nature trail leaflet and following green markers walk into the woods. Walk on through the woods, changing to purple then yellow waymarks to follow the path past The Strid and out over a footbridge into an open field. Turn right across the stone bridge disguising a water pipe and on the far side turn right again. Walk downstream through a wood of predominantly beech and oak trees. Cross a wooden stile then right along the road for about 130yd, over a road bridge then right along a grassy path signposted to Cavendish and Bolton Abbey. Continue downstream beyond a wooden bridge (cross only if calling at the Pavilion for refreshments). Climb up to the road again. Follow it, over a ford, then right as signposted to Bolton Priory. Cross the river, either by the footbridge or the Friar's Stepping Stones if the river is low enough and walk up to the abbey ruins. Follow the path to the left and away from the abbey to a hole in the high boundary wall. Go through it and turn left, back along the road to the village.

A SCENIC CAR DRIVE

Through Wharfedale 100 miles
As there is only one road through Wharfedale, the B6160, this drive has been designed to also cover the Washburn Valley, part of

PLACES TO VISIT AROUND WHARFEDALE

Barden Tower
On B6160, $2^3/_4$ miles north-west of Bolton Abbey
Artist's study open, art courses held.

Bolton Abbey
A69, $6^1/_2$ miles east of Skipton
Ruined Augustinian priory.

Grass Wood Nature Reserve
B6160 near Grassington
Woodland on limestone habitat.

Kilnsey Crag
On B6160, $4^1/_2$ miles north-west of Grassington
A dramatic overhanging limestone crag.

The Strid and Bolton Woods
Access from B6160
Deep narrow gorge with water worn formations. Nature trails. Small fee.

Upper Wharfedale Museum
Grassington, on B6160 8 miles north-west of Bolton Abbey
Farming and industrial life of Upper Wharfedale.

White Wells
Ilkley Moor
Private house, but arrangements can be made to view the history and geology display.

Nidderdale and in order to create a circular tour, the route enters Upper Wharfedale by way of Wensleydale and remote Bishopdale. The drive starts and finishes at Ilkley. Drive down the A65 to Otley and turn left along the B6451, through the Washburn Valley, over the A59 and on to Summer Bridge, where a diversion can be made to Brimham Rocks (National Trust). Left along the B6165 to Pateley Bridge (Panorama Walk, cafés etc). Right on the B6265, then by unclassified roads north through Kirkby Malzeard to Masham (pubs, cafés). Left along the A6108, past Jervaulx Abbey and through Middleham (castle, cafés, pubs, shops) to Leyburn. Left by the A684 along Wensleydale to Aysgarth (waterfalls, museum, cafés, pub). Minor road south to West Burton in Bishopdale (interesting unspoilt village); right on the B6160 through Cray (Warning: steep descent by narrow road) into Buckden (pub). Valley road through Kettlewell (pubs, cafés), past Kilnsey (pub, waterpark), to Threshfield (interesting village) and maybe divert to Grassington (interesting village, pubs, cafés, shops). Continue by the B6160 to Bolton Abbey (interesting ruins, restaurant, café etc). Cross the A59 and turn left on the A65 in Addingham, Ilkley is about 2 miles further down the road (shops, hotels, pubs, restaurants, museum, walks on Ilkley Moor).

Morris dancers at the Cavendish Pavilion, Bolton Abbey

The River Wharfe, Otley

8
AIREDALE

On first sight it would seem that the River Aire starts its life as the stream issuing from the letterbox shaped hole at the foot of Malham Cove. Surely it is in a direct line below Malham Tarn, which undoubtedly is the true parent of industrial Yorkshire's major river. Nature however, has other ideas and has arranged for a complicated switch to occur out of site and below ground. The stream flowing from Malham Tarn disappears undergound at Water Sinks immediately south of the tarn, only to reappear as the quiet spring known as Aire Head about half a mile south of Malham village. The stream issuing from the foot of Malham Cove started as an insignificant pair or runnels west of the Littondale road. The Aire has not always flowed below ground and at one time a waterfall higher than Niagara poured over the lip of Malham Cove. Local records seem to indicate that the fall dried up some time in the late eighteenth century, although there is no factual proof of this.

It is strange to find surface water and especially a lake in limestone country. The reason for it is that patches of Silurian slate, which is impervious to water, occur throughout Craven and the particular patch above Malham holds this tarn. Other examples of this slate can be found at a considerably lower level around Horton in the Ribble Valley. Although of the same geological age, the reason for such a marked shift is due to a massive downward movement of the earth's crust, known here as the 'Mid-Craven Fault'. The actual fracture can be traced by the line of dramatic cliffs including Malham Cove and Attermire Scar above Settle.

Beef cattle graze Malham Moor, but it is the sheep which provide the real income to the area. They have been the mainstay for

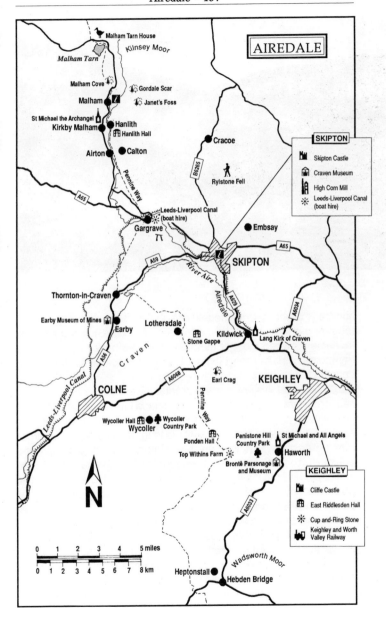

Malham Cove

hundreds of years, from the early times and later when huge flocks roamed the fells, founding the fortunes of Fountains Abbey. This monastery owned most of the land in the surrounding district, but Fountains Fell is the only tangible link with an order which prospered until the Dissolution.

While Fountains Fell is made of gritstone and grows a plentiful but sour grass, the land to the east of the upland farm at its foot, Tennant Gill, stands on limestone. Here the grass is much shorter, but sweeter. Limestone makes the whole long complex line of summits running east towards **Kilnsey Moor** as a maze of outcrops and boulders. This is a fascinating area for the birdwatcher or botanist, and especially the fossil hunter. The land is almost free of visitors so be careful not to break a bone on the often slippery limestone. A few public footpaths, which can be followed by careful navigation, cross the heights between Malham Moor and Littondale.

Malham Tarn and its house are owned by the National Trust and the estate has been devoted to the study of flora and fauna of the area. Malham Tarn House is used as a centre by the Field Studies Council and courses are held there for a variety of student bodies. Once a shooting lodge, the present use for the preservation of wildlife

Tennant Gill Farm near Malham

has encouraged an increase in the bird population, especially wild-fowl which visit the lake during their nesting season.

By using two quiet stretches of road round Tarn Moss, and then a footpath, Malham Tarn can be circumnavigated in a couple of hours, but it is a fair bet that the walker's footsteps will be slow along the side of the tarn, especially in spring when the birds congregate and begin their courtship rituals.

Charles Kingsley stayed at Malham Tarn House and was so inspired by the scenery that he made it the backcloth for his novel *The Water Babies*. He also used the magical aspect of the mysterious pool at the foot of Malham Cove, which became the place where the water babies made their home.

During the formative years of the world, tremendous upheavals took place and today it will be difficult to imagine the cataclysmic earthquakes which rent the face of the earth and reversed the relative heights of land in the Craven area. Nowhere along the Mid-Craven Fault is this so evident as at Malham. Land at the foot of Malham Cove started on the same level as the summit of Fountains Fell with the cove marking the fracture line of the fault. On top of **Malham Cove** is a remarkable limestone pavement, a wide expanse of clefts in the bare rock made by the action of water working its way down through weaker sections of this soluble rock. The clefts or 'grikes' are often filled with varieties of ferns such as hart's tongue fern and dog's mercury: plants normally living in shaded woodland and associated with the ground cover of ash woodland which covered most of the fells before the last Ice Age. The flat parts between the grikes are known as 'clints'.

In a field below the Cove, ruined walls at right angles to the path are themselves prehistoric and were built by the first men who settled in this sheltered and fertile little valley. Lynchets on either side of the valley beneath the Cove and clapper bridges across the beck also speak of man's long occupation of this sunny place. Despite being one of the most popular villages in the dales, **Malham** retains an unhurried rural charm. The Yorkshire Dales National Park Authority are to be congratulated on the way they have resisted attempts to commercialise Malham, and yet at the same time the village caters admirably for the needs of visitors. Malham is a very nice place in which to live as well as visit — not an easy combination to achieve.

The National Park Authority has provided a large car park and a very useful information centre on the edge of Malham village. Malham has attracted visitors for many years. Wordsworth and his sister Dorothy spent some time in the area in 1807 and the line 'Where young lions crouch' from his sonnet, composed after the visit, aptly sums up the feel of the crags and precipices of the cove and its neighbours. Malham has many more visitors than it did before the bridge by the green was widened. This was necessary to cope with motors rather than pack-horse traffic for which it was first built. Even older than this is Moon Bridge, an ancient clapper bridge a little way upstream by the side of Beck Hall, where on a sunny day the attraction of the river and cream teas can be irresistible.

A pack-horse road which crossed Malhamdale can still be followed most of its way on footpaths or by a little-used road. This is the route which climbs out from Settle by way of Attermire Scar and crosses Kirkby Fell by Nappa Cross before calling in on Malham. Next it crosses the bridge and climbs across Gordale and steeply back to the moors, where it becomes Mastiles Lane and so eventually down into Wharfedale by the side of Kilnsey Crag.

Lead was mined above Malham but the only visible remnant (except for the occasional blanked off shaft here and there) is the lonely chimney to the right of the Littondale road — all that survives of the smelt mill for the area. Mining of a different kind went on below Pikedaw Hill, west of Malham, where zinc in the form of calamine (zinc carbonate) was extracted from below ground.

About a mile north-east from Malham, along the road towards Mastiles Lane, is to the breathtaking spectacle of **Gordale Scar**. Here a collapsed cave system has formed a narrow gorge with towering and overhanging cliffs on either side. Most visitors will not care to emulate the rock gymnasts performing over their heads and in fact most people turn back at the point where the waterfall rushes down its tufa buttress. Tufa is rock which is made from deposits of limestone held in suspension in the stream; as the water flows over existing rocks it leaves behind minute amounts of lime to form a porous 'reconstituted' stone. Footholds on the buttress to the left of the waterfall make it easier to climb than first impressions might show and in fact the scree slope above is probably more difficult to anyone wearing footwear other than boots. To the walker's right of the scree slope the river pours through a natural window in the rock wall.

Below Gordale Scar and across the road the river tumbles over another tufa outcrop. This one, known as **Janet's Foss**, is a perfect gem set amongst shady trees and mossy rocks. Standing by it on a sunny day it is easy to believe the local legend that Janet, a fairy queen, lives behind the outcrop.

There is a walk from Malham (8 miles, 4 hours) which visits all the main features described so far. It starts by the bridge and follows the river downstream for a little way to a gate where a signposted path leads left into Gordale, alongside the stream and through Wedber Wood. Janet's Foss lies at the head of the wood which is set out as a nature trail with plaques explaining the natural features. Above Janet's Foss the path climbs up to and crosses the road before entering the meadow below Gordale Scar. As mentioned earlier the best way up the waterfall is to climb the buttress on the left (when facing); above it a scree slope leads to a field dotted with limestone outcrops and boulders. Pass through this field on a path of springy turf to the road. Turn right along the road and walk to Malham Tarn, but afterwards steps must be retraced until a path is seen diverging on the right. Follow this back to the road where a right-hand turn and then left beyond a gate leads down past Water Sinks (where the river disappears underground), and into a dry valley leading to the top of Malham Cove. The way down is to walk (with care) to the right, across the limestone pavement to its far end and after crossing a stile on the

Gordale

left follow zig-zags down into Malhamdale and back to the village.

The Pennine Way which has followed the Aire from Eshton Moor and through Malham village, climbs the Cove, but instead of following the interesting dry valley above it, takes a parallel course along Trougate to the Tarn. Beyond, the route is semi-artificial, wandering through fields to Tennant Gill and then up to Fountains Fell and across intervening col to Penyghent hill.

After the dramatic scenery around Malham, the character of Airedale quickly changes to the lush pasture which has made Craven's dairy farms so famous. On either side of the river are two ancient villages. **Hanlith** to the east was founded by the Angles, and its hall built in 1668 retains a Jacobean flavour despite later alterations. Westwards is the upper valley's main village, **Kirkby Malham**, where the dale's first church (St Michael the Archangel) was founded in the eighth century. Outside it is a preaching cross and a set of stocks which look as though they could still be put into use today. Oliver Cromwell is supposed to have witnessed three marriages in the church and there is a signature which looks like his on the register, but there is nothing else to authenticate his visit to this valley during the long and bitter northern campaign in the Civil War.

The next two villages almost mirror their upstream neighbours in their positions east and west of the river. **Calton** is on a hilltop to the east and was home for 'Honest' John Lambert, one of Cromwell's generals. **Airton** is linked more closely to the river, which once powered the former linen mill now converted into flats. Airton was a Quaker stronghold and still holds links with this gentle faith.

Strategically placed in the Aire Gap, **Gargrave** straddles the A65 ❋ as well as being served by the railway and a canal. Transport throughout the ages has passed through this village. Prehistoric man used the Aire Gap to cross the Pennines on an established trade route between Ireland and Scandinavia, and the Romans followed by building a road from Ribchester to link in with their main north-south arteries on either side of York. A battle associated with the legend of King Arthur is supposed to have taken place somewhere in this gap through the Pennines, but its site is unknown.

As the Yorkshire wool trade developed, improvements to the roads between the sheep-rearing areas and factory towns followed. In 1753 the turnpiking of the Keighley to Kendal road made it much easier for wool to be brought from Westmorland to industrial West Riding. A few years later waterways were promoted which were intended to link Liverpool with the east coast at Hull. In 1770 an Act

Cottages at Town Head, Malham

of Parliament authorised the building of a canal between Liverpool and Leeds. Work progressed rapidly on the lower stretches, but it was not until 1790 that the full length was opened, with the completion of the difficult stretch on either side of Gargrave. Canals fell into disuse with the advent of railways, for by 1876 the Leeds to Carlisle railway was in operation.

Today motor traffic speeds through Gargrave on surfaces far smoother than the builders of the turnpike ever envisaged. The railway is still open, but is frequently the cause of commercial head-shaking in sections of the British Rail management. The canal, which has not carried any commercial traffic since 1954, has benefited with the increasing popularity of canal cruising. During the holiday season the locks around Gargrave are in almost constant use as pleasure craft climb up to Craven and down to Skipton. Throughout the centuries Gargrave has, in its time, seen a great deal of traffic of one kind or another. Traffic has not always been friendly though. The Roman villa south-east of the village was found, during recent excavations, to have been sacked in the third century. The villa (SD 939535) is on private land, but can be seen from the lane running from the side of the church towards the railway line. The Scots also created much mayhem when they visited Gargrave in 1318 on a cattle raiding excursion. Walkers enjoying one of the most pastoral sections of the Pennine Way, pass through Gargrave on their way to Malham and the limestone regions of the Pennines.

Side valleys in the dales often lead to pleasant surprises for those who try to avoid the more crowded places. When, as often happens, Malham is overcrowdered and the traffic crawls through Skipton, the little **Winterburn Valley** above Gargrave will provide a haven of peace and quiet. Few roads and pathways traverse this valley but those that do are worth following. No villages occupy the main valley but its tributary gives anchorage to three which are very close together. **Cracoe** is the first, mostly industrialised and providing homes for quarry workers and lorry drivers, but Hetton and Rylstone are more attractive places. **Rylstone Fell** to the east provides some excellent walking and good rock climbing on the gritstone edge of the moor. Being part of the Chatsworth estate, concessionary access has been granted to the fell except during grouse shooting or at times of high fire risk.

The low, elongated hummocky hills on either side of the Leeds-Liverpool Canal below Gargrave are made up of boulder clay left behind by retreating glaciers after they breached the Aire Gap during the last Ice Age.

Craven is shaped roughly like an inverted south-west pointing 'V', with agriculture gradually giving way to industry the closer one gets to Lancashire, but even so there is still much delightful and unspoilt countryside to find. East of Thornton-in-Craven the gentle heights of Pinhaw Beacon (SD944472) and neighbouring Kelbrook Moor are a blaze of purple heather in August and September during the grouse shooting season. Heather, being the staple diet of grouse, is encouraged, and so there is the side benefit of a wealth of rich colour in late summer.

Earby never quite succumbed to the growth of industry as did the other cotton towns further south beneath the slopes of Pendle Hill. Elizabethan stone houses can still be found in odd corners, often alongside modern factories. One such building, the seventeenth-century grammar school, has been preserved as a lead mining museum by the Earby Mines Research Group. The collection of mining mementoes ranges from clogs and miner's hats, to working models and a unique ore crusher from Providence Mine near Kettlewell. As it is run by a voluntary society the museum's opening times are restricted.

On the edge of Lancashire's cotton domain and a mile or two outside Colne, is the unique living museum of **Wycoller**, a village which started life over eleven centuries ago as a hill settlement, and in the eighteenth and nineteenth centuries enjoyed a mini-boom as an industrial hamlet. This boom was short lived, as it was based on handloom weaving, and with the advent of mechanical power, industry moved to the more open spaces of Colne and the Calder Valley. Wycoller Hall was used by Charlotte Brontë as Ferndean Manor in her novel *Jane Eyre*. Slowly the hall and village fell into decay until 1950, when the Friends of Wycoller came into existence and the decay was halted. But it took until 1973 to bring about any true preservation, when the area was designated a Country Park and Conservation Area. Apart from providing a small visitor information service and generally tidying up the ruins and paths, the authorities have had the foresight to leave Wycoller for the visitor to explore and discover its delightful facets. Car parking is kept outside the village and one must walk in to enjoy the area. Several paths follow the valley as far as the Haworth road and there are numerous permutations on a theme to provide round trips for walkers.

Mastiles Lane

Moving back into Yorkshire along the A6068 towards Airedale, the industrial township of **Cowling** and its satellite Ickornshaw hold a tenacious foothold to the industrial twentieth century. The moors south of the road are sour and with little interest, but **Earl Crag** is worth visiting if only to view the curious towers known respectively as Wainman's Pinnacle and Lund's Tower.

Sheltering beneath the bulk of Elslack Moor is **Lothersdale**, a village of quaint and interesting houses, which manages the almost impossible task of remaining relatively prosperous without losing any of its character. The woollen mill provides work for most of the inhabitants of Lothersdale, and still retains its waterwheel although power is now from the more modern and reliable source of electricity. Persecuted Quakers sheltered here during the reign of King Charles II; their quaint Meeting House, with its peep-hatch gallery is still used. Charlotte Brontë used Stone Gappe the attractive Georgian house to the east of the village for Gateshead Hall in *Jane Eyre*.

The most southerly of Yorkshire's lead mining districts and by chance the last to be developed is between Lothersdale and Conon-ley. Here a single but rich vein occurs beneath a gritstone layer. While lead had been mined for centuries around this district, it was not until

PLACES TO VISIT IN AND AROUND MALHAM AND SKIPTON

Earby Museum of Mines
Earby A56, 6 miles south-west of Skipton
Large collection of Yorkshire Dales mining equipment, working models, mineral samples, etc. Limited opening.

Gordale Scar
$1\frac{1}{2}$ miles east of Malham
Deep limestone gorge formed by a collapsed cave system.

Janet's Foss
1 mile east of Malham
Cascade over a moss-grown tufa block at the bottom of a wooded dell. Nature trail.

Malham Cove
$\frac{1}{2}$ mile north of Malham
Limestone amphitheatre with water-worn pavement on higher level.

Malham Tarn
2 miles north of Malham
Moorland lake, bird/nature sanctuary. Ideal bird watching area. Roadside car parking. Refreshments, car parking and information centre available in Malham.

Skipton
Castle
Eleventh century, restored by Lady Anne Clifford between 1650-75 and still in excellent repair. Open to the public.

Craven Museum
Situated in High Street close to the castle, exhibiting a collection of Craven mementoes. Open most afternoons.

High Corn Mill
Mill Bridge
Still producing corn by the power of two waterwheels. Open to the public.

Leeds-Liverpool Canal
Open to pleasure craft. Boat hire from Gargrave and Skipton. Busy set of locks near Malham road on outskirts of Gargrave.

Yorkshire Dales Railway
Embsay, $1\frac{1}{2}$ miles north-east of Skipton
Length of track and a good collection of steam locomotives. Regular steam days.

1830 that serious development took place, producing some 150,000 tons of ore in the period up to 1876. The engine house and smelt mill chimney are still in very good condition and have been preserved in a joint venture by the Earby Mines Research Group and the Crosshills Naturalist Society.

Dales and industry both meet and co-exist in **Skipton**, where miles of sewing cotton are produced. The dales farmer and his wife come down to market to shop alongside visitors out for the day from nearby towns and cities. Good wholesome food is traditionally offered by the many inns lining, or not far from, the High Street. Skipton has long been a major market town at the crossroads of routes justifying its claim to be the 'Gateway to the Dales'. Certainly it is ideally situated as a tourist centre, especially since new by-pass roads were built, removing the frequent snarl-ups in the High Street. The town was established long before the Normans built a castle here and recorded the name 'Sceptone' or 'Sheeptown'. The *Domesday Book* lists the land around Skipton as Crown land which was later granted to Robert de Romille.

In 1138 William Fitzduncan, nephew of King David I of Scotland, attacked the castle but was conquered in his turn by Alice de Romille whom he married in 1152. Peace reigned over Skipton for several centuries, during which time the Clifford family took over the castle as protectors against the Scots. In 1642, during the ownership of the indefatigable Lady Anne Clifford, the castle was held by Sir John Mallory and 300 men for 3 years against Cromwell's troops. Starvation eventually forced their surrender on 21 December 1645. Lady Anne could not return to her castle until 1650 and it took the next 25 years until her death in 1675, to rebuild the castle to its present appearance. It was during this period that she also undertook the repair of her other properties throughout the North. The imposing gateway to the castle with its Clifford motto 'Desormais', roughly meaning 'Henseforth' is a lasting memorial to Lady Anne's work. The castle is a private house, but open to the public for most of the year.

An exhibition of life in Old Craven is on show in the Craven Museum in Skipton town hall below the castle, together with relics of the 3-year siege during the Civil War and even older finds. A 'living' museum can be found nearby at High Corn Mill on Ellerbeck where flour is still produced by two power generated waterwheels. The mill is as old as the town, one on the same site having been mentioned in the *Domesday Book*. Skipton parish church watches over the comings and goings at the top of Masket Street. Though greatly 'improved' in the Victorian era, much of the fabric dates from seventeenth-century restoration by Lady Anne Clifford, after the severe damage it sustained along with the adjoining castle during the Civil War.

The Springs branch of the Leeds-Liverpool Canal ends in Skipton at a busy basin; its almost constant movement of pleasure craft is only a short distance from the market. Skipton has its own 'private' moor to the east of the town where a network of paths remain from the time when people from the remote farm houses scattered over the moor, walked to and from Skipton to sell their produce at the market. **Embsay** is on the A59, 2 miles outside Skipton, the headquarters of the Yorkshire Dales Railway Society who have preserved a section of the old Ilkley to Skipton line. Lack of line has not deterred the society from collecting a large number of locomotives and rolling stock which are steamed regularly, especially at summer and Bank Holiday weekends.

Ever-increasing industrial towns line the Aire and the clear waters of Malhamdale are more and more polluted as the river approaches Leeds. High up to the east is Rombald's Moor and as previously seen in the chapter on Wharfedale, even though many tracks cross the moor from one valley to the other, few paths actually go round. However it is possible to walk from Silsden to Riddlesden on recognised rights-of-way.

Kildwick is the last true 'Dales' village in Airedale, an ancient place founded by the Angles who named it 'Childwic'. The church, often referred to as the Lang Kirk of Craven, is 176ft long, one of the longest in Yorkshire. The present building is sixteenth century, but its foundations are much older. Another old Kildwick structure is the much altered bridge across the Aire, which dates from the fourteenth century. The imposing manor house is Elizabethan, now tastefully converted into an hotel and restaurant and for 300 years was the home of the Currer family.

On no account should **Keighley** be written off as just another industrial town. Its art gallery in Cliffe Castle is worth visiting, as is its modern town centre, if only to see the Neolithic 'cup-and-ring' stone, uprooted from its true place on the moors to make an unusual town centre feature. Just outside Keighley on the Bradford road is East Riddlesden Hall, built in 1642, which boasts a magnificent banqueting hall and one of the finest timbered barns in the north of England.

In 1867 a railway line was opened to link the industrial mill towns of the Worth Valley to the main line at Keighley. This branch line continued to serve the scattered communities of the valley until 1962 when it was no longer considered an economical proposition. With the growth of nostalgic interest in steam engines it was a heaven sent opportunity. Members of the Keighley and Worth Valley Railway Preservation Society banded together for the specific purpose of bringing the line back to life and especially to run it as a commercial venture by using steam locomotives. A great deal of work was necessary both to bring the line and rolling stock up to the high standards required by the Ministry of Transport and more importantly, to raise the necessary cash to fund the venture. Money was needed not only to purchase the line, but also to buy the right to use Platform 4 on Keighley station. At 2.35pm on Saturday 29 June 1968 the hopes and ambitions of all the many people who had worked towards re-opening the line were realised, when a beflagged train, drawn by two locomotives pulled away from Keighley station. Since then the society has run steam trains every Saturday, Sunday and Bank Holidays and on certain weekdays in summer. The whole venture continues to be operated by enthusiastic volunteers and the profits are ploughed back to help buy new rolling stock and maintain the line. The full range of equipment is fully preserved and on view in the station yards of Haworth and Oxenhope. Film and television companies have been quick to realise the scenic potential of the Worth Valley Line and have used it many times, the best known being both the TV and screen versions of E. Nesbit's *The Railway Children*.

Clapper bridge above Malham on Mastiles Lane

PLACES TO VISIT AROUND THE WORTH VALLEY

Haworth
Brontë Parsonage and Museum.
Memorabilia of the Brontë family, paintings, manuscripts, costumes, etc.

Keighley
East Riddlesden Hall
On A650, 1 mile south-east of Keighley
Manor house and great barn. National Trust.

Cup-and-Ring Stone
Centre piece of Keighley market place. Prehistoric symbolic carving uprooted from nearby moorland.

Keighley and Worth Valley Railway
Steam railway from Keighley BR Station to Oxenhope. Trains run every weekend March to October, Bank Holidays and daily in July and August.

Penistone Hill Country Park
$1/_2$ mile south-west of Haworth

Wycoller Country Park
Off Haworth road 3 miles from Colne.

A trip on the Worth Valley Line can be included in a visit to **Haworth**, if only as a pilgrimage to the parsonage home of the Brontë sisters, daughters of the Reverend Patrick Brontë who was curate of Haworth's Church of St Michael and All Angels. Here is where Anne, Charlotte and Emily wrote their novels, set so often amongst local buildings and places. Even without its links with the Brontës, Haworth would be worth visiting for its evocative atmosphere which recalls the nineteenth century; from its cobbled Main Street to the gritstone houses laid out in a planners' nightmare. One must forgive the slight air of commercialism which has made traders link the name of Brontë to almost every saleable item, they have a living to make after all.

Penistone Hill above the village has been made into a Country Park and is ideally situated for picnics, or gentle wandering along the edge of the moors. In late summer the sheer enjoyment of the acres of heather recalls the love Yorkshire composer Delius had for the rolling moors and open skies of his native county. This is the sunny view of Yorkshire, rather than the sullen impetuousness of the Brontë sisters, more fitted to a wild stormy day when the dripping clouds cover everything.

A walk that Brontë devotees will follow is the one to **Top Withins Farm**, or Wuthering Heights (4 miles, 2 hours). The farm, now a ruin, is a typical hill farm made uneconomical when reservoirs were built on good valley bottom land. Emily enlarged the building in *Wuthering Heights*, but on a wild and foggy day late in the year, it is not difficult to people it with the ghosts of Catherine and Heathcliff. The path to Top Withins starts at the cross roads between the Country Park and Lower Laithe Reservoir.

The Pennine Way route passes Top Withins and 2 miles further on is **Ponden Hall**, also with Brontë associations. This house is reputed to be Thrushcross Grange in *Wuthering Heights*. The building has been preserved with a lot of care and attention given to the spacious rooms, with their massive oak beams and wide stone fireplaces. Pennine Way walkers and seekers of Brontë lore can all enjoy Ponden as its main use today is to provide food and accommodation.

Following the Pennine Way southwards the route crosses the watershed from the Aire into the last of the mid-Pennine valleys, the Calder. Although no longer dales' country and heavily industrialised around the actual river, the **Calder Valley** offers an amazing variety of lonely moors, deep wooded valleys and unspoilt villages with a heritage which seems to have remained almost unaltered since the eighteenth century. Then, industrialisation meant handloom weaving in tiny cottages; cottages which are still identifiable by the rows of windows in their attic rooms.

A pack-horse trail crossed Widdop Moor from Burnley to Halifax and a tiny inn on the Hebden Bridge to Colne road offered them shelter. Below the Pack Horse Inn, Hebden Water leads down to a lovely wooded valley. In it Hardcastle Crags have, on occasions, served as the setting for a traditional open-air parliament for Swiss nationals living in Britain. **Hebden Bridge** with its terraced cottages appearing to defy gravity makes an ideal centre for Calderdale, or perhaps the visitor will stray to Heptonstall high on its hillside. **Heptonstall**, with its Easter Pace Egg competitions, whose traditions are lost in the mist of time, is one of Yorkshire's most rewarding villages for visitors interested in the history of the domestic weaving trade. Across the valley is **Mankinholes**, dominated by the obelisk on Stoodley Pike, erected to commemorate the defeat of Napoleon in 1814. It has collapsed twice and been restored each time.

A long distance path known as the Calderdale Way roughly

follows the watershed of all the tributaries of the Calder. It visits many fascinating places and crosses quiet moors and offers 50 miles of interesting walking which can easily be split into 7 days splendid walking. Perhaps you may care to try it?

SELECTED WALKS

Malham Cove and Gordale Scar 5 miles • Moderate/Strenuous • 3 hours
From the centre of Malham, cross the hump-backed road bridge, then left along the lane past the Youth Hostel. Follow a waymarked path through fields, then left down to the stream and over a clapper bridge. Turn right along a path to Malham Cove and left up a stepped path. Climb a stone stile and turn right across the limestone pavement. **(Warning: Take extra care on the broken surface of the pavement, especially along the edge of the cove, and in wet or windy weather)**. At the far end, climb a ladder stile and bear right uphill on a waymarked grassy path. Cross ladder stiles on both sides of the road and follow another grassy path downhill as far as Gordale Bridge. Cross the bridge, go left through a gate to follow a path up to Gordale Scar; return to the bridge. Go through a gate on the left at the far side of the bridge, down to Janet's Foss. Follow the waymarked woodland and field path back to Malham.

Cracoe Fell 6 miles • Strenuous • 3 hours
(Do not attempt this walk during grouse shooting, or at times of high fire risk. If in doubt, ☎ Bolton Abbey 227, or Grassington 752748). From Skipton end of Cracoe village, turn left, and left again along a narrow winding lane. Right at the T-junction along a track towards the open fell. Go through a gate and bear left away from a sheep pen. Zig-zag uphill on the trackless moor, aiming towards the prominent skyline pinnacle. Climb a ladder stile behind the pinnacle and turn right, by the side of a gently descending moorland boundary wall. Go through a gap in the wall and descend to the right on a recessed track marked with blue topped stakes. Turn right at a track junction, then over a stile to follow a fieldpath signposted to Cracoe. Right through a narrow gate opposite Rylstone Church. Follow the path across one field, through another gate and along a leafy lane to Cracoe.

The Leeds-Liverpool Canal and the Pennine Way from Gargrave
7¹/₂ miles • 3-3¹/₂ hours • Easy
Walk along the Malham road from the centre of Gargrave and turn left along the canal towpath. Climb up to the main road, turn right along it,

then left along a side road. Go through a wooden stile on the left and right along the towpath. Cross the canal at Bridge 165, to walk along the opposite bank, following its contour-hugging course through fields. Go under the A59, turn right across the next bridge (number 160) and walk past East Marton Church. Cross the A59 in front of Cross Keys Inn. Follow the lane down to and over the canal following 'Pennine Way' signs; bear right away from the canal. Still following 'Pennine Way' signs for a little over $1\frac{1}{2}$ miles, cross a series of grassy fields. Join a farm lane; follow it to the right, then over a railway bridge. On the far side cross a stile on the right and walk diagonally across the fields to Gargrave school. Turn left along the access lane, past the church, over the River Aire where the main part of Gargrave is to the right.

A SCENIC CAR DRIVE

Around Airedale 58 miles

As a number of narrow, winding single track roads are used on this drive, great care and attention should be made to road conditions at all times and consideration given to other road users.

From Skipton follow the A65 to Gargrave, and take the valley road north to Malham (car park, pubs, cafés, Malham Cove, Gordale Scar, Janet's Foss, short walks, information centre), and turn right over the hump-backed bridge. Left beyond the Youth Hostel, steeply uphill and left to Malham Tarn (small car park, view point, wildfowl, short walks). Ahead and across Malham Moor, then steeply downhill to Settle (pubs, cafés, shops, museum, walks). A65 to Gargrave (pubs, shops, cafés, riverside strolls), and south by unclassified road to Broughton. Right for a quarter of a mile along the A59, then left by minor roads through Elslack and across Carleton Moor to Lothersdale (pub, interesting mill). Minor road into Crosshills, left on the A629 to Kildwick (restaurant, interesting church), to Skipton (pubs, shops, cafés, restaurants, castle, museum, interesting church, markets).

The Yorkshire Dales Railway at Embsay

USEFUL INFORMATION FOR VISITORS

Appleby Castle

Appleby, on the A66 Penrith-Brough road
☎ (07683) 51402
Norman keep set in attractive gardens.
Examples of Roman armour and medieval furniture.
Rare Breeds Survival Trust Centre.
Open: Easter Friday to Easter Monday 10.30am-5pm; May to September, daily 10.30am-5pm. Special party rates by arrangement. Free car park. Picnic areas.

Barden Tower

Barden, Wharfedale, on B6160 $2^3/_4$ miles north-west of Bolton Abbey
☎ (075672) 616
Eleventh-century hunting lodge above the River Wharfe. Part of the building is still inhabited and offers accommodation and refreshments.
Open: artist's studio, daily May to October, by appointment other times. Drawing, painting and etching courses held at certain times.

Barnard Castle

(English Heritage)
Barnard Castle, on the A67 in the centre of the town
An imposing Norman stronghold on the precipitous north bank of the River Tees.
Open: mid-March to mid-October (weekdays) 9.30am-6.30pm (Sunday) 2-6.30pm; October to March (weekdays) 9.30am-4pm (Sunday) 2-4pm; also Sunday, April to September 9.30am-6.30pm. Charge for admission.

Blanchland Abbey

Blanchland on the B6306, 8
miles south of Hexham
Remains of a fortified twelfth-
century abbey incorporated into
various buildings within the
village. The Lord Crewe Arms
was once the abbey guest
house.

Bolton Abbey

Wharfedale, 6$^1/_2$ miles east of
Skipton, approached via A69
Attractive riverside ruins of
Augustinian priory.
Open: to the public at all times.

Bolton Castle

Castle Bolton, Wensleydale,
4$^1/_2$ miles north-east of
Aysgarth on Reeth road
Fourteenth-century castle
which was besieged by the
parliamentary troops in the Civil
War. Public rooms now used
as a restaurant.
Open: March to mid-November,
daily 10am-5pm.

Bowes Castle

(English Heritage)
Bowes on the A66, 4 miles
south-west of Barnard Castle
Massive twelfth-century stone
keep built on site of Roman fort
of *Lavatræ* to command the
eastern access to Stainmore.
Open: daylight hours.
Free admission.

Brough Castle

(English Heritage)
Brough, 16 miles north-east of
M6 junction 38
at the junction of A685 and A66
Norman keep built on the site
of a Roman fort.

Clitheroe Castle

Clitheroe, Lancashire
Ruins of medieval castle in
public gardens. Free access
during daylight hours.

East Riddlesden Hall

(National Trust)
On A650, 1 mile south-east of
Keighley
☎ (0535) 607075
Seventeenth-century manor
house and banqueting hall.
Great barn.
Open: April to October, Wed-
nesday to Sunday, Bank
Holiday Monday (closed Good
Friday) 2-6pm; June, July,
August 11am-6pm. Educational
visits, Thursdays and Fridays
all season by appointment.

Egglestone Abbey

(English Heritage)
Approached by Rokeby Park
road 1 mile south of Barnard
Castle.
Picturesque ruin set on a hill
above the south bank of the
River Tees. The greater part of
the thirteenth- to fourteenth-
century nave survives.

Open: mid-March to mid-
October, weekdays 9.30am-
6.30pm, Sunday 2-6.30pm;
October to March, weekdays
9.30am-4pm, Sunday 2-4pm.
Free admission. Guide book
available.

Fountains Abbey and Studley Royal
(National Trust)
3 miles south-west of Ripon off
B6265 to Pateley Bridge
The largest monastic ruin in
Britain with landscape gardens.
Open: October to March, daily
(except Christmas Eve and
Christmas Day) 10am-4pm;
April to June and September,
daily 10am-7pm; July and
August, daily 10am-8pm.

Jervaulx Abbey
On A6108 between Leyburn
and Masham
Twelfth-century Cistercian
abbey, almost completely
obliterated by Henry VIII, but
the ground plan and a number
of carved stones still remain.
Beautiful setting on the banks
of the River Ure.

Knaresborough Castle
Castle Yard, Knaresborough
☎ (0423) 503340
Home of Plantagenet kings,
later sacked by Cromwell
during the Civil War.
Open: Easter weekend, Spring
Bank Holiday, then from late
spring holiday to 30 September.

Marrick Priory
Swaledale, $1/_2$ mile south-west
of Marrick village
Reached by stone causeway
from Marrick village. Tranquil
situation on the River Swale.
Exterior only, not open to the
public.

Middleham Castle
(English Heritage)
Situated in Middleham on
A6108 Leyburn to Ripon road
Impressive ruin of twelfth-
century castle, which once was
the home of King Richard III.
Open: mid-March to mid-
October, weekdays 9.30am-
6.30pm, Sunday 2-6.30pm;
October to March, weekdays
9.30am-4pm, Sunday 2-4pm.

Richmond Castle
(English Heritage)
Richmond, North Yorkshire
Massive Norman keep founded
in 1071 by Alan Rufus.
Open: mid-March to mid-
October, weekdays 9.30am-
6.30pm, Sunday 2-6pm;
October to March, weekdays
9.30am-4pm, Sunday 2-4pm.

Ripley Castle
$3^1/_2$ miles north of Harrogate on
A61

☎ (0423) 770157
Home of the Ingilby family. The nearby village has a strong French atmosphere
Open: gardens, April to mid-October, daily 11am-5.30pm. Castle, April to May, Saturday and Sunday 11.30am-4.30pm; June to mid-October, daily (except Monday and Friday) 11.30am-4.30pm; Bank Holidays in season 11am-4.30pm.

Rokeby Park
Off A66 about 3 miles south-east of Barnard Castle
Palladian house built in 1735. Paintings and unique collection of needlework. The ruins of Mortham Tower are within the grounds.
Open: throughout the summer.

Sawley Abbey
(English Heritage)
Sawley, on the A59, 3 miles north-east of Clitheroe
Ruins of medieval monastery. Free access during daylight hours.

Skipton Castle
Centre of Skipton town
Eleventh-century castle, restored between 1650-75 by Lady Anne Clifford. Maintained by local organisation.
Open: all year (except Christmas Day and Good Friday) weekdays 10am-dusk, Sunday 2-6pm (or dusk if earlier).

Whalley Abbey
Whalley, on A59 4 miles south of Clitheroe
Manor house used as a retreat centre. Attractive flower gardens, gift shop and craft centre.
Open: Easter to October, weekdays 11.30am-4.30pm, Sunday 1-4.30pm.

ACCOMMODATION

Wherever you find accommodation in the Yorkshire Dales you will find a warm welcome and a hospitality which is known throughout the world. In 1981 the first ever comprehensive *Accommodation Guide* was published by the Yorkshire Dales National Park Committee in conjunction with the Yorkshire Dales Tourist Association.

Simple and group accommodation is available at Youth Hostels and Bunk House Barns throughout the dales. For details, contact:

YHA (England and Wales)
Trevelyan House
8 St Stephens Hill
St Albans
Herts AL1 2DY
☎ (0727) 55215

The YHA Accommodation Guide also available from MPC.

Some Tourist Information Centres, such as Settle, operate a 'Book-a-Bed' service. For a small fee they will find you the right sort of accommodation.

Information on accommodation outside the Yorkshire Dales National Park is obtainable from tourist boards as listed below:

Northumbria Tourist Board
9 Osborne Terrace
Jesmond
Newcastle upon Tyne NE2 1NT
☎ (0632) 817744

North-West Tourist Board
The Last Drop Village
Bromley Cross
Bolton
Lancashire BL7 9PZ
☎ (0204) 591511

Yorkshire and Humberside Tourist Board
312 Tadcaster Road
York YO2 2HF
☎ (0904) 707961

ARCHAEOLOGICAL SITES

Bremetennacum
Ribchester on B6245, 4 miles north of Blackburn
Roman fort with only the perimeter wall visible and partially excavated granary.
Open: during daylight hours.

Hanging Walls of Mark Anthony
Kirkland, 9 miles north-west of Appleby, NY652322
Fine examples of prehistoric cultivation terraces.

Ilkley Moor
Ilkley Moor has innumerable prehistoric remains, and a glance at a map will indicate this fact.

Swastika Stone
SE095470
An enigmatic carving on a prominent rock.

Twelve Apostles
SE126451
Stone circle approached by path from White Wells to Baildon.

White Wells
SE109468
Bath house erected by eighteenth-century philanthropist for the inhabitants of Ilkley.

Long Meg and Her Daughters
Little Salkeld, 4$^1/_2$ miles north-east of Penrith NY571372
A huge oval stone circle with twenty-seven of a probable

sixty stones still standing. Long Meg is the tallest stone, 10ft high, with symbolic cup-and-ring carvings.

Virosidum
Bainbridge, Wensleydale, SD937902
Roman fortification visible on prominent mound east of Bainbridge village.

Whitley Castle
B6292, 2 miles north of Alston, NY695487
Excellent example of a well fortified Roman fort.

BIRD WATCHING

Courses in bird watching are organised by:

Bird Guide
Ashville
Rose Bank
Burley-in-Wharfedale
West Yorkshire

Field Studies Council
The Malham Tarn Field Centre
Settle
North Yorkshire BD24 9PU

YHA
Trevelyan House
8 St Stephen's Hill
St Albans
Herts

BOATING AND SAILING

Derwent Reservoir
Derwentdale
Club and day sailing.
Picnic areas.

Knaresborough
Rowing boats available for hire throughout the summer months on the River Nidd.

Leeds and Liverpool Canal
Pleasure boats available for holiday hire from:

Black Prince Narrowboats Ltd
Silsden
Steeton
☎ Steeton 53675

British Waterways
Bank Newton Lock
Gargrave
☎ (0756) 78428

Pennine Cruisers
Coach Street
Skipton
☎ (0756) 5478

Snaygill Boats
Skipton Road
Bradley
Skipton
☎ (0756) 5150

Yorkshire Dales Hire Cruises
Bank Newton

Gargrave
Skipton BD23 3NT
☎ (0756) 78492

Semer Water
Countersett, Raydale, 1 mile
south of Bainbridge, via A684
Popular picnic area with
unofficial small craft use.

BUILDINGS AND GARDENS OPEN TO THE PUBLIC

Opening times are subject to
alterations so check locally for
further details.

Browsholme Hall
Bashall Eaves, Near Clitheroe
☎ (025486) 330
Home of the Parker family
since 1507. Tours conducted
by members of the family.
Open: Easter, Spring Bank
Holiday and 1 week either side
of Summer Bank Holiday.
Parties of at least four by
appointment from mid-May to
end of September.

**Constable Burton Hall and
Gardens**
$3^1/_2$ miles east of Leyburn on
A684. Georgian hall. Gardens
open to public, but the hall by
appointment only.

East Riddlesden Hall
A650, 1 mile north-east of

Keighley
Seventeenth-century manor
house. Tithe barn, fishpond,
grounds. Art gallery. National
Trust.

Harlow Car Gardens
Harrogate, on south-west edge
of town approached from
B6162
Run by the Northern Horticultural Society. The gardens
specialise in testing new
varieties of fruits and vegetables as well as flowers and
shrubs. Free coach and car
parks.

Markenfield Hall
Off the A61, $1^1/_2$ miles south-
west of Ripon
Moated manor and farmhouse.
One time home of the Marken-
fields who lost everything for
supporting the abortive 'Rising
of the North' in 1569.

Newby Hall
Newby, 4 miles south of Ripon
on the Boroughbridge old road
☎ (0423) 2583
Magnificent hall with landscaped gardens. Built in 1690s,
enlarged and redecorated in
1760s by Robert Adam.
Open: to the public during
summer months. Gardens and
restaurant, Easter and April to
October 11am-5.30pm, every
day except Monday, but open

Bank Holiday Mondays.
Hall and train: April to October,
every day except Monday. Also
Easter and Bank Holiday Mondays, 1-5pm, plant stall, steam-
boat, children's playground,
steam railway (miniature).

Norton Conyers
Near Wath, 3$^1/_2$ miles north of
Ripon off A61
Fine Jacobean house and
garden. Open: all year, Monday
to Friday; April to October,
Saturday and Sunday
2-5.30pm. Garden centre and
refreshments.

Parcevall Hall Gardens
Skyreholme, near Appletree-
wick, 10 miles north of Ilkley
Secluded gardens in Trollers
Ghyll. Open: Easter to October,
daily 10am-4pm.

Stonyhurst College
Hurst Green, 4 miles from
Clitheroe
☎ Stonyhurst 345
Catholic public school founded
in 1593, but main building
dates from 1594.
Open: to visitors by prior
appointment.

COUNTRY PARKS AND VISITOR CENTRES

Beacon Fell Country Park
8 miles north of Preston and
signposted from Longridge,
SD568429
Conifer woods, forest walks,
viewpoint, picnic areas,
refreshments.
Open: all the year.

Bowlees Visitor Centre
Bowlees, Upper Teesdale, on
B6277, 3 miles north-west of
Middleton-in-Teesdale
Visual display of natural history
of Upper Teesdale. Attractively
laid out museum in converted
chapel. Picnic site nearby.
Open: summer months only.

Cove Centre
Malham
☎ (07293) 432
Craft workshops, café.
Open: throughout the year.

The Dales Centre
Grassington, near Skipton
☎ (0756) 752312
Holiday accommodation.
Caving and climbing instruc-
tion. Slide shows and other
events in the evenings.

How Stean Gorge
10 miles north-west of Pateley
Bridge, Nidderdale
☎ (0423) 75666
Narrow gorge near the head of
Nidderdale, skilfully laid out
with walks and footbridges.
Children's play area. Car park.
Open: all the year.

Kilnsey Water Park

Kilnsey, near Skipton
☎ (0756) 752150
Trout hatchery, picnic site, freshwater aquarium, fishing. Open: all year, daily 9.30am-5pm.

Lightwater Valley Country Park

3 miles north of Ripon on the A6108
☎ (0765) 85321
Miniature railway, visitor farms, adventure playground, old time fair, boating, golf, 'hellslide'. Fruit picking in season. Restaurants and gift shop.
Open: April and May, Easter week, weekends and Bank Holidays; June, July and August, daily; September, weekends 10.30am-3.30pm.

Penistone Hill Country Park

Haworth, $1/_2$ mile south-west of village
Open moorland on edge of village.

Rare Breeds Survival Trust Centre

Appleby Castle, Appleby, on A66 Penrith to Brough road
☎ (07683) 51402
Collection of rare breeds of domestic farm animals, wildfowl, pheasants, poultry and owls. Beautifully laid out grounds. Free car park. Picnic areas and tea rooms.
Open: Easter Friday to Easter Monday 10.30am-5pm; May to end September, daily 10.30am-5pm. Special party rates by arrangement.

Slurring Rocks Country Park

Hardcastle Crags, Hebden Bridge, SD988291
Attractive wooded valley and gritstone gorge. Refreshments nearby.

Whorlton Lido

4 miles south-east of Barnard Castle
On privately owned picnic site. Has narrow gauge railway on south bank of River Tees.

Wycoller Hall

Off Haworth Road, 3 miles from Colne
Was used by Charlotte Brontë as Ferndean Manor in *Jane Eyre*.

Wycoller Visitor Centre

Off Haworth Road, 3 miles from Colne
Sensitive preservation of an unspoilt hamlet.

CYCLE HIRE

Cycle hire is usually available at daily or weekly rates. For more information *Cycling in the*

Yorkshire Dales (R. Harries, MPC) gives a mile by mile account of routes and tour planning with a comprehensive list of cycle hirers.

Hawes
Dales Cycle Hire
☎ (09697) 487

Ingleton
Richard's Cycles
The Square
☎ (0468) 41094

Settle
Settle Cycles
Duke Street
☎ (07292) 2216

Wharfedale
The Dales Centre
Tennant Arms
Kilnsey
☎ (0756) 752301 or 752312

DALES RAIL AND BUS SERVICES

A fully integrated rail and bus service operates on certain dates throughout the summer based on the Leeds to Carlisle line with connections from Preston and Blackburn to Hellifield. Intermediate stations of Settle to Carlisle line are open for Dales Rail. Information is also available from the Yorkshire and Humberside Tourist Board, Northumbrian Tourist Board and North-West Tourist Boards (see under Accommodation for addresses and telephone numbers). There are organised walks planned each year, timed to start and finish with convenient trains and buses. By careful use of the Dales Rail Time Table more ambitious routes may be planned. Further details can be obtained from Yorkshire Dales National Park Committee Information Centres, or:

British Rail

Pennine
☎ (0756) 215

Settle
☎ (07292) 3536

Skipton
☎ (0756) 2543

United Automobile Services Ltd
☎ (0765) 2093

West Yorkshire Road Car Company
☎ (0756) 5331

D. Whaites
12 High Hill Grove
Settle
☎ (07292) 3235

Dales Rail
Yorkshire Dales National Park
Colvend
Hebden Road
Grassington BD23 5LB
☎ (0756) 752748

Friends of Dales Rail
c/o 3 Rochester Terrace
Leeds LS6 3DF

FISHING

Most rivers with game fish are
privately owned, but fishing
permits can be bought locally.
Rod licences are issued by the
various water authorities
(addresses below), who also
allow game and coarse fishing
on reservoirs and stretches of
river under their control. Each
authority publishes a descrip-
tive leaflet.

Owners of other lakes and
millpools, such as Malham
Tarn and Foster Beck Hemp
Mill near Pateley Bridge, issue
day tickets.

The useful *Northern
Angler's Handbook* covers
details of all fishable waters
and is on sale at bookshops
and Yorkshire Dales National
Park Information Centres.

Northumbrian Water
Northumbria House
Regent Centre

Gosforth
Newcastle NE3 3PX
☎ (0912) 843151
River areas: Tees, Wear,
Derwent, Tyne, Aln, Coquet,
Wansbeck.

North-West Water Authority
Rivers Division
PO Box 12
New Town House
Buttermarket Street
Warrington WA1 2QG
☎ (0925) 53999
River areas: Ribble, Lune and
Eden.

Amenity and Recreation Officer
Yorkshire Water Authority
Rivers Division
21 Park Square South
Leeds
☎ (0532) 440191
River areas: Aire, Wharfe,
Nidd, Ure, Swale.

GOLF COURSES

Allendale
Alston Moor
Appleby
Barnard Castle
Bedale
Catterick
Clitheroe
Harrogate
Keighley
Knaresborough
Masham

Richmond
Sedbergh
Settle
Skipton
Whalley

HORSE RIDING AND PONY TREKKING

Caton School of Equitation
Quernmore Road
Caton
Lancaster
☎ (0524) 770694

Fitton & Son
Bank Newton
Gargrave
☎ (0756) 243

Kilnsey Trekking Centre
Grassington
☎ (0756) 752861

Sinderhope Pony Trekking
  Centre
Broadgate
Sinderhope
Allenheads
Northumbria NE47 9SH
☎ (043485) 266

West Park
Lunedale
Middleton-in-Teesdale
Co Durham
☎ (08334) 380

LONG DISTANCE FOOTPATHS AND WALKS

The Calderdale Way
A walk following the approximate bounds of the Calder Valley watershed, linking public rights-of-way and permissive paths. Can be completed in five easy stages. 50 miles total length.

Coast to Coast Walk
From St Bees Head in Cumbria to Ravenscar on the Yorkshire Coast, coincides with both the Pennine Way and the Dales Way above Ribblesdale.

The Dales Way
A pleasant valley and fell walk of several days duration, starts at Ilkley in Wharfedale and finishes at Windermere.

The Ebor Way
Links the Dales Way and the Cleveland Way; passes through the historic city of York.

The Pennine Way
This route starts at Edale in Derbyshire and finishes at Kirk Yetholm in Scotland, passing through the area described in this book.

The Ribble Way
Follows the course of the Ribble, from the source to its estuary.

MARKET DAYS

Appleby — Saturday (cattle: Monday, Friday).
Barnard Castle — Wednesday.
Clitheroe — Tuesday, Saturday (cattle: Monday, Tuesday, Friday).
Gisburn — (cattle: Tuesday, Thursday).
Hawes — Tuesday.
Ingleton — Friday.
Kirkby Lonsdale — Thursday.
Kirkby Stephen — Monday.
Knaresborough — Wednesday (cattle: Thursday).
Leyburn — Friday.
Middleton-in-Teesdale — Tuesday.
Richmond — Saturday.
Ripon — Thursday.
Sedbergh — Wednesday (cattle: Friday).
Settle — Thursday.
Skipton — Monday, Wednesday, Friday.

MUSEUMS

Beamish North of England Open-Air Museum

Stanley, Co Durham, off A693 Stanley to Chester-le-Street road
☎ (0207) 231811
A 200-acre open-air museum of northern life, where buildings from the region have been rebuilt and furnished as they once were, with a 1920s town street with shops, houses, pub etc; a northern colliery with mine and pit cottages; a working farm and a NER station and reconstructed steam locomotives. Working electric trams.
Open: Easter to mid-September, daily 10am-6pm; mid-September to Easter, daily (except Mondays) 10am-5pm. Last admission always 4pm.

Bedale Hall Museum

Bedale, DL8 1AA
☎ (0677) 23131
Georgian ballroom with fine Italian plaster ceiling and rare scarfe jointed pine floor. Museum displays local art and crafts, tradesman's tools, clocks, coins, weights and many other interesting objects. Seventeenth-century hall.
Open: May to September, 10am-4pm or by appointment.

Bowes Museum

Barnard Castle, $1/_2$ mile from town centre on Whorlton road.
☎ (0833) 37139
Collection of national importance housed in a French-style *château*. It includes paintings by El Greco and Goya and extensive collections of furniture, pottery, porcelain and tapestries. Administered by Durham County Council.

Open: weekdays, May to September, weekdays 10am-5.30pm; October, March and April 10am-5pm; November to February, 10am-4pm; Sunday, summer 2-5pm, winter 2-4pm. Closed one week Christmas and 1 January. Charge for admission.

Brontë Parsonage and Museum

Haworth, Keighley
☎ (0535) 42323
Many original manuscripts and personal memorabilia of the Brontë family.
Open: April to September, 11am-5.30pm; October to March 11am-4.30pm; Closed 24, 25, 26 December and for 3 weeks in February.

Clitheroe Castle Museum

Castle Hill, Clitheroe, Lancs
☎ (0200) 24635 or 25111
Small museum devoted to life in the nineteenth century. Museum contains an important collection of carboniferous fossils and a selection of items of local significance.
Open: Easter to October, daily 2-4.30pm and Bank Holidays 11am-4.30pm.

Craven Museum

Town Hall, High Street, Skipton
☎ (0756) 4079
Collection illustrating history

and archaeology of Craven.
Open: April to September, Monday, Wednesday, Thursday and Friday 11am-5pm, Saturday 10am-12noon and 1-5pm, Sunday 2-5pm; October to March, Monday, Wednesday, Thursday and Friday 2-5pm, Saturday 10am-12noon and 1.30-4.30pm. Closed Sundays and Tuesdays.

Earby Museum of Mines

School Lane, Earby, on A56, 6 miles south-west of Skipton. A large collection of Yorkshire Dales lead mining equipment.
Open: Thursday evenings 6-9pm and Sunday afternoons 2-6pm.

Georgian Theatre Royal and Theatre Museum

Victoria Road, Richmond
☎ (0748) 3021
A unique fully operational Georgian theatre and adjacent museum which links modern productions with 'the good old days' through hand bills and costumes, etc.
Open: May to September, weekdays 2.30-5pm, Saturday and Bank Holiday Monday 10.30am-1.30pm.

Green Howards Regimental Museum

Trinity Church Square, Richmond

☎ (0748) 2133
Memorabilia of this famous
Yorkshire regiment since its
formation in 1688.
Open: April to October, week-
day 9.30am-4.30pm, Sunday
2-4.30pm; November and
March, Monday to Saturday
10am-4.30pm; February
Monday to Friday 10am-
4.30pm. Closed all December
and January.

Harrogate Art Gallery

Victoria Avenue, Harrogate
☎ (0423) 503340
Permanent collection of many
fine oil and water paintings,
including paintings by Turner
and Constable.

Ilkley Art Gallery
and Museum

Ilkley, in centre of town
☎ (0943) 600066
Museum on the site of Roman
fort, and many artefacts from
this are on display.
Open: daily 10am-6pm. Closed
Monday (except Bank Holiday
Mondays.)

Isurium

Boroughbridge off A1 (Dere
Street) 7 miles south-east of
Ripon
Roman fort with several
preserved tesselated pave-
ments.
Small museum on site.

Killhope Wheel Lead Mining
Centre

$2^1/_2$ miles west of Cowshill on
A689 in Upper Weardale
☎ (091) 64411 ext 2354
A restored lead crushing mill,
with a 34ft-high waterwheel.
The areas best preserved lead
mining site. Exhibition about
lead mining and life of the
miner housed in one of the
restored buildings.
Open: April, May, June and
September, daily (except Mondays) 10.30am-5pm; July and
August, daily; October weekends and Wednesday; November to end of March by appointment for parties.

Museum of North Craven Life

Victoria Street, Settle
☎ (0468) 61163 or (04885) 414
Display of man in the countryside around Settle since
prehistoric times. Also temporary exhibitions, guide cards,
demonstrations and lectures.
Open: May to June, Saturday,
Sunday 2-5pm; July to September, daily (except Monday)
2-5pm; October to April,
Saturday 2-5pm.

Museum of Steam

Caravan site off the A682, 2
miles south of Gisburn
☎ (02005) 322
Small collection of steam
driven vehicles, including

showman's engines, all steamed during the summer. Open: at all reasonable times. Free admission. Access for coaches.

Nenthead Mines and Museum

A689, 5 miles south-east of Alston
Reconstructed mining area and processing plant. Trails, interpretive plaques.

Nentsberry Mining and Farming Museum

Open-air collection of mining equipment, farm implements. Narrow gauge mine railway, play area, picnic site.

Nidderdale Museum

Old Council Offices, Pateley Bridge, Nidderdale
Recently enlarged with several shop displays, Victorian living room and solicitor's office.
Open: all year, every Sunday; Easter to October, weekends 2-5pm; Whitsun to October, daily.

Old Court House

Adjacent to Knaresborough Castle
Fourteenth-century building with a reconstructed court room scene of 1602 including figures dressed in period costume.
☎ (0423) 503340

Old Court House Museum

Castle Yard, Knaresborough
☎ (0423) 503340
Museum of local history with original Tudor court.
Open: 1 April to 30 September; October to March, Sunday only, 1.30-4.30pm.

Pig Yard Museum

Castle Hill, Settle
Exhibitions of items of archaeological interest found locally.
Open: by appointment only. Write to the curator.

Richmondshire Museum

Ryders Wynd, Richmond
Museum of bygone Richmond's county before its amalgamation with Yorkshire. Includes the veterinary surgery from the BBC production of *All Creatures Great and Small*, a story which is set in the nearby dales.
Open: 21 May to 24 September, daily 2-5pm.

Swaledale Folk Museum

Reeth Green, Reeth, Swaledale
☎ (0748) 84373 (evenings only)
A museum of agricultural life and mining in bygone days of this area.
Open: Easter to September, daily 10.30am-6pm.

Upper Dales Folk Museum
Station Yard, Hawes
☎ (09697) 494
Exhibition of life on dales farm based on the Marie Hartley and Joan Ingilby collection. Located in the goods shed of the old railway station.
Open: Easter or 1 April to September, Monday to Saturday 11am-1pm and 2-5pm, Sunday 2-5pm; October, Tuesday, Saturday and Sunday only.

Upper Wharfedale Museum
The Square, Grassington
☎ (0756) 752800
Displays of dales farming and industry of the past; also included are veterinary equipment and a mineral collection.
Open: April to October, daily 2-4.30pm.

Wakeman's House Museum
Market Square, Ripon
One-time home of the wakeman, a medieval guardian of the town. The custom of blowing the wakeman's curfew horn is still maintained. House is also an information centre.
☎ (0765) 4625
Open: summer months only and daylight hours.

White Wells
Ilkley Moor
Display of natural history and geology. Accessible only on foot.
Open: summer, Saturday, Sunday and Bank Holiday Monday 2-6pm, or by prior arrangement.

The Yorkshire Museum of Horse Drawn Carriages
Aysgarth, Wensleydale, north of the A684
One of the most comprehensive collections of horse drawn vehicles used by the country squire and his estate.

NATURE RESERVES

Gouthwaite Reservoir Nature Reserve
Nidderdale, 4 miles north-west of Pateley Bridge
Bird sanctuary not freely accessible to general public, but many birds can be seen from the roads and trackways surrounding the reservoir.

Grass Wood Nature Reserve
Wharfedale, 1$1/2$ miles north-west of Grassington
Ash woodland on limestone. Owned and maintained by the Yorkshire Wildlife Trust Ltd. Parties by arrangement only.

Upper Teesdale National Nature Reserve
A botanically unique area of 8,600 acres. The area around

Cauldron Snout is accessible to the general public and a nature trail on Widdybank Fell allows visitors to see some of the rare plants flowering in their season. Field studies are based at Moor House.

NATURE TRAILS

Aysgarth Falls Nature Trail
$1/_4$ mile east of Aysgarth, GR010887
Nature trail starts from National Park Information Centre and follows wooded river bank above a series of attractive waterfalls.

Clapdale Wood (Reginald Farrer Trust)
$1/_2$ mile north of Clapham
Trail is in memory of Reginal Farrer (1880-1920), authority and collector of alpine plants. Himalayan shrubs and trees are featured in the trail.

Gibson's Cave Nature Trail
Bowlees, Upper Teesdale. Access from B6277, 3 miles north-west of Middleton-in-Teesdale
Nature trail starts from Bowlees Visitor Centre car park and picnic area. Interesting short walk through wooded valley.

Hardraw Force
Rear of Green Dragon Inn, Hardraw, near Hawes
Natural amphitheatre and highest above ground waterfall in England.

Ingleton's Waterfalls Walk
Follows a series of natural waterfalls on the River Greta.

Janet's Foss Woods
1 mile east of Malham village, SD912634
Trail laid out with explanatory plaques in woodland below Janet's Foss Waterfall.

Salthill Quarry Geological Trail
Near Clitheroe, Lancs
Abandoned limestone quarry with unique fossil evidence. Nature conservancy booklet available.

Sedbergh Town Trail
Short interpretive walk around Sedbergh.

Sedgwick Geological Trail
Lower Garsdale
Short ($1^1/_2$ hours approx) trail laid out on Longstone Common, crosses Dent Fault where the complex folds of Lake District rocks meet the horizontally bedded Carboniferous limestone and Yoredale shales of the Pennine Dales.

Trail in memory of Adam Sedgwick (1785-1873) father of modern geology.

Spring Wood Nature Trail
Whalley, near Clitheroe, SD741361
Mixed woodland. Picnic site.

The Strid and Bolton Abbey Woods
Wharfedale, approached from B6160, SE077553
Several trails of varying length start and finish at the Cavendish Pavilion. Refreshments.

Valley Walks
Ilkley, Wharfedale
Short waymarked routes from $^1/_2$ mile to $3^1/_2$ miles.

Weelhead Syke Nature Trail
Cow Green
(off B6277 Upper Teesdale)
Trail starts from scenic car park above Cow Green Reservoir. Open moorland, semi-alpine and tundra plants.

ORGANISED HOLIDAYS AND COURSES

Birdguide
Ashville
Rose Bank
Burley in Wharfedale
West Yorkshire LS29 7PQ

The Dales Centre
Grassington
☎ (0756) 752757

Field Studies Council
Malham Tarn Field Centre
Settle
North Yorkshire BD24 9PU
☎ (07293) 331

HF Holidays Ltd
142 Great North Way
London NW4 1EG
☎ (081203) 3381

YHA
Trevelyan House
8 St Stephens Hill
St Albans
Herts AL1 2DY
☎ (0727) 55215

Yorkshire Dales Adventure Centre Trust Ltd
Gildersleets
Giggleswick
Settle
☎ (079292) 5359

OTHER PLACES OF INTEREST

Alston Market Cross
Alston, A686, 19 miles north-east of Penrith
Covered market stand in main street. Highest market town in England.

Aysgarth Falls
$1/_4$ mile east of Aysgarth
A series of stepped falls for 1
mile on either side of the
Aysgarth to Carperby road.

Brimham Rocks
(National Trust)
Near Pateley Bridge, access
from B6265 or B6165
Moorland area dotted with
natural sculptures made from
weather-worn gritstone. Car
park on perimeter. Trails
indicated on information boards
lead past most of the formations. Information centre and
refreshments at Brimham
House.

Buttertubs
On Thwaite to Hawes road, $2^1/_2$
miles south of Thwaite
Shallow potholes easily
accessible from roadside. Car
park and information panels.

Cauldron Snout Waterfall
Upper Teesdale, below Cow
Green Reservoir. Access from
Cow Green car park

Dropping Well
Knaresborough
☎ (0423) 862352
Petrifying well adjacent to
Mother Shipton's Cave.
Objects placed in the well are
coated with stone over a period
of several months.

Ebbing and Flowing Well
Buckhaw Brow, on A65 1 mile
north-west of Settle, SD803654

The Fall's Walk
Ingleton
Delightful wooded ravines and
waterfalls. Footpath, steeply
stepped in places makes an
interesting $4^1/_2$ mile long
circular walk.
Small admission charge.

Fort Montague
Knaresborough
Eighteenth-century house
carved from solid rock overlooking the River Nidd.
Open: to the public during the
summer months.

Gaping Gill
3 miles north-west of Clapham,
SD751727
Impressive pothole. Local
caving club erects a winch-
borne chair during spring and
August Bank Holidays.

God's Bridge
2 miles west of Bowes on A66.
Approach $1/_4$ mile south of
Pasture End Farm, NY957127
Natural limestone bridge
spanning River Greta.

Gordale Scar
$1^1/_2$ miles east of Malham
village, SD915642
A deep limestone gorge formed

by a collapsed cave system.
Popular rock climbing area.

Hardraw Force

Access behind Green Dragon
Inn, Hardraw, 1 mile north of
Hawes, SD868914
Highest above ground waterfall
in England. Band concerts in
summer. Small entry fee.

Hawes Ropeworks

Near to Station Yard, Hawes
☎ (09697) 487
A working ropeworks specialising in animal halters, church
bell ropes, bannister and
barrier ropes. Shop etc.
Open: Monday to Friday 9am-
5.30pm (closed $1/_2$ hour lunch),
Saturday in most school
holidays, 10am-4pm (summer),
closed Sunday.

High Corn Mill

Mill Bridge, Skipton
☎ (0756) 2883
Corn mill still using the power
of two waterwheels.
Open: Wednesday, Saturday
and Sunday 2-6pm.

High Force

Upper Teesdale. Access from
B6277 High Force Hotel,
NY881284
Small fee.

Janet's Foss

1 mile east of Malham village,
SD912634
Cascade over a moss covered
rock at the bottom of a wooded
dell.

Kilnsey Crag

Wharfedale, $4^1/_2$ miles north-
west of Grassington on B6160,
SD975679
Impressive overhanging
limestone crag dominating the
landscape.

Low Force

Upper Teesdale, on the B6277
1 mile north-west of Newbiggin,
NZ904279

Malham Cove

$1/_2$ mile north of Malham village,
SD896641
Natural limestone amphitheatre
with water-worn pavement on
high level. Remains of ancient
field system below. Explanatory
notices nearby.

Malham Tarn

2 miles north of village
A unique moorland lake and
bird/nature sanctuary. Residen-
tial courses in all aspects of
natural history run by the Field
Studies Council at Malham
Tarn Field Centre.

Mother Shipton's Cave

Knaresborough, on south bank
of river and approached from
B6163

☎ (0423) 862352
Reputed home of the fifteenth-century witch who prophesied many modern inventions.

Norber Boulders
1 mile north-east of Clapham via A65
Silurian slate boulders left on white limestone pedestals, by the retreating Ice Age glacier.

Ribblehead Viaduct
6 miles north-east of Ingleton near the B6255, SD760795
Carries the Settle to Carlisle railway over some of the wildest upland country in England.

Shambles
Settle
Interesting group of old houses and shops on the east side of the market square. Naked Man Café on opposite side of street.

Stainforth Bridge and Force
(National Trust)
Below Stainforth on B6479, SD817672
Elegantly arched pack-horse bridge and attractive waterfall nearby.

The Strid
Wharfedale, 2 miles north-west of Bolton Abbey, SE063565
Dramatic narrow cleft through which flows the River Wharfe.

Many interesting water worn rocks.
Warning: Do not attempt to jump across The Strid, the river is very deep and fast.

SHOW CAVES

Opening times tend to vary and often depend on the weather or the number of visitors. Check locally for up-to-date information.

Gaping Gill
3 miles north-west of Clapham, SD751727
Local caving clubs organise winch descents, Spring and August Bank Holidays.

Ingleborough Cave
1$\frac{1}{2}$ miles north of Clapham, approached by footpath through Clapdale Wood
☎ (04685) 242
Open: March to October, November daily and February, daily (except Monday and Friday); December and January, Thursday, Saturday and Sunday.

Mother Shipton's Cave
Knaresborough, on south bank of river approached from B6163
☎ (0423) 862352
Reputed home of the fifteenth-

century witch who prophesied many modern inventions.
Open: most of the year.

Stump Cross Caverns

On B6265, Pateley Bridge to Grassington road, 5 miles west of Pateley Bridge. Easy access from road
☎ (0423) 752780
Fine stalactite and stalagmite formations. Visitor centre, café and gift shop.

White Scar Cave

1 mile north-east of Ingleton on B6255, access from road
☎ (0468) 41244
Ample car parking.
Open: February to November, daily, weather permitting.

SHOW SPORTS AND EVENTS

The exact dates vary each year and details should be checked with information centres. A weekly listing of activities taking place in Craven and around the Dales is published in the *Craven News* every Thursday under the heading 'Diary Dates'. Autumn shows take place at Wolsingham, Egglestone and Stanhope.

Allendale New Year's Eve Fire Ceremony, New Year's Eve.

Heptonstall Easter Pace Egg Play, Easter.
Three Peaks Race, April.
Gaping Gill Winch Descents, Bank Holidays.
Hardraw Band Contest, May.
Farm Open Days (check with National Park leaflet).
Arkengarthdale Sports and Sheep Show, May.
Street Market, Austwick, May.
Swaledale Festival, May.
Wensleydale Horse Show, May.
Tan Hill Sheep Show, May.
Penygent Race and Gala, Horton-in-Ribblesdale, June.
Grassington Festival, June.
Appleby Horse Fair, June.
Hawes Sports (horses and sulkies), June.
Bainbridge Sports (motor-bikes), June.
Hawes Gala, June.
Masham, Great Traction Engine Rally and Steam Fair, mid-July.
Hebden Sports, August Bank Holiday Monday.
Malham Show, August.
Reeth Show, August.
Burnsall Sports, third Saturday August.
Grassington Exhibition, August.
Kilnsey Show, Tuesday after Bank Holiday Monday, August.
Leyburn Show, August Bank Holiday Saturday.
West Witton Feast and Burning of Bartle (St Bartholomew),

Saturday nearest 24 August.
*Upper Wharfedale Agricultural
Show*, August.
*Wensleydale Agricultural
Show*, August.
Swaledale Agricultural Show,
Muker, September.
Horton Show, September.
Morcock Show, Lunds, Sep-
tember.
Redmire Feast, September.
Nidderdale Agricultural Show,
Pateley Bridge, September.
Three Peaks Cyclo-Cross,
September.

SKIING

Cross Country
From Dufton Youth Hostel

Indoor Ski Slope
Catterick

Winter Ski Slopes
Allendale
Allenheads
Cross Fell
Upper Teesdale
Weardale
Westgate

SPORTS CENTRE

Coulthurst Craven Sports
Centre
Sandylands
Carleton New Road
Skipton BD23 2AZ
☎ (0756) 5181

STEAM RAILWAYS

**Keighley and Worth Valley
Railway**
Haworth Station
Haworth
Keighley
West Yorkshire
☎ (0535) 43629 (talking
timetable)
Steam line operated by preser-
vation society between
Keighley British Rail Station
and Oxenhope near Haworth.
Steam trains run every week-
end, March to October, Bank
Holidays and daily July and
August.

**South Tynedale Railway
Preservation Society**
Alston, on A686
☎ (0498) 81696
Narrow gauge railway along
part of the old branch line
towards Haltwhistle. Trains at
weekends Easter to September; daily during summer.
Shop, café, tourist information,
parking at Alston Station.

Yorkshire Dales Railway
Embsay, $1^1/_2$ miles north-east
of Skipton, access from A59
☎ (0756) 4727
Short length of track and good
collection of steam
locomotives. Steam trains run
on Sundays and Bank Holi-
days. Easter to September,

plus Tuesdays in July and August. Also a number of special events.

SWIMMING POOLS

Grassington
Upper Wharfedale School

Ingleton
Heated open-air, summer season

Settle
Next to Settle Middle School
☎ (07292) 3262

Skipton
Aireville Park
☎ (0756) 2805

TOURIST INFORMATION CENTRES

Information is also available from the Yorkshire and Humberside Tourist Board, Northumbrian Tourist Board and North-West Tourist Boards (see under Accommodation for addresses and telephone numbers).

Askrigg
Market Place
☎ (0969) 50441

Barnard Castle
43 Galgate

☎ (0833) 38481 (weekdays),
☎ 37913 (Sundays/Saturdays)

Bentham
Station Road
☎ (0468) 61043

Burnsall
Car Park Kiosk
☎ (075672) 295

Harrogate
Royal Baths Assembly Rooms
Crescent Road
☎ (0423) 65912

Horton-in-Ribblesdale
☎ (07296) 333

Ingleton
Community Centre Car Park
☎ (0468) 41049

Ilkley
☎ (0943) 602319

Kirkby Lonsdale
☎ (0468) 71603

Leyburn
Central Garage, Market Place
☎ (0969) 84373

Pateley Bridge
☎ (0423) 711147

Reeth
Swaledale Folk Museum
The Green
☎ (0748) 84373

Richmond
Friary Gardens, Queens Road
☎ (0748) 3525

Settle,
Town Hall
☎ (07292) 3617

Skipton,
Town Hall Car Park
☎ (0756) 2809

USEFUL ADDRESSES

British Mountaineering Council
Crawford House
Precinct Centre
Booth Street East
Manchester M13 9RZ
☎ (061273) 5835

British Tourist Authority
Information Centre
Lower Regent Street
London W1

Camping and Caravanning
  Club
11 Lower Grosvenor Place
London SW1W 0EY
☎ (071828) 1012

Caravan Club
East Grinstead House
East Grinstead
Sussex RH19 1UA
☎ (0342) 26944

Cyclists Touring Club
59 Meadrow
Godalming
Surrey GU7 3HS
☎ (04863) 7217

English Heritage
PO Box 1BB
London
W1A 1BB
☎ (071973) 3000

English Heritage
North Office
Arnhem Block
Carlisle Castle
Carlisle CA3 8UR
☎ (0228) 31777

HF Holidays Ltd
142 Great North Way
London NW4 1EG
☎ (081203) 3381

National Trust
36 Queen Anne's Gate
London SW1 1HS
☎ (071222) 9251

Outward Bound Trust
Chestnut Field
Regent Place
Rugby CV21 2TJ
☎ (0788) 60423/4/5

Ramblers Association
1-5 Wandsworth Road
London SW8 2XX
☎ (071582) 6878

Yorkshire Wildlife Trust
20 Castlegate
York YO1 1RP
☎ (0904) 59570

Youth Hostels Association
Trevelyan House
St Albans
Herts AL1 2DY
☎ (0727) 55215

YORKSHIRE DALES NATIONAL PARK INFORMATION CENTRES

Aysgarth Falls
☎ (09693) 424

Clapham
☎ (04685) 419

Colvend
Hebden Road
Grassington
Skipton
North Yorks
B23 5LB
☎ (0756) 752748

Hawes, Station Road
☎ (07293) 363

Sedbergh, Main Street
☎ (0587) 20125

RECOMMENDED FURTHER READING

Bonser, K.J. *The Drovers*
(Macmillan, 1970)
Calderdale Way Association.
The Calderdale Way, (1978)
Cowley, W. *Farming in
Yorkshire* (Dalesman, 1972)

Duerden, N. *Portrait of the
Dales* (Hale, 1978)
Hartley, M. and Ingilby, J. *The
Yorkshire Dales, Life and
Tradition in the Yorkshire
Dales*
Harries, R. *Cycling in the
Yorkshire Dales*
(Moorland, 1989)
Hoole, K. *Railways in the
Yorkshire Dales*
(Dalesman, 1975)
Hopkins, T. *Pennine Way,
North, Pennine Way, South*
(Countryside Commission,
Ordnance Survey and Aurum
Press)
Hoskins, W.G. *English
Landscapes* (BBC, 1973)
Lousley, J.E. *Wild Flowers of
the Chalk and Limestone*
Collins, 1950)
Mitchell, W.R. *Wild Pennines*
(Hale, 1976)
Pennine Birds (Dalesman,
1973)
Mitchell, W.R. & Joy, D. *Settle-
Carlisle Railway*
(Dalesman, 1969)
Poucher, W.A. *The Peak and
the Pennines*
(Constable, 1966)
Raistrick, A. *Green Roads in
the Mid-Pennines*
(MPC, 1978)
Old Yorkshire Dales
(David & Charles, 1967)
The Pennine Dales
(Eyre & Spottiswoode,
1968)

Malham and Malham Moor (Dalesman, 1971)

The Pennine Walls (Dalesman, 1973)

Lead Mining in the Mid-Pennines (Bradford Barton, 1973)

The Lead Industry of Wensleydale and Swaledale: Vol I *The Mines* (MPC, 1974) Vol II *The Smelting Mills* (MPC, 1975)

Buildings in the Yorkshire Dales (Dalesman, 1976)

Simmons, E.G.(Ed) *Yorkshire Dales National Park* (HMSO, 1971)

Sims, L. & Darmon, C. *Through the Carriage Window Number one-Leeds-Settle-Carlisle* (Dalesman, 1989)

Speakman, C. *Transport in Yorkshire* (Dalesman, 1969) *The Dales Way* (Dalesman, 1970)

A Yorkshire Dales Anthology (Hale, 1981)

Spencer, Brian *Walk the Dales — 40 Walks in the Yorkshire Dales* (John Bartholomew and Son Ltd)

Further Walks in the Yorkshire Dales (John Bartholomew and Son Ltd)

Stephenson, T. *The Pennine Way* (HMSO, 1969)

Wainwright, A. *Pennine Way Companion* (Westmorland Gazette, 1969) *Walks on the Howgill Fells* (Westmorland Gazette, 1968) *Walks in Limestone Country* (Westmorland Gazette, 1968)

Wood, G. Bernard *Yorkshire Villages* (Hale, 1971) *Yorkshire Dales National Park Plan* (Yorkshire Dales National Park, 1976)

Wright, G.N. *The Yorkshire Dales* (David & Charles, 1986) *View of Northumbria* (Hale, 1981) *Roads and Trackways of the Yorkshire Dales* (MPC, 1985)

Some of these books are out of print. Your local library should, however, be able to obtain a copy.

INDEX